W9-AOD-843

Twayne's International Studies and Translations Program

GERMANY

Seven Years of My Life

FRITZ REUTER

Seven Years of My Life

TRANSLATED FROM THE LOW GERMAN
WITH INTRODUCTION AND NOTES

BY

Carl F. Bayerschmidt

Twayne Publishers • Boston, Massachusetts
In cooperation with
The Germanistic Society of America

Library of Congress Cataloging in Publication Data

Reuter, Fritz, 1810-1874.
  Seven years of my life.
  Translation of Ut mine Festungstid.
  "Twayne's international studies and translations program."
  Published in cooperation with the Germanistic Society of
America.
  1. Reuter, Fritz, 1810-1874. I. Title.
PT4848.R4U513   839'.4'8209 [B]   74-10854
ISBN 0-8057-5740-6

Contents

Introduction

Fritz Reuter, the greatest of all Low German dialect writers,[1] was born on November 7, 1810, in the small town of Stavenhagen in the eastern part of Mecklenburg-Schwerin, near the Prussian border. His father, Johann Georg Reuter, served as mayor, registrar, and judge in this small agricultural community, which at the beginning of the nineteenth century numbered no more than 1,000–1,200 inhabitants. In the years which followed the Seven Years' War (1756–63) Mecklenburg had made a good recovery from the devastation brought upon the land by Swedes and Prussians alike. From 1806 to 1813, however, the country suffered even greater hardship and destruction during the period which came to be known to all Mecklenburgers as the "Franzosentid" (period of French occupation).

After Napoleon's decisive victory at Jena in 1806 French forces under the leadership of Marshals Murat, Soult, and Bernadotte pursued a part of Prussia's defeated army into Mecklenburg and thus this country too became involved in the war. During the French occupation robbery and pillage became commonplace and Stavenhagen itself was plundered in 1806. Both duchies, Mecklenburg-Schwerin and Mecklenburg-Strelitz, like Prussia and many other German states, were forced to join the Confederation of the Rhine under Napoleon's protectorate. Of more than 2,000 men who were conscripted from Mecklenburg to take part in Napoleon's campaign against Russia less than one hundred came home again.

After Napoleon's defeat in Russia the dukes of both Mecklenburgs were among the first to renounce the alliance with France and in the War of German Liberation which followed (1813–15) Mecklenburg troops under Marshal Blücher played a significant part in defeating Napoleon and throwing off the French yoke. At the Congress of Vienna in 1815 the two Mecklenburg duchies were raised to the status of grand duchies.

With the coming of peace, however, there also came a period of economic depression which lasted until the early 1820s. The coastal towns of Mecklenburg were able to recover from the wounds of war through improved business and commerce, but the inland rural communities were brought close to ruin due to falling grain prices and an almost complete lack of road facilities for the transport of agricultural products. It was therefore fortunate for Stavenhagen that it had such an energetic and capable leader as Johann Reuter. He was a tireless worker who served as mayor of the town for over thirty years. Johann Reuter could well boast that the rising sun had never found him resting in bed. He was able to acquire extensive land holdings and at times provided work for as many as one hundred people. He introduced grains previously unknown in North Germany, built his own mill and brewery, and thus helped the small town to survive these difficult years.

I   Boyhood and University Years (1810−1834)

It was in Stavenhagen, which was virtually cut off from the rest of the world, that Fritz Reuter spent his boyhood years. He knew of the "Franzosentid" and the War of German Liberation from the accounts of older people. His imagination was stirred by these tales, but the events themselves were too far removed to interfere with the happiness of his early years. In his reminiscences *Meine Vaterstadt Stavenhagen (My Hometown Stavenhagen)* he has drawn a delightful picture of the life and people he knew at the time when he was growing up in this small provincial town. Mecklenburg is a flat but fruitful land abounding in green meadows, hundreds of lakes, and beautiful woods. As a boy Fritz Reuter was free to wander through the streets of the town and explore the surrounding countryside to his heart's content. Later in life he recalled his frequent visits to the beautiful park in nearby Ivenack, well-known throughout Mecklenburg because of the magnificent grove of thousand-year-old oaks growing there.

In his early years he did not have the benefit of a formal education. His mother, an invalid who died when Fritz was sixteen years old, taught him to read and write and awakened in him an interest in literature and in all that is beautiful in life. From his father he received instruction in geography and the rudiments of mathematics, and in addition he was given private lessons by a succession of theological students living in Stavenhagen. Of these tutors he once remarked that it was unfortunate that he could remember neither what they had tried to teach him nor even their names. It was also unfortunate that in his training Fritz was not subjected to a more rigid discipline, so essential for a young boy of his outgoing and carefree nature. However, his father was too much occupied with his many duties and responsibilities to supervise the boy's education properly. Fritz was therefore for the most part left to his own devices and as a result never acquired any systematic learning habits.

It was Mayor Reuter's fond hope that his only son should some day succeed him as the chief administrator in Stavenhagen, and so in the spring of 1824 he was sent to a school in Friedland in Mecklenburg-Strelitz, near the Pomeranian border, in order to prepare himself for university study. Fritz was a pupil in Friedland for four years (1824−28) and then from the spring of 1828 until the autumn of 1831 he attended a newly organized school in Parchim in the western part of Mecklenburg-Schwerin. At neither school did he acquit himself very well. Although highly intelligent he was never able to find any satisfaction or enjoyment in the regimentation of school work. To a certain extent his inadequate preparation may have been responsible for this, but above all he lacked the necessary diligence and perseverance to carry out any school assignment which held no interest for him. He achieved his best results in German composition and drawing, but not in any of the subjects on which his father placed greatest value. Indeed, Fritz would have preferred to study art rather than pursue his academic studies, but that was not what his father had in mind for him. It was primarily because art was not part of the curriculum in Parchim that his father had had Fritz transferred to that school.

There was another reason, however, for the boy's unhappiness in school. His father had so little confidence or trust in him that he arranged for informers to report to him on the progress and activity of his son. In Friedland it was a cousin of Fritz who made these reports. Later, when Fritz was at the university, and even when he was imprisoned, his father found ways to receive such secret information. Without doubt the father had his son's best interest at heart, but it was his mistake to think that he could mold the lad in his image and make plans for his future without making any concessions to the boy's own wishes. The father's letters to his son contain admonitions and reprimands, and the son's answers are filled with excuses and promises to improve, although with time the boy must have realized only too well that they were promises he would be unable to keep. Fritz never lost his respect or love for his father, but after his mother's death the rift between the two became ever wider until there was nothing left but disappointment for the father and discouragement and at times despair for the son.

In September, 1831, Fritz passed the examination qualifying him for admission to the university and he was enrolled at the University of Rostock to study law. Both the university and the course of study were his father's choices. Fritz enjoyed the freedom of university life in Rostock, but the semester spent there was a complete waste of time as far as his law studies were concerned. When he returned home he could hide from his father the unpleasant fact that he had incurred some debts, but not the truth that he had learned nothing. Mayor Reuter, however, was determined that his son continue his studies. Many of Fritz's friends were planning to study at the University of Jena, and Fritz was able to convince his father that the reputation of the law professors at Jena was far superior to that of the professors at Rostock. His father gave him permission to study at Jena, but remained firm in his demand that he complete his studies within three years.

In the spring of 1832 Reuter arrived at Jena, the picturesque university town located in the valley of the Saale. He quickly became involved in the gay student life with its good fellowship, dueling, and drinking bouts. For a short time he was even enthusiastic about his law studies and his professors, for in his first letter from Jena to his father he wrote, "Now I am here, and here I am supposed to study — yes, under such guidance and with such lectures one has to learn, whether he wishes to or not." However, before long his enthusiasm slackened and he began to attend the lectures less and less regularly.

Reuter joined the *Burschenschaft* or student society "Germania" which had been founded at Jena in 1815 by a group of students, among them Karl Horn, one of his former teachers in Friedland. These young students, many of whom had fought in the War of German Liberation, were imbued with the liberal ideas of national unification and political freedom. The Holy Roman Empire had come to an inglorious end in 1806 and it was therefore one of the primary tasks at the Congress of Vienna (1814—15) to remake the German lands into the semblance of a state. Under the presidency of Austria and with Prince Metternich as its chief negotiator, the German Confederation consisting of thirty-nine states came into being, but in the hands of reactionary rulers the Confederation became merely a powerful instrument for the suppression of all liberal tendencies. Perhaps nowhere in Europe was the reactionary movement with strict political and religious censorship more pronounced than in Germany during this period which came to be known as the Age of Metternich. The diplomats at Vienna completely rejected the reforms in the area of political and civil liberties already instituted by Ministers Von Stein and Von Hardenberg and also proclaimed by Wilhelm von Humboldt in the field of education and by the German philosopher Johann Gottlieb Fichte in his famous *Addresses to the German Nation*. The princes of the smaller German states had earlier promised their subjects constitutional reforms, but now for the most part they were unwilling to grant any privileges that impinged upon the sovereignty that they enjoyed as members of the German Confederation.

In the beginning the *Burschenschaft* at Jena was not a wild revolutionary group. Its members were not interested in the overthrow of existing conditions nor were their aims directed against the ruler of any particular state. They were political idealists who were filled with love for their country and who hoped to attain their goal of political freedom and national unification through the moral elevation of the younger generation and through the establishment of a well-ordered society.

On October 18, 1817, a group of approximately 200 members of the Jena *Burschenschaft* invited all Protestant university students to attend a meeting at the Wartburg, overlooking the city of Eisenach. The exact date was not without its significance, as it was the fourth anniversary of the Battle of Leipzig (1813) and the tercentenary of the Reformation (1517). At this assembly a united national organization, the *Allgemeine Deutsche Burschenschaft* was founded and the society adopted as its official colors those of the Jena *Burschenschaft* (red-black-gold). At the conclusion of the meeting symbols of the Reaction, a pigtail, a corporal's cane as well as a number of books of reactionary content, were thrown to the flames. This might have been interpreted merely as an outburst of student enthusiasm, but Prince Metternich considered the act a serious threat to the security of the state.

By this time there were certainly many hotheads and even fanatics in the *Burschenschaft*. In 1819 one such crazed student, Karl Sand, murdered the German writer August von Kotzebue, who was believed to be an agent of Tsar Alexander I of Russia and who was detested by the students for his reactionary propaganda. Such an act was enough to make even the liberal-minded Von Hardenberg question the advisability of granting a constitution to the German people. As a result of this mad deed a conference of ministers of the German states was convened at Carlsbad. Their resolutions, later ratified by the Diet of the German Confederation in Frankfurt, provided for uniform press censorship and police supervision of all universities for the purpose of suppressing all liberal agitation. The *Allgemeine Deutsche Burschenschaft* was dissolved and political clubs prohibited as the government took strong action against all demagogues ("Demagogen"), as these liberal students were called. Secretly, however, the *Allgemeine Deutsche Burschenschaft* continued its existence and in 1827 it was officially reorganized in Jena.

German efforts for political freedom and national unification were given further impetus by the revolutions in France and Belgium in 1830 and by the popular uprisings in Poland in 1830–31. At a meeting of the *Allgemeine Deutsche Burschenschaft* in Frankfurt in September, 1831, it was decided that members of the society should be obligated to resort to violence and to take part in a revolution if it had as its purpose the goals of the *Burschenschaft* — freedom, justice, and unity. Thus when Reuter came to Jena in the spring of 1832 the *Burschenschaft* was at the height of its political development. Shortly thereafter, on May 27, 1832, a mass demonstration of 30,000 members of the liberal bourgeoisie took place at the castle of Hambach near Neustadt in the Rhenish Palatinate. To fiery revolutionary speeches the masses responded with shouts of "Down with princes!" and "To arms!" Popular uprisings occurred in many towns throughout Germany.

Because of the tense political atmosphere dissension arose among members of the *Burschenschaft* at Jena resulting in a split between the politically-minded "Germanen" and the conservative "Arminen."[2] Reuter joined the former group and he must certainly have been aware of the revolutionary tendencies of the "Germanen," although when questioned later he denied having such knowledge.

On the other hand, he also knew with what patriotic idealism the *Burschenschaft* had been founded. He had probably learned of this through the association with his friend and former teacher, Karl Horn, the founder of the society. In Reuter's defense it must be said that at no time did he hold any office in the society or make a speech at any of its assemblies. He did not become involved in any of the brawls between "Germanen" and "Arminen," because violence was not part of his nature. In his literary works, all of which are characterized by a spirit of conciliation, he has revealed his great compassion for the poor and oppressed. It was the conviviality and joy of student life that interested Reuter most. All of his friends, many of them Mecklenburgers like himself, were members of the "Germania" and under the circumstances it would have been difficult for him not to become a member also. Little did he know at that time what tragic consequences membership in the *Burschenschaft* would have for him.

At Christmas, 1832, students from the universities of Heidelberg, Würzburg, Erlangen, and Giessen at a gathering of the *Allgemeine Deutsche Burschenschaft* in Stuttgart voted not only to support popular uprisings, but also to take the initiative for revolution into their own hands. There were no members of the Jena *Burschenschaft* present in Stuttgart, but when reports of the meeting came to Jena, there were further outbreaks of violence between members of the liberal "Germania" and the conservative "Arminia." Militia was brought in from Weimar and both societies were dissolved. Henceforth the only student colors permitted in Jena were those of the Saxon state.

Fritz Reuter decided to leave the university, especially when one of his friends was summarily expelled. He himself was given a statement testifying to his good behavior while at the university. On February 18, 1833, he went to Camburg in neighboring Saxony-Meiningen where he remained until April 20.

He had no desire to return home, remembering only too well the unpleasant meeting with his father the previous spring after the wasted semester in Rostock. For six weeks he did not even write to his father until he learned from friends in Jena that his father had had notices placed in newspapers requesting him to return home immediately. On March 17 Fritz wrote to his father and explained in great detail why he wanted to continue his studies at the University of Munich. It is not too surprising that in a second letter he expressed his complete distaste for the study of law. His father, however, rightly concerned for his son's safety, ordered him home, and early in May Fritz finally returned to Stavenhagen. There he learned the reason for his father's greatest worry. On April 3, 1833, while Fritz was in Camburg a group of about fifty fanatical students had planned to storm the very seat of the reactionary government, the Diet of the German Confederation in Frankfurt. The leaders thought they would have the support of the working classes and farmers in and around Frankfurt. But no such help materialized and when armed troops appeared the uprising was easily put down. Investigations revealed that the plot had originated at several universities, among them Jena, and the government immediately proceeded to arrest all members of the *Allgemeine Deutsche Burschenschaft*. About 2,000 "demagogues" were arrested in all states of the German Confederation, and in Prussia alone over 200 students were brought to trial by the Supreme Court by 1836.

Reuter was, of course, included on the government's list of wanted students and he was therefore in danger of being arrested wherever he might be. However, Mayor Reuter felt that his son would be safe enough at home, and indeed no attempt was made by the Mecklenburg government to arrest him.

Fritz Reuter spent the summer and fall of 1833 at home. Both he and his father must have thought that the danger of his being arrested had now passed. They felt that nothing had happened to him in Mecklenburg, and so he would be safe elsewhere too, even in Prussia. At the beginning of October he arrived in Berlin to resume his studies there in the winter semester. However, he was not accepted at the university and furthermore he learned that one of his friends from the Jena "Germania" had been arrested. He left hurriedly for Leipzig in Saxony, but there too he was refused admission to the university. Once again his father urgently summoned him home. He left Leipzig for Berlin, where he arrived on October 27, 1833. Instead of continuing immediately to Stavenhagen Fritz unwisely remained in Berlin and was arrested on the night of October 31. He was taken to the city jail where he was thrown together with vagabonds and common thieves. He was subjected to constant questioning, but he stoutly denied that he knew anything of the political tendencies of the "Germania." He did not consider the "Germania" a forbidden society because the students had worn their colors openly.

Every effort of his father to have him freed on bail or extradited to his native Mecklenburg proved to be in vain. On New Year's day 1834 Reuter was transferred to the magistrate's jail in Berlin where further hearings were conducted by one of the most bitter enemies of the *Burschenschaft*, Criminal Councillor Heinrich Rudolf Dambach. He was again questioned repeatedly from January to July, but conceded only that to his knowledge the sole purpose of the "Germania" had been the physical and moral preparation of its members to become loyal and patriotic citizens. He continued to believe that he would be freed, because he was not a Prussian, had never studied in Prussia, nor had he ever committed any crime against the Prussian state. However, on October 3, 1834, the Minister of Justice decreed that Reuter as a member of the "Germania" was guilty of a crime against the Prussian state, and since he had been arrested in Prussia he was subject to the jurisdiction of that state. For eleven months Reuter was imprisoned in a small dark cell which was so damp that his boots rotted away. The window was covered with tin reinforcement so that his eyes suffered from the poor light, and at times he was forced to sleep on a straw sack.

On November 12, 1834, Reuter was transferred to the military fortress at Silberberg in Silesia. Here he was fortunate enough to be reunited with some of his friends from Jena. The officers in command treated the prisoners humanely, but Reuter's health had suffered from the harsh treatment in Berlin. The food was poor and insufficient, since the prisoners were given an allotment of only five talers a month. Furthermore, Silberberg was located 2,000 feet above sea level and the winter there lasted nine months of the year. In their depressed state of mind and impaired health the prisoners had recourse to the hard liquor distilled in Silesia, and for Reuter alcohol soon became a necessity. Had he been given some hope of freedom it is quite likely that he would not have fallen victim to the recurring attacks of dipsomania against which he had to fight so courageously all his life.

However, the years 1835 and 1836 passed and still the prisoners were left in ignorance of their fate. Finally on January 28, 1837, they learned of the verdict which had been passed down by the Supreme

Court about a half year earlier, on August 4, 1836. Of the 204 students tried, thirty-nine, including Reuter, were condemned to death. At the same time he learned that by a decree of King Frederick William III of Prussia on December 11 his sentence had been commuted to thirty years of fortress imprisonment.

Reuter was extremely disheartened to learn of this cruel sentence, especially since he knew that other students who had been extradited to Mecklenburg as well as those who had been arrested in their native states were then already at liberty after having served short sentences of from six months to two years.

His health continued to remain poor and a physician testified that he was in danger of losing his eyesight if detained in the damp casemates of Silberberg any longer. As a result he was transferred to the fortress of Gross-Glogau on the Oder toward the end of February, 1837.

It is at this point that Reuter takes up the account of his years in prison. *Ut mine Festungstid (Seven Years of my Life)* was not published until twenty-five years later, in 1862, but probably for that very reason he was able to look back with a certain objectivity on those years which had brought him so much anguish. He does not hide his bitterness, but he is able to find light in the shadows and diffuse the entire account with a humor and spirit of reconciliation which are the marks of all his literary works.

II   The Road Back (1840–1874)

In August, 1840, Reuter was finally released from prison through the general amnesty decreed by King Frederick William IV of Prussia. He returned to his home in Stavenhagen, but whatever joy he might have felt in his newly-won freedom was tempered by the realization that the time of his imprisonment represented seven lost years of his life. As the reader can see from the final pages of *Ut mine Festungstid* he was discouraged and completely at a loss to know what the future might hold for him. While in prison he had made attempts to read some technical books in the field of agriculture and applied chemistry, but in spite of his great interest in farming he had no practical experience in such work. During these seven years he had also painted many excellent portraits, but with all his artistic talent he knew that here too he lacked the proper training to achieve success in this field. He had regained his freedom, but his health was broken and in addition he was still a periodic drinker.

Mayor Reuter saw the only hope for his son's future in a continuation of his law studies, and so in October Fritz, once again acquiescing in his father's wish, became a student, this time at the University of Heidelberg. This ill-fated plan, however, was doomed to failure from the beginning. Fritz was now thirty years old, but no more interested in academic study than he had been years earlier in Rostock or Jena. The other students, all younger then he, were at first impressed by the fact that they had in their midst a "revolutionary demagogue" who had once been sentenced to death by the Prussian government, but they soon found out that his accomplishments were not in keeping with what one might have expected in a man of his age. More and more they avoided the "loner" who would periodically drink himself into a state of complete stupor. Learning of his son's hapless condition Mayor Reuter had a city official of Stavenhagen sent to Heidelberg with the authority to escort his "disturbed" son to the mayor's brother, Ernst Reuter, pastor of the small parish of Jabel near Stavenhagen. Johann Reuter did not even wish to see his son, whom he now looked upon as a drunkard and a hopeless failure.

From the middle of July to the end of March, 1841, Reuter spent many happy hours in the home of his uncle in Jabel. Here the bewildered student found a haven in the company of the kindly pastor, his friendly wife and their five lively daughters. All gave him the warmth and love which he had so sorely lacked in his own home. Outdoor activity restored his health and the happy life in the parsonage revived his spirits. He endeared himself to his cousins with the many poems he wrote for them in celebration of special occasions. At this time there was no indication that he would become a writer, but nevertheless in Jabel he was able to observe many individual types, such as the forester Schlange and the beloved sexton Suhr, who were later to appear as characters in his anecdotes and humorous novels.

Early in 1842 Reuter's father was able to secure a position for him as "Volontär" or apprentice without salary on the estate of Franz Rust at Demzin near Stavenhagen. This marked the beginning of Reuter's "Stromtid" or farming period. Rust was a university-trained and widely traveled man who was happy to associate with a man of Reuter's intelligence and discuss with him topics of a literary, political, or cultural nature. He could not treat Reuter, a man of thirty-two years, as an ordinary apprentice, and therefore wisely assigned to him tasks which would give him pleasure and at the same time a certain amount of practical experience in agriculture and husbandry, for it was still Reuter's hope that he might some day own his own land or at least become the manager or overseer of a large farm, possibly even of a grand-ducal estate.

Reuter thoroughly enjoyed his "apprenticeship" because of the valuable training he received from a warmhearted friend, but there were other reasons too why the four years spent at Demzin were of such importance for his rehabilitation and for his future career. Through Rust he became acquainted with members of the liberal bourgeois party who raised their voices in opposition to the noble landowners and the special privileges granted them. In a journal to which Reuter made anonymous contributions the weapons of satire were employed to attack many political and social injustices. For two numbers of the journal (1846–47) Reuter wrote a sharp satire, *Ein gräflicher Geburtstag (The Birthday of the Countess)*, in which he described a birthday celebration he had witnessed several years earlier. He raised the question whether God or the countess had been honored more on that occasion. The central theme of the account was Reuter's criticism that Mecklenburg was still without a constitution in spite of the promises made by the Diet of the German Confederation.

In Demzin Reuter also had much opportunity to make sketches of many people who seemed to him to be interesting subjects. They included drawings of farmers, teachers, preachers, merchants, farm laborers, inspectors, schoolchildren, doctors, shepherds, and all the people who make up the population of a small Mecklenburg community and give it its special character. During his imprisonment Reuter had not been able to associate with many people and only later did he realize that when one is shut off from outside influences and impressions he gets to understand himself all the better. It was probably for that reason that he now likewise learned to observe other people more carefully and thus make such interesting character studies. In Demzin just as in Jabel he continued to write anecdotes of all kinds, but merely for the benefit of his intimate friends.

Here he also met Luise Kuntze, a governess in the large family of a neighboring pastor, who was a frequent visitor in the Rust home. Luise was later to become his wife, but at this time Reuter had no means to support himself, much less a wife. In March, 1845, Reuter's father died and by the terms of the will Reuter and his two half-sisters were each to receive 4,750 talers, but Reuter was to receive his share only if he were able to abstain from alcohol for a period of three years. Otherwise he should receive only the interest on the capital, and even that should be lost if he were to marry.

This was a severe blow to Reuter. He had always believed that his father was a wealthy man and that he would inherit enough money to establish himself on his father's estate or elsewhere as a tenant farmer. Now that hope was shattered. In these circumstances Luise, Franz Rust, and the latter's brother-in-law, Fritz Peters, proved to be the steadying influences in his life. For the greater part of the next four years Reuter lived with his "best friend" Peters at a farm near Treptow, a small Prussian town across the border from Stavenhagen.

In 1848 he returned to Stavenhagen with the intention of giving private instruction in secondary-school subjects, since his hometown had no school at that level. He was unable to receive such permission from the authorities, but his stay was not without importance for his literary work, because he became a member of a "Reformverein," and later in his most important novel *Ut mine Stromtid (My Years as a Farmer)* he gave a delightful description of the meetings of such a radical civic society, many of which had sprung up in towns throughout Mecklenburg in the politically turbulent year 1848. He was appointed to represent Stavenhagen at two meetings of "Reform" societies in Güstrow and he also served as a delegate from Stavenhagen at the special session of the provincial diet in Schwerin.

However, he also had to earn a livelihood and so in 1850 at the suggestion of his friend Fritz Peters he returned to Treptow (Prussia) and was there granted permission to give private instruction in various subjects including gymnastics, drawing, mathematics, history, geography, English, Greek, and other foreign languages. It seems ironical that he who had once been forced to swear an oath that he would never again return to Prussia should have applied for Prussian citizenship, but he did so because without such naturalization he would have been in danger of being expelled from Prussia at any time.

He thus became a Prussian citizen in March, 1851, and now nothing stood in the way of his marriage, since his half-sisters, realizing what a beneficial influence Luise had upon him, had agreed that he should receive the interest due him in the amount of approximately 240 talers per year, even though he should marry.

In June, 1851, Fritz and Luise were married and that year marked the beginning of Reuter's career as a writer of Plattdeutsch or Low German literature. Until that time he had written only some political satire and occasional verse, but all had been written in High German with the exception of a few instances when for obvious reasons he had Mecklenburg peasants make use of their native dialect. By comparing the High German version of the *Stromtid*, which was not published until 1949, and the Low German *Ut mine Stromtid* one can immediately note the difference in Reuter's style. His High German is precise, but stiff and stilted in contrast to the smooth flow of his Low German dialect. As a humorist it was quite natural that Reuter should have told his Mecklenburg stories in the Mecklenburg dialect. He was born and brought up in Mecklenburg and had spoken Low German all his life. At the university and in prison he had associated with Low German speaking friends. Above all, he wrote for and about the people he knew best of all, those of Mecklenburg and Pomerania. He himself thought that to write such stories in High German would be like dressing a street urchin in ermine.

The Reuters spent five happy years (1851–56) in Treptow. They became acquainted with some of the most distinguished families in town, and spent much time with their good friends Fritz Peters and his wife in nearby Thalberg. Luise recognized the great potential which Fritz had as a writer and encouraged him in his work. For the first time since he had left home as a schoolboy of fourteen years Fritz now had a home of his own and he enjoyed the comfort and feeling of security which his loving wife could offer him.

Every evening after giving 6–8 hours of private instruction he would sit down for a couple of hours and write *Läuschen un Rimels (Rhymed Anecdotes)*. Reuter had always been known among his friends as a good storyteller; now he began to put these tales and anecdotes into writing. They are all humorous little stories dealing with real people he had known. For the most part he writes about the peasantry, but there are also tales about the bailiff, the sexton, the pastor, the teacher, the schoolchildren, etc. They are concerned with the colorful world of everyday life with all its manifold joys and also its problems. He doesn't hesitate to poke fun at the stupidity and foibles of his characters, but there is no bitterness to his humor. These are all his kind of people and he describes them just as they are. He adds a personal touch to his stories by introducing names of specific people and places, so that everyone could recognize himself or his neighbor in these anecdotes. Indeed, the personal element is everywhere evident in Reuter's works. Whenever he was among a group of friends he would often begin his stories by saying, "When I was in the magistrate's jail," or "When I was 'studying' at Silberberg. . . ."

If he was sometimes at a loss for additional material, he would ask among his circle of friends if anyone knew a good story with an interesting point. More often than not the jovial Judge Schröder, who was also a good storyteller, would then supply him with such a humorous story. Otherwise Reuter would take his material wherever he could find it — from newspapers, journals, or old books — for it was not so much in his choice of material as in the mere telling of the tale where Reuter reveals his special narrative skill.

In November, 1853, with the help of a loan of 200 talers from Judge Schröder the volume of *Läuschen un Rimels* was privately printed and dedicated to Fritz Peters. The edition of 1,200 copies was sold out after six weeks and a second edition appeared soon thereafter.

The *Läuschen un Rimels* were well received in Mecklenburg and Pomerania, but their popularity did not extend beyond Low German speaking territory. Nevertheless, they brought great personal satisfaction to Reuter, because now for the first time he was aware of his calling as a writer. Their success inspired him to write *De Reis' nah Belligen (The Journey to Belgium)*, which he called a "poetic tale," but which is in fact an extended "Läuschen." It is a story of two peasant youths who with their fathers set out from home on an educational trip to Belgium, which at that time was reputed to be the most advanced in scientific methods in agriculture. The four get only as far as Berlin and the trip as described consists of a series of comic situations in which the naive and unsuspecting peasants become involved. All is told within the framework of a serious love story. Fritz Swart, one of the boys, is in love with Dürten, the sexton's daughter. His mother, a robust and energetic peasant woman, is opposed to the union, but by the time the travelers return from their brief journey she has been won over and the story ends with a happy peasant wedding.

Fritz Swart, his father, his friend Karl Witt, and the sexton are characters familiar to the reader from *Läuschen un Rimels*. These and all other figures with the possible exception of Fritz himself, who is somewhat colorless, are portrayed in very realistic fashion, just as they would be seen through the eyes of peasants. The two threads of the narrative — the incidents of the journey and events at home — are woven together to form a harmonious and unified picture. Especially interesting is the manner in which Reuter creates a certain mood or atmosphere. There is a lyric quality to the language in which he describes the various sounds of birds in the woods or the individual tone of each instrument of the orchestra at the wedding. There is also a reflection of Reuter's own happy married life in the last two lines of the story:

> To whom God would grant a happy life
> To him he gives a good and loyal wife.

In April, 1856, Reuter moved to Neubrandenburg, at that time the largest and most important city in Mecklenburg-Strelitz. It was clear to him that the city with its historical background and delightful natural surroundings had many advantages over Treptow. Here there were publishing houses and book stores, both very important for an author, and a larger circle of outstanding scholars, among them the brothers Franz and Ernst Boll, authorities in the field of Mecklenburg history. At first it was Reuter's intention to continue giving private lessons in Neubrandenburg, but soon his writing took up all his time, so that the seven years spent in this town were the most productive in his entire life.

It was chiefly through his association with the Boll brothers that Reuter turned to a social problem which had always interested him, one which certainly offered no opportunity for humorous portrayal — the plight of the Mecklenburg laborers on the estates of the noble landowners. Legally, serfdom had been abolished in Mecklenburg in 1820, but in the middle of the nineteenth century peasants were still in fact bound to the soil just as they had been in the Middle Ages.

The servant of a noble landowner was not permitted to marry unless his master granted him a place to live ("Hüsung"), and the master, if he wished, could arbitrarily refuse him the right to establish his own home.

This is the theme of Reuter's tragic poem *Kein Hüsung (No Place to Live)*, which was published in 1857. The servant Johann is refused "Hüsung" and is thus unable to marry Marik. When horsewhipped by his master, Johann in a fit of rage stabs his tormentor to death with a pitchfork and escapes to America. Marik is cruelly treated both by the feudal lord and his bigoted wife, becomes insane and commits suicide. Years later Johann returns to find his son and to take him away to freedom in the New World.

It was not surprising that the Mecklenburg Junkers looked upon *Kein Hüsung* as a bitter indictment of themselves, and the literary critics called the poem a shameful misuse of the freedom of the press written in defiance of all authority by a man with no feeling for his fatherland. Conditions as described by Reuter in this poem are completely true, but it is also true that *Kein Hüsung* is a tendentious work in which all characters are portrayed as entirely good or entirely evil. Reuter said he had written it with his heart's blood and he considered it his best work. He looked upon Johann not as an individual but as a representative of his class living in a land of despotism and tyranny. Perhaps this is the chief weakness of the poem, because in order to make this point Reuter has ennobled both Marik and Johann to the degree that they are no longer typical Low German peasants. The unsatisfactory ending also tends to make the reader overlook the fact that the poem has many dramatic situations with excellent dialogue and individual passages in which the lyrical quality of Reuter's language is seen at its best.

As close as *Kein Hüsung* was to Reuter's heart it also reveals that his strength did not lie in tragic or sentimental themes. In 1859 he returned to the humorous narrative and published *Ut de Franzosentid (In the Year 1813)*, which together with *Ut mine Festungstid* (1862) and *Ut mine Stromtid* (1862—64) must be considered one of his three greatest prose narratives.

The scene of the *Franzosentid* is Reuter's hometown of Stavenhagen in February, 1813, during the French occupation. At that time the author was only three years old and therefore too young to have experienced the events as they are related in the story.

However, from relatives and friends whose memories of the occupation were still fresh he must have heard again and again tales of Germany's humiliation and of the conditions which prevailed in Stavenhagen at that time. With a few minor exceptions the characters in the story were real people whom Reuter knew very well, even though from a somewhat later date. It is in the delightful portrayal of these characters that Reuter shows his greatest skill. Each figure is described with vivid clarity, much in the manner of Dickens or Thomas Mann. In the "castle" we see the tall and distinguished ducal administrator (Amtshauptmann) Joachim Weber and his devoted wife, whom he treats with the greatest gentleness, and in the Rathaus we meet the resolute mayor with his invalid wife and son, who is none other than the author himself, pictured as a young boy of about 10−12 years. There is also the miller Voss who is ensnared in all kinds of problems; he has lost both sons in the war, is in danger of losing his mill, and is finally unjustly arrested by the French colonel. However, he is saved by his daughter Fiken, who is just as bright and alert as he is stupid and phlegmatic. The miller's servant, Friedrich Schult, and the Councillor Herse are two of the most colorful characters in the story. The former, a patriot with intense hatred of the French, is the central character of the story. He is an unselfish and resolute man of action who always knows how to be of help when the need is greatest. Councillor Herse is impressed with his own importance, but nevertheless he wins the reader's sympathy, especially since all his efforts to do good result in failure.

The events as described are for the most part true. In letters which he later wrote to his son Amtshauptmann Weber stated that Reuter had given a faithful account of everything just as it had happened. In 1878, when Kaiser William I attended a dramatic presentation of the *Franzosentid* he stated, "I remember those times very well, and that's exactly the way things were."

Nevertheless, it is to Reuter's credit as an artist that the *Franzosentid* is no more than a combination of *Dichtung und Wahrheit* (Poetry and Truth). He has made many changes in chronology and details to suit his artistic needs. The excitable and corpulent Mamsell Westphalen, for example, was not the housekeeper for the Amtshauptmann at the time of the story, since she did not enter his service until 1815. Furthermore, Friedrich Schult — his real name was Müller — was not the miller's helper, but actually worked for

Mayor Reuter in various capacities from 1818 to 1844.

Reuter has taken the liberty of adding his own personal touches in describing all characters in the story. It is as though he had constructed a building according to the architect's specifications, but the internal design of the building is the work of the author, for it was Reuter's ability to survey a comic situation in its totality and to give form to the story through the slightest shifting or altering of details. He was writing about a time when the German nation was at its lowest ebb. The year 1813 brought great hardship to Mecklenburg, which suffered from the ravages and plundering of French troops returning from Russia. However, Reuter wanted to write an "entertaining story" and there is a note of reconciliation in the final chapter when the French colonel returns to Stavenhagen to visit the Amtshauptmann. Reuter has tried to banish the memory of those days by throwing a ray of sunlight into what could otherwise have been a somber setting. Because of the warm glow of his humor the reader thinks less of the events themselves than of the many quaint characters and lovable people who enliven the pages of the *Franzosentid*.

In 1860 Reuter published *Hanne Nüte un de lütte Pudel (Handsome Hans and the Little Curlyhead)*, a lyric epic about the love of a young journeyman blacksmith and the daughter of a simple cottager. He called it a "story about birds and people" in which he hoped to depict the bright and cheerful side of country life in contrast to the gloomy social picture as seen in *Kein Hüsung*. Talking birds or animals who protect young lovers is a fairytale literary motif with which Reuter was familiar. However, Reuter's birds are no supernatural beings, but creatures endowed with human understanding, virtues, and weaknesses just as in the Low German beast epic *Reinke de Vos (Reynard the Fox)*. In his youth Reuter had learned something of the sounds and movements of birds from one of his four godfathers, "Uncle" Herse, the same quaint character who was given such a comic role in the *Franzosentid*. This interest in bird life was already evident in some passages of *De Reis' nah Belligen*. He was also familiar with a local folk legend which told of birds that were instrumental in solving a murder and bringing the perpetrator of the crime to justice. Reuter was aware of the fact that the murder story intruded too crassly on the lyric and idyllic scenes of the poem. Nevertheless, in spite of this weakness *Hanne Nüte*,

Reuter's last poetic work, is also his best. Critics were quick to praise the high quality of the poetry and humor in the early part of the work, as for example in Reuter's description of children at play or of Hanne's leave-taking from pastor, sexton, and parents as he departs from home. Public readings of such passages by professional actors contributed in no small way to the remarkable success and popularity of *Hanne Nüte*.

When *Ut mine Festungstid* appeared in 1862 Fritz Reuter was already a German author of renown. His works, because they were written in Plattdeutsch, were at first limited to Low German readers in North Germany, but now they were read in Upper Germany also. It was the observation of Jakob Grimm, the great German scholar, that each new book of Reuter's was better than the preceding one. *Ut mine Festungstid* was republished in a new edition each year for seven consecutive years and his earlier works were likewise republished in new editions.

With literary success for Reuter there came also financial success. He was happily married and found great satisfaction in his work and contentment in his status as a free and independent man. To a large extent all of his works are reflections of his own experiences, but none is more autobiographical than *Ut mine Festungstid*. More than twenty-five years had passed since the time of his imprisonment. The fire of hatred which he had felt for his tormentors was extinguished. He no longer called out for vengeance, but as a political rebel, which he had been and still was, his hatred of the Reaction and all injustice flared up again as he wrote of this sad chapter in his life. However, because he was an artist he was able to tell his story in a dispassionate way combining the serious with the humorous. To produce a well-constructed and harmonious work he could not give a complete factual report of the entire period of his imprisonment. Parts had to be omitted, as for example the entire Silberberg period, and parts had to be modified (Dömitz) out of consideration for people who were still living. He tried to bring light into the shadow, although at times, as he said years later, it was difficult to do so. His contemporaries, however, could only admire the spirit of a man who had not forgotten the suffering and torment of his imprisonment, but who could look back on this time and recount his experiences with such warmth and humor. It had been the most critical period of his life, and that his body and soul had not been crushed is in itself a testimony to the strength of his character and of the inner harmony which he had found in his life.

Reuter's longest and best known work, *Ut mine Stromtid* (*My Years as a Farmer*), appeared in three volumes published over a period of as many years (1862−64). The enthusiastic reception given this novel by the public was almost without parallel for its time, and as a result Reuter's name became known far beyond the borders of his own country. In Germany in the year 1906 more copies of *Ut mine Stromtid* were printed than of any other book.

Like most of Reuter's works this novel too is of an autobiographical nature, although the author appears only briefly and incidentally in the third volume. As far as its form is concerned, *Ut mine Stromtid* is a historical novel extending from the years of economic depression in Mecklenburg in the early 1820s to the politically turbulent 1840s and then continuing for another eighteen years after the revolution of 1848. It is a realistic novel which draws a vivid picture of social and economic conditions in rural Mecklenburg during these years, and yet the work transcends all time limitations because Reuter was more interested in the members of this peasant society then in the events themselves. During the ten years of his "Stromtid" as well as through extensive travel in his native Mecklenburg he had become well acquainted with members of the landed nobility and the farmhands and supervisors employed on such estates (Pümpelhagen in the novel) and also the tenant farmers of the grand ducal lands (Rexow). These two classes of society together with the pastor and his wife at Gürlitz represent the three chief groups around which the action of the novel revolves.

Dozens of other figures are also introduced; however, because they are all part of the Mecklenburg homeland which Reuter knew so well and loved so much. He once said that he could never be happy any place where Low German was not spoken. One may search for the prototypes of these characters from among Reuter's friends and acquaintances, but whether or not he can specifically identify them is less important than the fact that all represent types which were well known to the author. He has described them just as they are, men, women, and children of flesh and blood, with all their virtues, but also with their failings, for he knew from his own experience that there is nothing infallible in human nature. Indeed, it is in the portrayal of the idiosyncrasies and foibles of some of his characters that Reuter reveals one of his greatest talents. However, his humor rarely deteriorates into caricature and it leaves no scars, for he had compassion for all mankind and a clear understanding of the difficult lot of the Mecklenburg peasants.

Of the many characters in the novel certainly the most important is "Uncle" Bräsig, one of the best-known figures in all German literature. Bräsig is the catalyst who weaves together the episodic threads of the novel into a harmonious pattern. As a retired overseer of a large estate, Bräsig is well informed in all practical matters of husbandry and the energetic and capable old man is quick to be of help to others whenever necessary. He is a loyal friend who is gifted with a delightful sense of humor, solid common sense, and a homespun philosophy which never fails him. Bräsig always seems to have the answer to any problem which may arise and sometimes he even appears on the scene like the "deus ex machina" of the classical Greek drama.

Reuter has put much of his own thinking into this beloved figure, but Bräsig's language is certainly his own. Whereas most of the other characters speak Low German, Bräsig speaks a peculiar mixture of High and Low German known as "Missingsch." He is a man of some education and therefore he likes to intersperse his Low German with High German words, but unfortunately his use of arbitrary sound laws results in forms which are neither High nor Low German. His misuse of foreign words, usually French, likewise produces original but humorous constructions. However, Bräsig always has enough self-assurance not to let himself get perturbed by such errors.

At the conclusion of the novel Reuter writes, "Many a person might ask: Where are Pümpelhagen and Gürlitz and Rexow located? — Well, on the map he will look for them in vain, and yet they are to be found in our German fatherland, and I would hope that they are to be found in many places. — Wherever there is a nobleman who doesn't pretend to be better than his fellow man and who looks upon the lowliest of his workers as his brother — there one will find Pümpelhagen. — Wherever there is a pastor who is not so proud that he expects all people to think as he does, who makes no distinction between rich and poor, and who not only preaches, but also steps into the breach with word and deed when held is needed — there one will find Gürlitz. — Wherever there is a villager who is industrious and who feels the urge to improve his knowledge and for whom the common weal is more important than his own material gain — there one will find Rexow. — And wherever these three villages are united through the love of good women and of happy and healthy children — that's where these three villages are located side by side."

The third volume of the *Stromtid* was published after Fritz Reuter and his wife had moved from Mecklenburg to Eisenach in 1863. They had visited Thuringia on earlier occasions and had been charmed by this lovely area in the green heart of Germany. Luise was particularly anxious to leave Neubrandenburg because she believed that too much of the convivial life with his friends there was harmful to her husband's health.

From June, 1863, to Easter, 1868, the Reuters rented a Swiss chalet at the foot of the Wartburg. With the tremendous sale of his books he was then financially in a position to purchase a plot of land at the edge of the woods between the town of Eisenach and the Wartburg. Here the Reuters had a splended villa built with beautiful landscaping and an extensive garden where they spent six happy years until Reuter's death on July 12, 1874.

Before he left Neubrandenburg Reuter was awarded a doctorate *honoris causa* by the University of Rostock, and in Eisenach many further honors were bestowed upon him. In 1866 he was decorated with the Gold Medal for Arts and Sciences by the Grand Duke Friedrich Franz II of Mecklenburg, and in the following year he was awarded the Tiedge Prize for his novel *Ut mine Stromtid.* Among other decorations, none of which he ever wore, was that of the Bavarian Maximilian Order awarded to him by King Ludwig of Bavaria in 1872.

In Eisenach Reuter's health, which until then had been quite robust, began to fail. He found it necessary to pay frequent visits to various health spas, but such cures were effective only for short periods. His literary output could not begin to match that of his most productive years in Neubrandenburg. He had always been reconciled to the fact that a time of diminished strength would inevitably come, and for that reason he hesitated to publish anything which would be inferior to his earlier works.

Nevertheless, the reading public looked forward to each new book by Reuter. One of these, *De Urgeschicht von Mecklenborg (The Ancient History of Mecklenburg),* remained a fragment and was not published until after his death. It is a travesty of the chronical style so popular in historical studies of the seventeenth and eighteenth centuries. In this work Reuter satirizes social, political, and religious conditions in Mecklenburg,but the satire is too vague and the humor too forced. In contrast to a novel a chronicle offers no opportunity for an organically developed tale. New motifs have to be found and new characters introduced. Reuter's strength as a writer lies in the humorous delineation of character and not in the invention of material. Humorous writing, however, is dependent on the feeling of attachment and sympathy which the author can create for the characters he introduces, but because of the constantly changing characters which appear in the *Urgeschicht* the reader does not become sufficiently acquainted with any of them, as he usually does in Reuter's earlier works. Reuter was probably aware of this weakness, because he decided against publication, even though the first part of the *Urgeschicht* was ready for the press in 1864.

Reuter's best novel from the Eisenach period is *Dörchläuchting* (*His Excellency*), published in 1866. *Dörchläuchting* is a historical novel which has as its setting Neubrandenburg around 1780, during the time of Duke Adolf Frederick IV of Mecklenburg-Strelitz. However, it is to a large extent autobiographical, because it is a literary souvenir of the happy years Reuter spent in that city from 1856 to 1863. Many tales about the comical and whimsical regent, such as his everlasting fiscal problem or his fear of thunderstorms were current in Neubrandenburg, and Reuter had good opportunity to hear these stories from his friends as they sat around the table in the Ratskeller or in the tavern "Die goldene Kugel." For verification of the historical material which Reuter thus gathered he was indebted to his friends, Franz and Ernst Boll, who had also been of help to him in the writing of the *Urgeschicht* and *Hanne Nüte*.

Duke Adolf Frederick IV, the uncle of Queen Louise of Prussia, ruled over Mecklenburg-Strelitz from 1752 to 1794. He was very much interested in the arts and sciences and did much for the beautification of Neubrandenburg, where a beautiful palace and theater were constructed during his reign. He was a very popular ruler, as may be seen by the fact that he was addressed as "Dörchläuchting," a diminutive form of endearment for the formal "Durchlaucht," and although he may have had his quirks and peculiarities, he was by no means the simpleton as portrayed by

Reuter. Even Franz Boll criticized Reuter for the irresponsible way in which he had made a caricature of this kindly and well-meaning prince.

However, if Reuter has failed to produce humor in his portrayal of "Dörchläuchting," he has been all the more successful in introducing many other figures, especially those drawn from the everyday life of Neubrandenburg in his own time around 1860. The hilarious description of the drinking bout in the tavern or of the folk festival in the Nemerow Forest just outside the town once again reveal Reuter's humor at its best. He was not a student of history, nor did he pretend to be. There are therefore many anachronisms in the novel, but if Reuter had adhered to the historical truth, *Dörchläuchting* could not possibly have been the delightful story it is.

Although *Dörchläuchting*, which was published shortly after the end of the Austro-Prussian War, is not one of Reuter's better works, it turned out to be a tremendous success. Three editions with a total of 13,000 copies were sold within a few months. Reuter was proud of the fact that "in Thuringia and Saxony as well as in Upper Germany everyone is now reading Low German."

From March 26 to May 12, 1864, the Reuters traveled with about a hundred other people on an organized tour which took them from Trieste to Constantinople, Corfu, Smyrna, Athens, Venice, Padua, Verona, Innsbruck, and back to Munich. From the experiences of the trip he hoped to gather material for another novel, and indeed after many delays *De Reis' nah Konstantinopel (The Trip to Constantinople)* finally appeared in 1868. Reuter realized that it was very much inferior to his earlier works and in this judgment critics concurred, so that he decided that it would be preferable to "take leave of his friendly reading public rather than to treat it to some overripe pears."

Reuter thus wrote very little of lasting value during his Eisenach years. From his extensive correspondence, however, we can see how much he was concerned with political events as they were unfolding in his country. To a friend who had been imprisoned with him he wrote, "If one will just read between the lines, he will see that I have always remained loyal to my beliefs; the ideas which once almost placed my young head on the executioner's block are now still running through my old head." He had, however, become more mature in his political thinking. He was still a liberal democrat, but not a revolutionary political thinker like such of his contemporaries as Ferdinand Freiligrath or Georg Herwegh.

Before leaving Mecklenburg he had joined the newly founded National Association (*Nationalverein*), a liberal organization which was forbidden in Mecklenburg-Schwerin, but after he had left Mecklenburg and moved to Thuringia he began to realize how politically backward his Low German homeland was. Some agrarian reforms had been made, but the condition of the peasants on the manorial estates was still deplorable. Some improvement had also been made in city constitutions, but because city charters were based on different laws, utter chaos prevailed in this area too. Because of restrictive measures and also because of their own indolence the Mecklenburgers, according to Reuter, had no political understanding whatsoever. In other German states, however, there was also much political confusion, so that Reuter was now moved more by national patriotism than by political reform from within.

Years of reaction had followed the 1848 revolution, and although the efforts of the Frankfurt Parliament to establish a "constitutional" empire had failed, it had nevertheless given the impulse to the idea of national unification in Germany. Reuter saw a sign of such national unity in the Austro-Prussian victory over Denmark in 1864 following the Schleswig-Holstein dispute, and again in Prussia's decisive victory over its former ally, Austria, in the Seven Weeks' War of 1866. In the latter war many of the battles were fought at Langensalza, Dermbach, and Salzungen, all in the vicinity of Eisenach. Transports of soldiers were constantly coming through Eisenach, and the Reuters cared for many of the wounded in their own home. To his friends in Mecklenburg he sent a stirring appeal for contributions of money and food to help the wounded on both sides. At that time he had a good opportunity to observe the splendid discipline of the Prussian army and the exemplary behavior of its soldiers. He rejoiced in the Prussian victory because he realized that in this conflict Germany's unity, freedom, and religion were at stake. He felt that the events of 1866 offered clear proof that the students of the *Burschenschaft* had by no means deserved the label of "fools" and "fanatics" given them during the terrible Metternich-Russian era of Prussian history under Frederick William III.

In July, 1866, Reuter still expressed fear of a Bismarck-Junker government. He looked upon a regime under Bismarck as minister-president as a terrible misfortune, but he was convinced that despite such a temporary interlude German unification would nevertheless eventually be attained. However, on October 5, 1866, in a letter to the Boll brothers he wrote, "I have become a Bismarck enthusiast. Not the victory of German arms — that in itself could be terribly misused — but Bismarck's concessions to the liberal party, the pressure which he exerts upon the king, his break with the Junkers, his check on the absolute power of the reigning family, and the wailing of our petty Mecklenburg feudal lords — those are the true *signora temporis*."

Reuter sent Bismarck a set of his collected works with an expression of thanks that the dreams of his youth and the hopes of his advanced years — the unification of Germany — had been realized. Bismarck answered, "What youth hoped for has not as yet come to pass, but it bodes well for the present, if Germany's chosen national poet, who was prepared to sacrifice his life for that freedom, can look to the future with such assurance."

Reuter lived to see the establishment of the German Empire in 1871. After the defeat of the French army he wrote to a German army captain, "I fell on my knees and thanked God that everything turned out so well. It has even turned out much better then we poor fellows ever dreamed of. As I now look back I see that everything we impetuous young students were unable to achieve at that time has now gradually come to pass after all."

Fritz Reuter has remained the Mecklenburg writer par excellence. He was a child of his time with his roots in Low German soil. He did not write of kings and great heroes, but of the common people of the small towns and the peasants in the country, people whose lives just as his own were conditioned by the same events which put their stamp on the entire era. Perhaps it was Reuter's personality more than anything else which contributed to the tremendous popularity of his works both during his lifetime and after his death. People felt that they could identify with him. His life was typical of their own and what had happened to him might just as well have happened to them.

But Reuter is more than a Mecklenburg writer; he is also a writer who belongs to the whole German nation. After he had moved to Eisenach he often expressed his annoyance and vexation with political and social conditions in his own state. This was not because he loved Mecklenburg less, but because he loved Germany more. In his youth he had been imprisoned for seven years by the Prussian government. Since that time, however, a new Prussia had come into being, one which through many political, military, economic, and educational reforms had assumed leadership among all German states. The German Empire was thus established under Prussian hegemony. It is a mark of Reuter's character and patriotism that he could erase the memory of the injustice he had suffered at the hands of that state which had now achieved what had always been his own political goal — national unification.

I   *The Fortress of Glogau*[1]

CHAPTER 1

"**M**Y, what experiences a man like that must have had!" said old "Uncle" Rickert — he was still living then — after listening to his son Jehann, who had returned from a whaling trip and now at twilight was telling stories about icebergs and polar bears.

"My, what experiences a man like that must have had!" said old village mayor Papentin to his old friend Baumgarten, as they were going home in the evening from the tavern where Friedrich Schult had been reminiscing about the Battle of Leipzig.[2] "People like us can live to be seventy years old, but we never experience anything like that."

"You're right, my friend," said Baumgarten.

But I say the mayor is wrong! — The stream of no human life flows so evenly and smoothly that man is never dashed against an embankment and spun around like a top, or that people do not throw stones into the clear water. No, something happens to everyone, and moreover, something unusual happens to everyone, even though the flow of his life is completely dammed up, so that the coursing stream is turned into a quiet lake. He must simply see to it that the water remains clear, so that heaven and earth can be reflected in it.

Once upon a time the flow of my life was blocked off and turned into such a lake; for many long years it had to stand still, and even though the water was not completely clear and peaceful, and even though at times angry waves were raised, there were also times when heaven and earth could be reflected in it.

What does all this mean? — Nothing more than that they once locked me up for seven years. — Why? — The good Lord knows why! — I never stole or took anything that wasn't mine, nor did I ever lie or cheat.

I had already been imprisoned for three years. I had been condemned to death, but the sentence had been commuted, and in place of that they had given me thirty years of confinement in a military fortress.[3] No one can really understand the meaning of such a "gift" except a man who has already been imprisoned for three years and still has a long stretch ahead of him. If the future looked hopeless, the present looked even more so. To make matters worse, I had been transferred from one fortress to another. I had comrades where I had been,[4] good friends and acquaintances, but where I was going I would be alone.

On a bitter cold day I sat in a covered van; a gendarme sat beside me. The trip took three days. The man was friendly toward me, but I was freezing cold. The cold and the uncertainty as to the future chilled me to the bone. When a man is faced with a fate which he cannot alter, all his blood rushes to his heart and he freezes. The soldier in the heat of battle, the shipwrecked sailor under the scorching sun, the criminal on the scaffold, all shiver with cold.

We arrived at the new fortress. First of all, of course, we had to go to the provost marshal. The man was eating dinner. He got up, took the papers from the gendarme and read them. Then he motioned to his dear wife. She brought a clean plate, drew up a chair to the table, and the provost marshal asked whether I would be his guest. Most gladly! This was something special! May God bless the man for his kindness! I can't mention his worthy name here, because that might divulge other names, and I don't want to do that.[5]

We ate bratwurst and lentils. In all my days I have never eaten lentils that tasted so good; usually I don't care much for lentils.

The gendarme took his leave, and I was now in the hands of strange people in a strange place.

The provost marshal put his sword in the scabbard at his side and motioned to me; we were to leave. He went to the commanding officer [6] at the garrison headquarters, but the man wouldn't see me. That was a strange feeling. His name was one that commanded my respect. He was the brother of a man who in 1813 was revered by all people and under whose banner my favorite teachers and my own uncles had marched into battle.[7] On the gymnastics field I had praised his name in song, for to my mind this name was synonymous with courage and freedom, and yet just because in my own way I too had had the courage to seek this same freedom I had been sentenced to imprisonment in a military fortress. — And now the man with this illustrious name wouldn't even see me? I wasn't freezing any more now; I was burning with rage.

The provost marshal came out and told me that there had been some mix-up in the general administrative office. I was not supposed to stay here. I would have to be transferred, but for the time being I was to have a prison cell just vacated by a lieutenant who because of mental derangement had been removed to the military hospital.

An old man was called out of the guard house. He appeared with a bundle of keys and unlocked a door close by. We went up a flight of stairs, and then I stood in a small rectangular cell with dismal-looking windowpanes, naturally with iron bars. A shaky old table, a three-legged stool, a water pitcher, and a straw sack — that was the extent of the cell's furnishings.

The provost marshal left; Kähler, the old guard, kindled a fire in the stove and then he left too, but he locked the door after him, both at the top and at the bottom.

I now sat there all alone — oh, how very much alone! Being alone is a very nice thing, if one's heart is free and he can ask himself what meaning there is to his life, from what sources he derives his inner strength and what forces spur him on to action. It is very nice to let the past with all its joys and sorrows arise before the mind's eye and then to look ahead and dream of the future. However, if one asks himself these questions, he must also know the answers. The past with its joys and sorrows must be wiped out and completely forgotten. One must never look back, neither to those moments of happiness when his heart beat more quickly with joy, nor to those times when he was beset with fear and anxiety. He must always look ahead to the future just as toward a bright clear morning. But — as I say — his heart must be free, and all past sorrows must be forgotten. But my heart was not free; it was tied more securely in bonds and fetters than my body. Day in and day out, year after year, everything was the same; today was the same as yesterday, and yesterday was the same as the day before! Nothing was forgotten, and in the future there was nothing to look forward to but thirty years of imprisonment. Just let anyone try to look through thirty years of night into a bright clear morning!

I sat on my straw sack all alone, how long I don't know. What I thought about on that evening I don't remember either. I awoke from the rattling of keys — that will make every prisoner wake up, even though he is imprisoned for a thousand years. It was dark all around me; I had probably been sitting like this for a long time. My door was unlocked, and someone with a firm step entered my cell.

"Good evening! Don't you have any light here?"

I said I had none.

"Kähler," said the man, "put the lantern down and go fetch a candle!"

That was done, and then I saw a heavyset man of average height standing before me. He was wearing a military coat and a field service cap. He could have been between forty and fifty years of age, but looked strapping and robust. There was a certain resoluteness to his movements and he impressed me as a man who had been giving orders for a long time and who was used to making quick decisions.

I had gotten up and now stood before him.

"I am Colonel B.,[8] the second in command here," he said, "and I wanted to look in and see how you were."

I gave him what was supposed to be a polite answer, but it probably sounded somewhat less than friendly, because I wasn't in a mood to be courteous.

"You are not going to be able to stay here very long," he said. "You will soon be transferred again."

I answered that I knew that; the provost marshal had already told me.

"Why don't you have any light and why haven't you made yourself comfortable?" he asked.

I told him I hadn't unpacked as yet and hadn't thought about making myself comfortable.

"I understand," he said, "but don't let your troubles get you down. As long as you stay here, you will deal mainly with me, and I shall make every effort to lighten your burden, as far as my duty allows."

With that he turned around, nodded "adieu" and walked as far as the door. Then he turned about abruptly as though he had forgotten something, and asked me where I was from.

"I'm a Mecklenburger," I said.

"A Mecklenbörger?" he asked. He spoke a real good Plattdeutsch[9] except that his pronunciation had a slight Prussian accent, just like the Plattdeutsch that is spoken around Neu-Strelitz. "What town are you from?"

"I'm from Stavenhagen," I answered.

"From Stemhagen?" he continued; "what does your father do?"

"He's the mayor," I said. [10]

"How long has he been there?" he asked.

"Since the year 1805," I answered, now also speaking Plattdeutsch.

"Well, well," he mumbled. Then all of a sudden he seemed to get real inquisitive. "Tell me, is Sommer the baker still living?"

I asked him which Sommer he meant, because there were two bakers named Sommer. One of them was always called "Christopher Ghost," because he had such a deathly pallor, and the other was called "Schill-Sommer," because he had fought under Schill. [11]

"That's the one! That's the one!" he called out quickly. "Is he still living?"

"No," I said, "he died some years ago."

"Well, it had to happen," he said abruptly; "he liked his whiskey too much." He nodded "adieu" once again and left.

My sad thoughts were gone. The colonel's friendly manner and his kind words had done their part, but above all it was curiosity which helped to dispel my low spirits. The most trifling bit of news has great significance for a prisoner, but after all, this was something that could arouse anyone's curiosity. How did the colonel happen to be speaking Plattdeutsch? — Well, he might have come from Pomerania, but why did he suddenly show so much interest when I mentioned Mecklenburg? — Well, he might even be a Mecklenburger. At that time there were many Mecklenburgers in Prussia, but that type was above speaking Plattdeutsch. They spoke a horrible kind of High German, but still they preferred to murder this language rather than speak Plattdeutsch, because they considered it more refined. Yet this man had spoken Plattdeutsch with obvious pleasure, and what was more, he spoke it well. And what did he know about Stavenhagen, and what did he know about my father, and what did he know about Schill-Sommer? I racked my brains to find the answers to all these questions, but found none. However, as I threw myself on my straw sack to go to sleep, I said to myself, "Never mind! I don't exactly think you've come to the worst possible place."

The next morning I unpacked a chest which contained my few belongings. I pulled out all sorts of articles which travelers don't usually carry around with them: a hand-basin, a glass, a candlestick, and then my most precious piece of equipment, a coffee maker. Sergeant Kähler came and kindled a fire in the stove, I put a little pot of water on the fire, and when the water came to a boil, I took out a paper bag with ground coffee, and before long my coffee was prepared. Then I put on my good old dressing gown, which had once been badly singed on one side and on which I unfortunately carried no fire insurance, and then I put on my nice warm slippers, which had been patched together from pieces of cloth but which had just one fault: they weren't watertight. But what business did I have outside in the rain anyway? It was nice and dry where I was, and so in a way I felt pretty good. Then I unpacked my food supply: a half loaf of army bread, a piece of goat cheese and a tallow candle stub.

This last item to be sure wasn't food, but it was something I could use, and that's why I had brought it along, because if one is to manage on five silver pennies[12] a day, he has to economize as much as he can. Five silver pennies a day is a nice piece of change; it comes to sixty talers a year, but a prisoner, poor devil, is not in a position to look after his own interests, and therefore there are always people who steal from him, and there is nothing he can do about it. Five pennies would hardly have been enough if it hadn't been for my father, who helped me out now and then with a little subsidy. Even that, however, couldn't be too much, and whatever money actually came through was given to me only in dribs and drabs. But now my father didn't know where in the world I was, and so I had to write, but until I received an answer I had to manage on my government salary of five silver pennies, because Sergeant Kähler was a very nice old man, but he was not stupid enough to let anyone hit him for a loan. — Consequently, I wrote.

After I had finished writing my letter I stood by the window. I was in an altogether different frame of mind from the previous evening. A night of restful sleep makes one a different man. Furthermore, the sun was shining through my window, and fortunately the bars were not so close that they could prevent the sun's rays from shining in on me. I could see as far as the gate; carriages and also post-coaches and market wagons were driving in and a hearse was driving out — that was something I hadn't seen in three and a half years. I thought everything was beautiful, even the hearse. Country maids with milk pails and farm boys with wood were going to town,

the townspeople were going about their business, and old gentlemen
with warm fur-collared coats were out for a little stroll. Then there
came lovely little ladies with feathers in their hats and with green
veils from behind which there peered pretty red faces as fresh as
moss roses. They were all beautiful, every one of them! I didn't see a
single one who seemed to me anything but beautiful. Why was that?
— Well, I was twenty-four years old and for three and a half years I
had seen no women other than that fat old Frau Grehlen, who had
been a canteen woman with a Polish uhlan regiment thirty years
ago, and then our Korlin with her bleary eyes.[13]

I had no personal contact with all the people I saw out there. They
paid no attention to me, but I paid all the more attention to them
and after a few days I knew pretty well who they all were. The little
girl with the bright red dress was the daughter of the laborer who
came home every noon with ax and saw. Once he gave her some
money right in front of my window, and shortly afterwards she came
out of the green house on the right with a loaf of bread. I couldn't
see the sign on the house, but that was probably where the baker
lived. A few days later a couple of real sturdy boys were scuffling in
the street. A man with a white apron came out of the house and
broke up the fight. He was the baker and he gave one of the boys,
evidently his own, a box on the ears. The other rascal ran into the
neighboring house, where he was met head-on by a man with a
black leather apron, who promptly gave him a couple of whacks.
That had to be the blacksmith and his son.

And from the baker's house there came an attractive little girl as
neat as a pin and as white as a dove, and a sergeant of the guard
walked along with her for a short distance. Then he took hold of her
hand and began to talk to her very earnestly. She kept looking over
her shoulder toward her father's windows, and then all of a sudden
she blushed like a rose, pulled her hand away, and in a flash disappeared around the corner. — What business did the sergeant have
to speak with my baker's little daughter?

A little while later she came out again, and in the blacksmith's
door there stood a trim young fellow, but he was as black as a crow.
And the crow coughed and the little white dove looked about and
before long they were standing side by side and joking, and the
sergeant was pacing up and down before the stacked rifles,
clenching his teeth, stroking his mustache, and looking very angrily

at the two. How painful it was for him that crows and doves are fond of each other and that neighbors' children are in love!

No, I hadn't come to the worst place in the world, by any means!

The sight of people, even though one has no personal involvement with them, freshens the heart. But it is just like music; it must not become too loud. A beautiful soft melody soothes the heart, but if everyone all around is fiddling and tooting and beating the drum, then it hurts the ears and one longs for solitude.

One evening a few days later my Colonel B. came to see me again. This time I had a light in my cell. My candlestick looked very ostentatious standing there on the table; I had placed a half-penny candle on it. The colonel spoke High German to me; never again did he speak Plattdeutsch, and of course I didn't either. As he was leaving he said, "What a miserable candlestick you have here!"

I replied that it was all I had and after all it did the job.

"Do you have anything to read?" he then asked.

"Oh yes," I said, "I have Höpfner's *Institutions*[14] and Thibaut's *Pandects*[15] and a *corpus juris* and Ohm's *Mathematics*[16] and Fischer's *Hydrostatics*[17] and a few more such interesting books."

"Well," he said, "I don't read much fiction myself, but my daughter has a small collection of such light reading and I'll see to it that you are provided with something from her library." With that he left.

CHAPTER 2

IN the meantime a thaw had set in; the ice and snow had been washed away by a spring rain, and the spring breezes and the spring sun in turn had dried up the rain, and it really appeared as though everything were just about to shoot up and blossom, and in my heart a longing for the spring breezes and the spring sun was likewise beginning to shoot up and blossom to such an extent that I could hardly stand it behind my iron bars. I had written to the commandant's office and asked for permission to go out for a little walk in the fresh air, but had received no reply. But then why should I have written to the commandant's office where the man with the famous name was playing first violin? Why didn't I appeal to Colonel B.? Simply because no one gave me any advice or suggested any course of action. For a person who is free there are a thousand ways of getting something done. If he can't get it done one way, he'll get it done some other way, but for people like us there was only one way, and that way went through the prison door and crashed against lock and bolt.

But things were to get better than my faint heart had hoped for. Toward the end of February our good Lord saw fit to give me my Christmas present which I had not received during the Christmas season — for no one should believe that He bestows His gifts only on Christmas Eve. He distributes them the whole year through. A Christmas present may come on any given day, and the St. Nicholas who brings it may appear in any form. On this evening my St. Nicholas appeared in the form of a Prussian colonel and he came in through the door with a firm step.

"You have applied to the commandant's office for permission to go out for a walk," he said. "Your request has been granted. You will be allowed to walk on the ramparts of the fortress under the surveillance of a sergeant whom I shall select."

This was a good beginning and I could already feel the warmth of the spring sun. "And here," he added as he reached into his pocket, "is a letter from your father. It's a very friendly letter and he sends you money which I shall give to you as the need arises." — I held out my hand for the letter; this was really a good day.

The colonel went to the door and called, "Sergeant!"

The sergeant came, the colonel took a package from him, laid it upon the table and said, "Books for you." He took another package from the soldier and said, "And here are a couple of decent-looking candlesticks. Throw your old ones out the window! — Good night! — Kähler, from now on there is half a taler a day available to this gentleman for his needs!"

This was quite an evening! A letter from my father; money in all abundance; permission to go out for a walk the next day in the fresh spring air and get a close look at all the young girls. Now to open the first package! Goethe — *Faust* — *Egmont* — *Wilhelm Meister.*[1] And now the second package! Two beautiful little silver candlesticks. — Away with the old candlestick! But what was I going to do with my halfpenny candle stub? Put it on one of the new candlesticks? That would be the same as having a menial servant come riding up on a full-blooded steed! That would never do! "Kähler," I said — and I had become much taller because of my present affluence, and he had shrunk considerably — "Kähler, go buy me two candles, at a silver penny a piece."

Kähler was about to go. — "Wait a moment, Kähler!" I said; — "and then — and then — do you suppose I can get some beefsteak and some fried potatoes nearby? — No, never mind! — For two and a half years I've seen nothing but beef, except at Christmas, Easter, and Pentecost, when we got some bacon as a delicate morsel for the holidays. — What do you think, Kähler? Do you suppose I can get some roast pork. . .?" — Fortunately it occurred to me in the nick of time that I might ask for something better for my good money, and so I let all the finest dishes pass through my mind, because why should I be over-hasty in this matter? Well, finally I decided on roast rabbit. That's what it should be. I had now made up my mind. "All right, Kähler, roast rabbit it shall be!"

Kähler went as far as the door. — "Oh, one more thing! — I don't know whether we have enough money, but I would like . . ."

"What would you like?" asked Kähler.

"Well, I was thinking about a small bottle of wine. But just an inexpensive one," I quickly added, as I saw him scratching his head.

Finally he said, "No, we don't have enough money, unless . . ."

"Yes, I know," I interrupted, "unless I start chewing army bread again tomorrow. I understand, but even so I want the wine."

And so after half an hour I was sitting at the table with my roast rabbit and my small bottle of wine, and before me stood two beautiful sturdy tallow candles on the two silver candlesticks. Kähler had set the table very nicely and had even brought along a napkin.

— That was a wonderful Christmas Eve, and after Kähler had gone I read my father's good letter once again, and then I read in *Wilhelm Meister's Apprenticeship*, and when I came to the passage,

> Who never ate his bread with tears,
> Who never worn with care sat on his bed
> Through tear-filled nights. . . .[2]

then I felt as though I might be moved to tears at my own fate. And that was quite natural, because I had eaten my fill, and it has always been my experience that those people who have eaten their fill are most easily moved at another's misfortune. However, that's as far as it goes, because if it's a question of real help, then they are not available. Then it's the hungry who come to the aid of the hungry.

The next morning around eleven o'clock Kähler came up with Sergeant Altmann who had been assigned to take me out for a walk. We went out and walked along the ramparts of the fortress. Oh, how beautiful, how wonderful that was! To be sure, there was no tree that was greening, nor any flower in bloom; the fields and meadows still wore their old, faded, yellow-brownish dress, for their beautiful new green dress was still at the tailor's shop. Along with his best wishes the tailor sent the message that the dress would be ready in another week. However, if it was to be trimmed with flowers, then he couldn't have it ready in less than three weeks. He hoped that it would not be taken amiss that he did not deliver the message in person, because he was still sitting beside a nice warm stove some place in Italy or Turkey, or where I don't know. However, in his stead he was sending his own apprentice, a merry little fellow, who served as his courier. Well, this merry little fellow was the beautiful warm breath of spring with all its invisible beauty that brings so much joy to all hearts. —

And indeed I was happy. It was almost too wonderful. I didn't even need all those lovely radiant faces of the young girls I met on the ramparts to make me happy. For complete happiness I would have been satisfied with one, just a single one, who could take my hand and look into the world with me.

But how could Sergeant Altmann help it that he hadn't come into the world as a young girl? What fault of his was it that he had to mention Schnabel[3] just at that moment when I was thinking of grass and flowers and of freedom for myself and for my fatherland? Schnabel was a dangerous robber and murderer who was sitting in chains and bonds in the cell below mine. Yes, they had Schnabel now; he was condemned to death, thank God. A light was burning in his dark cell by day and by night, and a guard with drawn sword was standing in front of his plank-bed, for he had already escaped three times, since he was able to break the strongest Warsaw locks as though they were broom twigs or pieces of cord. But now they had put iron manacles on him; now he had to give up! Oh, good God, what had become of my beautiful spring day! Iron manacles! Some day I might be provided with iron manacles too!

Sergeant Altmann told me in all detail how Schnabel once put clothes on a dummy and placed it on his cot and then crept into the iron stove and waited there until the turnkey came in and started to talk to the dummy. Schnabel then jumped out of the stove and hit the turnkey over the head with the heavy stove lid, so that the man sustained a permanent injury. He then took two worthy citizens who were standing guard before his cell and slammed their heads together, so that they became mentally confused for the rest of their lives. Finally Schnabel reached the street and managed to escape. As Sergeant Altmann was telling me this, I felt like slamming his head against some one else's head so that he too would become mentally confused for the rest of his life. Just then we met a couple of ladies; one of them looked at me in a strange way, and as I turned around, I saw that she had stopped and was looking at me too.

What a friendly and beautiful face that was! How sad and lovely her beautiful eyes! And these eyes had looked at me! Which is more beautiful: a spring day or a pair of beautiful eyes? — because I don't want to talk about my sergeant and Schnabel any longer — Oh, I would say by all means a pair of beautiful eyes! One can look far and wide into a spring day like this — yes, far and wide — and it's beautiful; but the farther one sees the dimmer and mistier it becomes. But one can look into the eyes of a young girl — deeply and ever more deeply — and the farther one sees the clearer it becomes, and far down at the bottom, there lies heaven, and the wonder of heaven no human eye has ever seen.

"Who was that?" I asked. "Do you know the young lady?"

"Of course!" answered Sergeant Altmann, and he raised his hand to his shako as though in salute, "It's the only daughter of Colonel B., the second in command. He has no other children. — Schnabel has two children, who . . ."

"Do me one single favor," I said, "and leave Schnabel in peace."

"What are you saying?" replied the sergeant. "He can't be left in peace. The guard who stands watch in front of his cot is relieved every two hours, and that can't be done without some words being spoken. Besides, Schnabel says . . ."

"Let's go back," I said, as I continued to look at the girl in the distance. But I never looked into her eyes again. And that was good, because if one has been sitting in the shade for a long time and then suddenly looks into God's lovely sun, he can become blinded. Or if he has been groping around in a cellar and then comes out and looks into the blue sky, everything becomes blurred before his eyes, and he may become dizzy for the rest of his life.

The greatest misfortune, which to my knowledge has never been described in all detail by novelists, is that suffered by a poor, young, imprisoned student who falls in love with a commandant's daughter.[4] No one knows what that is like, but I do; I've been through it.

CHAPTER 3

THIS time I didn't suffer that misfortune; this time
Schnabel saved me. My sergeant didn't allow me sufficient time
to fall in love with the lovely girl. I was trying to draw a mental picture of the beautiful daughter of the commandant, as if seen in one
of those new contraptions called stereoscopes, when the sergeant
pulled away the sweet little maid from under the glass and replaced
it with Schnabel, iron manacles, fetters, shackles and all.

We came back to my cell and Kähler locked me up again in my
hole. There I sat and everything within me was alive and jumping,
not only veins and nerves, but every bone in my body.

Now this was the proper time to really fall in love, but it was also
time to eat. It's true that when a man is twenty-four years old, he is
very eager to fall in love, but he is certainly just as eager to have his
dinner. Kähler came in and placed some kind of stockpot on the
table, with mutton and peas and potatoes and cabbage and turnips.

"Well," I said, "you might have done well to leave out some of
this stuff. It looks too much like a mishmash to me." I could talk like
that, because after all I had a half taler to spend every day.

"You're right," said Kähler, "but I don't do the cooking just for
you. I have to cook for all the others too, and this was a special request of one prisoner who is going to celebrate tomorrow, because
today he learned that his death sentence has been revoked by the
king, and tomorrow Schnabel is going to be executed."

"Oh, no, not Schnabel again!" I shouted, jumping up and walking
to the window.

"Don't stand there," said Kähler. "Don't you see the crowd of
people out there? They all want to see Schnabel, and because that's
not possible, since he is sitting in a dark cell, they might take you for
him, and that can cause a big commotion."

Good God in heaven! What did I have to do with Schnabel? Did I
really look like a robber and murderer? I guess I did, because as soon
as I stood by the window, the crowd below began to shout, "Look,
there he is! Schnabel! Schnabel!"

I reeled back from the window. "Kähler," I asked, "do I look anything like that unfortunate creature?"

"God forbid!" he answered. "He's a tailor by trade and very scrawny, whereas you're very broad across the shoulders."

"We want to see Schnabel!" the people outside shouted.

I sat down on my straw sack, placed my head in the palm of my hand, thought for a long time, and then finally I said, "Kähler, as far as I know, I have never killed a man nor stolen anything from anyone."

"I believe you," said Kähler, "otherwise the colonel wouldn't be so friendly to you."

"Well, why is he so friendly to me?"

Kähler came up close to me and whispered into my ear, "He knows what it's like. He was once imprisoned too."

"What?" I exclaimed. "The second commandant has been imprisoned?"

"Yes, he was sentenced to four years, but the king freed him after six months."

"How did that happen?" I asked.

"Well," he said, "it's a very unfortunate story. I don't like to talk about it. Ask Altmann; he knows what happened."

"I have never been shown such friendliness," I said, "and that from a complete stranger."

"Maybe you're not such a stranger to him," he said. "After all, he is a fellow countryman of yours."

"Then he is a Mecklenburger?" I asked.

"Yes," said Kähler, "that may be the reason for it. There is a tailor living here in town who is a good friend of my son-in-law. This tailor comes from Friedland[1] in Mecklenburg-Strelitz, and he has often told us that the colonel was a fellow countryman of his and that he also used to know the colonel's parents, who were just ordinary crofters."

"But," I called out, "how in the devil's name did he get to be colonel?"

"Oh, that's easily explained. He has been in military service for a long time. As a young boy he joined Schill when the general was marching through Mecklenburg. Later he made his way to East Prussia and then went to Russia with the York regiment[2] in 1812. He took part in the campaigns of '13, '14, and '15 and then later when I was in Breslau he was a cavalry captain with the first dragoon regiment. There he was the butt of everyone's ridicule. All the officers in that regiment were of the nobility; he was the only commoner, and that's why they wanted to get rid of him. However, he held his own with them and refused to leave. Well, that went on for a while, but in the end they probably would have gotten the better of him, if it hadn't been for the little old hunchbacked general, Hans von Zieten.[3] He was a little fellow, but a real firebrand who was no man's fool, and he kept B. The officers realized that they were not meeting with any success this way, but they didn't give up; they tried something else. They sent a petition to the king, stating how unheard of it was that a commoner should be an officer in the oldest regiment in the entire Prussian state — that regiment which had faced the enemy at Fehrbellin."[4]

"That's very nice, Kähler," I said, "except that the gentlemen forgot that it was an apprentice tailor who was in command of the regiment at Fehrbellin."[5]

"I don't know about that," said Kähler, "that was before my time. All I know is that he was supposed to leave. But what did our most gracious king do then? — He didn't want to lose face with the officers and he didn't want to lose his cavalry captain either. So he had him promoted to major and at the same time raised to the rank of nobility. — What did our good colonel do then? He accepted the promotion to major, but declined the ennoblement. He had no desire to become a nobleman through the intrigues of his comrades. — Now, of course, he was treading on the king's toes; so he had to be transferred, and that's how he came to be second in command here, for everyone says that in spite of all that had happened the king still held him in high esteem.

"And I don't doubt it at all," Kähler added, "because there was that other ugly incident which took place later, when he stabbed a convict to death and was sentenced to four years imprisonment. It was again the king who then intervened and let him off with six months."

"What was that?" I asked.

"You'll have to ask Altmann about that; he was there. I'm an old man and have a wife and children, and I never talk about my superiors. Besides, the colonel has been good to me, and why should

I talk behind his back about things which have given him enough
gray hair and with which his soul must be burdened from morning
till evening? Because since that time he has been a greatly changed
man; anybody can see that."
Old Kähler left. Kähler was a fine man; that I could hear and see,
for he had become quite sad.
I reflected on the old man's story. — And so Colonel B. was a
Mecklenburger after all, a fellow countryman! He and Schill-
Sommer, both comrades! — One dead and buried, the other strong
and healthy, honored and respected. — Then Schnabel again came
to mind. We were comrades too, both condemned to death; he was
down below and I was up here, separated from each other merely by
a flimsy reinforced ceiling. We had both committed horrible crimes;
he had killed a couple of people, and I had displayed the German
colors at a German university in broad daylight.[6] We had received
the same sentence; he sat in the cell below in mental anguish and
the fear of death, but no one touched a hair of my head. Why was
that? What explanation was there for that?
"My dear friend," said Judge Schröder[7] years later when I told
him this story and put the question to him, "there's nothing more
simple than this: the king pardoned you, but not him."
"I wouldn't say he *pardoned* me," I answered. "By virtue of his
power as supreme judge and authority he commuted the sentence to
a fortress imprisonment.[8] What kind of judicial authority is that, if
it's based on power?"
"Well, you don't think that the King of Prussia[9] would have had a
hundred young people executed for such mere bagatelles, do you?"
he asked.
"Why not?" I replied. "If a Henry VIII[10] or a Peter the Great[11] or
a Nicholas I[12] or a crazy Karl of Brunswick[13] had been on the Prussian throne — why not?"
"The humanitarianism of the government and of the age protects
us from the abuse of capital punishment. There has to be capital
punishment; society must have the power to rid itself of such
beasts."
"Thanks for the compliment!" I say. "But, Judge Schröder,
nowadays humanitarianism is nothing but a counterfeit coin. Only
the kindhearted and the stupid will accept it, but those who go to the
marketplace and pass it off on others will never let themselves be

taken in. And as far as capital punishment and its usefulness are concerned, I just wish you had once been in the same boat with us. It's possible that your eyes would have been opened."

"You can't complain," he answered, "for the law expressly states that the attempt to commit high treason shall be punished as high treason itself. According to your own testimony the avowed purpose of your student society was: 'the establishment of a German form of government based on freedom for all people and the unification of all states.' Juridically this was understood as an attempt to commit high treason; correctly or incorrectly, I can't say." — N.B. this was after 1848 — "In any case the law is thus protected."

"Well, Judge Schröder, then I want to tell you something. In that case the law and humanitarianism are making fools of each other; either the law must do away with humanitarianism, or humanitarianism must get rid of the law. — The way things turned out, it was just a farce, a horrible farce! Not so horrible for us as for our old parents, for with this judgment much human happiness was destroyed. I'm against capital punishment, and who can blame me? Whoever has fallen into the water and almost drowned doesn't like the water. Anyone can fall into the water, not just I. I once saw a double-edged knife with which a lunatic had killed a man. I was struck with terror at the sight of that knife, and I'm just as terrified by a double-edged law which can be turned and twisted like a wet rag, especially when the law is placed in the hands of a madman. And the so-called referee in our case, Herr von Tschoppe,[14] who made use of all the documentary evidence in such a way as to find us guilty of the most horrible crime of attempted high treason, was a madman and he died as a madman. They should have locked him up. Thousands of families would have been spared untold misery and anguish. — After all what had we really done?

"Nothing, absolutely nothing. At our assemblies and in our closed meetings we had merely discussed such things which today are shouted with loud outcry on every street. We spoke about Germany's freedom and unification, but we were too weak to act and too stupid to write, and so we followed the old German custom: we just talked about it. However, that was enough for a clever judge like our 'Uncle' Dambach,[15] who didn't miss a single opportunity to further his own career. And so out of a harmless little sneeze they made a thunderbolt, and a death penalty was pronounced, although they didn't tell us on the basis of what evidence this decision was rendered.[16] They promised to give us this information later, but they conveniently forgot to do so, and so we learned nothing. Instead, the bigwigs, who at that time were at the tiller, were very quick to put into circulation all kinds of terrible stories about demagogues and regicides, — and yet — God forgive them! — they knew very well that they were all stinking lies! We were not allowed to choose our defense lawyers; they were selected for us. My lawyer,[17] who promised me that I would most certainly be extradited to Mecklenburg, my fatherland, never replied to any letter I wrote. — Don't take it amiss, Judge Schröder, that I've been carried away a little, but when I think about the usefulness of capital punishment and then also of the human kindness that was shown me in a court of law, then something within me rebels and my thoughts are thrown into confusion."

CHAPTER 4

THAT'S the way I spoke years later, but on that afternoon and that evening to which I have just referred, I was in no frame of mind to use my power of reason. I felt as though I were having a nightmare and my breath was almost choked off at the thought of that unfortunate creature below. Below me, separated merely by a flimsy reinforced flooring, stood death. It had not come unexpectedly like sleep in childhood years, nor had it come gradually. Suddenly it stood there in all its stark horror beside the bed of the murderer. It made no sound, it made no movement; it just pointed at pictures, bloody red pictures, one after another, and it didn't overlook a single one!

"Lights out!" the guard outside called up to my window. It was ten o'clock and now I had to sit in the dark. Darkness held no horrors for me. At the fortress where I had been,[1] I sat for years in a dark casemate. Down below, the storm winds howled and roared through the long subterranean corridor. At my left was the fortress church and in a dark hole behind me chained to the wall sat the robber and murderer Exner, about whom Pitavel has written.[2] I was not terrified then. At night I often walked through the church that in peacetime served as a depository for military uniforms. Along the walls there hung old white Austrian military coats; above each one there hung a shako and below each one there stood a pair of boots. The windowpanes had been removed, so that everything was well aired, and along the walls the coats under the shakos and above the boots floated and fluttered in the breeze, and it was as though the ghosts of the old Austrians, who had fallen in battle at Prague and Leuthen,[3] once again stood in rank and file and were marching in double-quick time. — I had seen that at midnight, but it hadn't terrified me.

But I was terrified now. I listened and listened for every sound that came up from below, and if anyone listens long enough, he'll hear something. All around me there was a moaning and groaning and the rustling sounds of something moving back and forth. — That was nothing, couldn't be anything; these sounds were merely my thoughts! Yes, but these thoughts had come from within me; they were very real. My ears seemed to hear them and my eyes seemed to see them. I was terrified.

That was a long night of torment! — And as we human beings are — in the end I thought only of myself and not of the poor wretch below me. I thanked God for the new day which for him would be his last.

Down below things began to stir; a wagon drove slowly up to the door, and shortly after, the wagon drove slowly away again. I didn't look out — I was too depressed.

In the afternoon Sergeant Altmann came to take me for a walk. "Don't be angry," he said, as he came into my cell, "that I didn't come this morning; I had to be present when Schnabel . . ."

"Shut up about Schnabel!" I barked at him.

The man was really taken aback by my quick temper, but before long he looked at me very calmly, for he was a noncommissioned officer of mature age who had already been through the mill. "Very well," he said, "if you don't care for my conversation, we can let it be. The only orders I have are to take you for a walk on the rampart. — Would you care to go now?"

We went along the rampart! The sergeant walked behind me about two paces to the side, as though he had me on a leash like a farmer taking his pig to market. — We walked the length of the embankment and then we came back again. Finally I could stand it no longer; I had done the man an injustice. He had had the best of intentions and I had been rude to him. So I turned about and said, "Sergeant, pardon me for my angry words. These last few days I have heard about nothing except Schnabel. I thought about him all night, so that I didn't sleep a wink, and so when you came into my cell and I was just beginning to think that the walk would make me think of something else . . ."

"Never mind," he answered, "I was just taken aback a little, because this was almost the identical response I got from the second commandant this morning. He was actually supposed to be in charge of the execution this morning, but he sent word that he was ill, and so when I reported back to him this morning in order to give him a detailed account of what had happened — because I had been present — he barked at me too and wasn't interested in hearing my report."

"Why not?" I asked.

"How do I know?" he answered. "Since that tragic incident with the convict the colonel has been a completely changed man. He used to be such a calm soul, but now he is quick-tempered and irritable and he seems to be disturbed by some inner restlessness."

"Well, is this incident with the convict a secret?" I asked. "Old Kähler also spoke about it, but he wouldn't give me any information."

"Old Kähler is chickenhearted," said Sergeant Altmann. "Every child around here knows what happened, and furthermore, a court decision was made in the case. I was on guard duty that night and later I had to testify at the trial. — It was on Christmas Eve and it is now a little more than four years ago. On that evening the convicts had requested and received permission to visit with one another and to have lights burning in the casemates. At first everything went very well; they ate and drank and sang together, but then they managed to get hold of some whiskey. Now these people are not used to whiskey, because they have only one and a half silver pennies for food per day, and since they need five pounds of army bread every three days, that doesn't leave them much for even the smallest amount of hard liquor.

"Well, it didn't take long before they were drunk and fighting among themselves. We went in and broke up the fight. If the officer of the guard, who was a very young lieutenant, had known with what kind of fellows he was dealing, he would have locked them up in their casemates and everything would have turned out well. Instead, he let himself be talked into giving them permission to stay together. That was a serious mistake and nothing good could come of it. — Before long the uproar was at high pitch again and so we had to intervene once more. This time, however, the situation had changed; they were no longer fighting each other; they were now beginning to close in on us. Our lieutenant did not want to accept the responsibility of using force, so he ordered us back and had the doors blocked, and there we stood with fixed bayonets and before us one hundred and fifty convicts in full rebellion. Our lieutenant didn't know what to do, so he sent an orderly to the second commandant in order to have him reestablish order.

"On that evening the colonel was also in the company of some convivial friends. He came immediately, to be sure, but one could tell that he had been at a party — and later that proved to be his undoing. — His face was very red as he pushed his way through the guards without saying a word, went straight up to the convicts and asked with a loud and angry voice what they wanted. — They wanted permission to leave their cells on that evening, they wanted to have better bread, they wanted . . . and now they all began to shout at the same time with demands for everything they wanted to have.

" 'Let one man talk!' called out the colonel.

"Then a tall fellow, a journeyman tailor, stepped forward. He had the leg of a chair in his fist and he shouted, 'We're not getting anything here through good behavior!' and he made for the colonel.

"However, he stood his ground without flinching, and as the tailor came closer the colonel kept repeating very quickly, 'Man, stay away from me! — Man, stay away from me! — Stay away from me or I'll . . .!' — With that he lunged at the tailor and the fellow fell dead at his feet.

"You see, sir, I was in battle as an artilleryman at Kulm[4] and I was the only man from the entire personnel of my battery who was not ridden down and stabbed to death by the Polish uhlans, but I wasn't frightened then, nor have I ever been so frightened as at that particular moment. I suppose that's because in battle one is prepared for anything, whereas at all other times one is taken by surprise.

"The convicts must have been frightened too, for without a word being heard they scurried away and each one returned immediately to his cell.

"The colonel stood there in complete silence as though rooted to the spot until the last of the convicts were again locked up. Then he turned about abruptly and without uttering a syllable walked through the group of guards. Then, as I heard tell, he went to the first commandant on that very night, surrendered his sword and had himself put under arrest.

"A court martial was held and I had to appear as a witness. Above all they wanted to know whether the colonel had been drinking. — How could I know? He had arrived in all haste, had spoken in all haste, had acted in all haste, and his face was quite red. — None of us could say more than that, but some from among those with whom

he had spent the evening must have testified otherwise. He was
sentenced to four years of fortress imprisonment.[5] And why?
Because a human life was involved, and a human life is not to
be taken lightly, even though it was a bad one — the life of a
convict who had been sentenced to twenty years for robbery and
theft."

A few days after I had heard this account, bad weather set in
again; my beautiful spring had let me down. I again sat behind my
iron bars, looked out into the storm and saw how the wind whirled
the snow around. A rather cozy feeling came over me when I saw the
poor devil of a sentry pacing up and down in front of the rifles and
tramping in the snow just to keep his feet warm. When the sun is
shining outside, and the birds are singing, and the flowers are
blooming, when all the world is happy and hearts beat a little more
quickly with joy, that's the worst time for a prisoner. The best time
for him is when the rain is pouring down and the storm rages and
whips up the snow with its gusty blasts.

Many years have passed since that time, but this stormy weather
still has the same effect upon me now as it did then. I can look out at
a storm for hours and feel comfortable and relaxed. It is as though
the terrible winds outside were my bad years; they rage about me in
vain, for they can no longer do me any harm. A certain sadness
comes over me that this stormy weather had to come in the
springtime of my life, but, thank God, it is a sadness without
bitterness, for our good Lord has given me a life full of warmth and
inner contentment.

I had now been at this fortress for approximately six weeks, and
was already beginning to hope that I might stay here, where conditions were not all that bad, but this hope, this springtime of my
future, had deceived me. One evening the Colonel came and told
me that he had received orders and that I was now to leave.

"Where am I going?" I asked.

"To Magdeburg," was his answer.

That was truly bad news! For us Magdeburg was Hell. A little bir-
die had already told me about that place. — But it couldn't be
helped; in two days we were to leave. The next day I sat down and
wrote to my father,[6] squared my account with old Kähler, said good-
by to Sergeant Altmann, packed my few belongings, and now I sat
there between the devil and the deep blue sea, in a helpless predica-

ment, because I couldn't do anything on my own behalf and had to wait to see what would happen.

The evening before my departure the colonel came in again and bade me farewell.

"I have arranged your journey," he said, "in such a way that you won't have to travel to Magdeburg by post-chaise. You will travel from town to town in short easy stages. I thought that you would prefer it that way."

The man had some common sense; he knew what was good for a prisoner. I thanked him and — why should I not admit it — big tears ran down my cheeks, as though I were taking leave of my best friend for evermore.

And he was a friend, and I never saw him again.

CHAPTER 5

E IGHT years may have passed; I had long since been set free. I had become a farmer[1] and I cut a very impressive figure in my top boots and knee breeches, and I walked around as though the whole world belonged to me. I was now twice as broad as I had been, and Bank the shoemaker, who was an old schoolmate of mine,[2] said, "Fritz, with the exception of Haufnagel the baker you have the fattest legs in the whole town. I'll be damned if I'll make you a pair of top boots for six talers!"

Free! Free! All this country air and country food, this breath of fresh air from morning till evening, and God's splendor as revealed in nature, there for everyone to have just for the asking. Activity without end; today this and tomorrow that, but everything in its proper time, so that it is in tune with nature. That's what makes the cheeks rosy and the mind fresh. It's an elixir for body and soul, and even though the old bones and muscles become tired and one is about to fall to the ground, the soul retains its strength and radiates the joyous love of life.

I bestow my blessings upon farming as a vocation; it made me healthy and instilled in me fresh courage. From this occupation one may not learn as much as from that most erudite cattle fodder that is served up at the universities, but nevertheless there is much to be observed, and if one is not too lazy and too shortsighted, and if he is able to relate his own work to the activities of the world about him, then he will find good food for understanding and common sense, and what he finds are green pastures, freshened by the blue heaven and by rain and sunshine, which will do him so much more good than the heavy pedantic cattle fodder of the universities and the stall-feeding of an office desk.

I was free and I was healthy! — I had gone to my hometown[3] to get some clover seed, for it was the spring sowing season and we were going to plant some clover in with the summer grain. — Well, a trip to the city takes up the better part of the whole day. I had quite a few errands to attend to and I had to pick up some articles which were not ready as yet, and so I still had some time to look at the old homesteads and visit some of my old friends. It was almost noon, and at noontime the townspeople of Stavenhagen in those days were accustomed to go to the post office, because the wife of the postmaster had the best beer for sale. Furthermore, since the mail from Berlin arrived at that hour, it was also the best time of the day to catch up on the news.

I came into the little room. I hadn't been there for a long time, but it was still the same as it had been. A small section of the little room was set off with a wooden railing. The postmaster[4] called this his "office," but it looked more like a rather large bird cage, and in this bird cage sat the postmaster and his son. However, they were not singing because — as far as I know — no grand-ducal postmaster sings during post office business hours, nor can he be expected to. The wife of the postmaster was still standing by the tile stove, just as she had in my boyhood days, whether it was in winter or in summer, but now the glaze of the white tiles was so worn from scrubbing and polishing that the stove had become red. The same pictures were still hanging in the room; a couple of pictures of "Old Fritz,"[5] a pictorial display of French military uniforms, and then a picture of General Kalkreuth.[6] Befitting the dignity of the post office, Kalkreuth had put on his very best full-dress uniform, and he stood there in a blue coat, a three-cornered hat, white trousers, and brightly polished pitch-black coachman's boots. His face had a healthy red color and his nose, as far as its length was concerned, left nothing to be desired. Among all pictures, however, he had the place of honor, for the postmaster had served with the Lithuanian dragoons under General Kalkreuth and still looked upon him as his commandant. Whenever the postmaster was in a happy mood and was let out of his bird cage after business hours, he sometimes drank a few of his red bitters and then walked up and down in the room with such splendid military bearing that it did one's heart good just to see with what a warm feeling of friendship the two old comrades in arms looked at each other. Kalkreuth said nothing, but the postmaster came to attention each time he marched past his chief of staff and called out, "You are my Kalkreuth!"

This was all to the credit of the postmaster, because he had once had a bad falling out with Kalkreuth, and Kalkreuth had discharged him from his service. However, the postmaster harbored no ill feelings, even though it had all been Kalkreuth's fault. It once happened that the postmaster, when he was still a sergeant major with the dragoons, had been dispatched by Kalkreuth to one of the general's estates to make an inventory — because the postmaster was very good in writing. — Everything went well until the postmaster came to the cows which also had to be listed. However, they had names which don't exist and which couldn't possibly be recorded, such as "Stripe" and "White Nose" and "Spot" and "Three-Tit" and what not! Furthermore, to the postmaster these names seemed too crude, and so he changed "Stripe" to "Juno," "White Nose" to "Minerva," and "Three-Tit" to "Venus," etc. — Kalkreuth had too little culture to appreciate this improvement and flew at the sergeant major in a rage, but the latter, in the certain knowledge that he was superior to the general in esthetic matters, wouldn't yield, and so they had this terrible falling out. Now a sergeant major has never been known to discharge a general, and since they could no longer remain together under these circumstances, the general discharged the sergeant major. — That was his good fortune; otherwise he would never have become postmaster in Stavenhagen.

After his discharge from the regiment things went rather badly for him at first, but he was a man who knew how to make a go of it; so he and his wife took up "dramatic art," as it is called nowadays. Whether he had ever heard of Stavenhagen when he was out in East Prussia, or whether he knew that there was supposed to be a very enlightened public here, I don't know. In any case, one fine day he turned up in my hometown and opened a theater in Almer's hall. Because he and his wife were the only members of the troupe, they produced only four-legged plays, which, however, were of the very best.

It happened just at that time that postmaster Toll[7] passed away and was buried. Now Stavenhagen couldn't exist without a postmaster, but the position was difficult to fill, because the salary was a paltry 120 talers a year. In spite of that the former sergeant major accepted the position as postmaster and administered it well to the very end of his days. He was a fine upright man, but he had no easy time making ends meet. He realized that he could not manage with 120 talers a year and so he had another bird cage constructed opposite his own bird cage, and in it he put his wife. That was the store, which had, as long as it existed, the best reputation among all the shoemakers in Mecklenburg because of its snuff. And why was that? Because the postmaster had a good nose for snuff himself, and with his own nose he could vouch for the excellent quality of his wares. In time a very handsome beer dispensary was added to the snuff trade, and when the grand duke helped him out a little with a small increase in salary, then no one was happier than he and she and Kalkreuth, and all three lived together in peace. Sometimes, however, when the bird became too merry and talked with Kalkreuth too much, she became angry. When he noticed that she had something to say, he flew into his bird cage, and say what she wished, he paid no attention.

And so I entered the post office to visit these good old people and to drink a glass of beer. "Good day, Madame postmistress!" I said in High German, because she would have taken it amiss if I had addressed her in Plattdeutsch, since she spoke only High German herself. It's possible that she still regarded herself as an actress, but it's also possible that she simply considered it below her dignity to speak Plattdeutsch.

"What's the news today?" I asked, for that was the eternal question which everyone asked her in those days, and for which she always had the answer, partly because of the post office and partly because of the store. But now the old lady stood by her stove and shook her head disconsolately.

"Oh, Fritz, I'm an old woman now and no one tells me anything anymore!" she said wiping her eyes with her apron.

Well, I felt sorry for her, and so just to console her I quickly fabricated a couple of betrothals and a couple of murders and a nice little fire, so that she might have something to be happy about.

That seemed to help; she became quite cheerful, and because she had nothing new to report, we talked about old times. At the same time a few words could be heard coming from the bird cage off and on, such as: "Good morning!" — "No, that's not the way it was." — "I don't have any time for that." — "Three fourths and an eighth, that's seven eighths — that will be three shillings." — "No, there's no mail for Jürgensdorp." — "Good morning, Herr Bold, good morning, Herr Braun!" — All these remarks were made according to which Stavenhagen resident happened to be passing by the peephole of his cage at that time.

And now they all came in: Otto Bold and Otto Braun and Risch the glazier and my brother-in-law Ernst.[8] Risch the glazier had purchased a pig, but when it was unloaded from the wagon, it was already dead. Otto Bold was explaining what had happened. The pig had been riding backwards and no pig can stand that; a pig has to ride frontwards. Otto Braun agreed with Otto Bold on that, because, as he explained, the anatomy of a pig is similar to that of a human being. Some people can't stand riding backwards, and it's therefore much more difficult for a pig, because a pig has so many more nerves than a man.

Otto Bold made a wager of a couple of steins of beer with Otto Braun that for each bushel of barley seed which he had just sown he would harvest a bushel more of grain than Braun, because he had harrowed his field very thoroughly. When he was asked how he had done that, he explained that he had had two horses with wooden harrows trample upon a small patch of ground for two and a half days. That's what he called a thorough job of harrowing.[9]

They drank the two steins then and there, and when they told the postmistress that one of them would pay for the beer at harvest time, she left the room in a huff, saying that she did not conduct her business in that way and that she was not interested in getting involved in such a dubious transaction.

Now the wagering was in full swing. As the post coach drove up to the door, my brother-in-law Ernst made a wager with Risch the glazier that on this day the postmistress would open up her "Holy of Holies," and Risch took him up on it.

The "Holy of Holies" of the postmistress was a tiny room behind the small post office proper. No one of the regular daily guests ever entered this room, and beer was never served there. The door was opened only when princes or counts or special guests arrived on the post coach. On such occasions the postmistress would stand at the door and practice her dramatic art by inviting her guests with gestures and curtsies. — Only twice in all my life was I ever able to steal a quick glance into this room, but it was very beautiful there. On the walls there hung pictures of maidens representing the four seasons: spring and summer with flowers and ears of grain on their Italian straw hats, and autumn and winter with hats of black satin, one with grapes and apples and berries, and the other with white feathers. They bore a remarkable resemblance to one another, just as sisters do. And indeed, they really are sisters, for they are all children of one and the same year.

These were all merely simple details and at times just foolish pranks, but for me these small details were important, because I knew the people who were involved, as for example, the postmaster in his bird cage. I could also laugh from the bottom of my heart at the foolish pranks, because I was free and healthy, and for a man who is free and healthy, humor doesn't have to be too subtle; good wholesome fun serves the purpose just as well.

All of a sudden it became very dark in the post office, as though a cloud were passing over. That was because Otto Bold was standing outside in front of the only window of the room, and Otto Bold had a back as broad as a barn door. Looking through the window was therefore out of the question. To find out who the new guests were, we had to wait until they came into the post office to purchase something to quench their thirst. —

First of all two pleasant commercial travelers staggered in and ordered a couple of steins of beer. Then there came a lovely young girl who was almost too shy to order a soft drink — she said the courier would pay for it. After her there entered a sturdy, energetic gentleman in a Prussian uniform. He went up to the young girl and asked, "Did you get it yet?"

"I'll get it in a moment," she answered.

The man spoke a few more friendly words to her and then turned to face us. He cast a quick glance at us, nodded to no one in particular, and then stood before Kalkreuth and looked into his bright blue eyes.

The postmistress took a key from her pocket, unlocked the "Holy of Holies," curtsied, and made a very charming gesture as if to say, "Would you care to look in?"

My brother-in-law Ernst had won the bet; the glazier had to pay.

"Thank you!" said the gentleman very curtly, looked into the "Holy of Holies," as though it were a matter of complete indifference to him, and then continued to occupy himself with Kalkreuth.

From where he was standing outside with his back to the window Otto Bold merely had to make a half turn toward the bird cage in order to call in and ask, "Who are they?"

From the bird cage came the answer, "Two for Malchin, one for Güstrow,[10] and one is staying here." Then there was added a postscript, which was supposed to be whispered, but which all of us could hear very distinctly: "General von Schuckmann."[11]

The man in the Prussian uniform evidently had just as sharp ears as we; he turned around, laughed, and then asked us, "Gentlemen, how far is it from here to Ivenack?"[12]

"If you take the carriage road, it's a good half mile," I said, "but by the footpath it's only a quarter of a mile, and besides, it's a very lovely walk. It leads through meadows and woods and at the other end you will come through the beautiful Ivenack deer park."

He thought about it for a moment, went out and spoke to the coachman who had lace braiding on his hat, returned and said, "I have decided to take the footpath, but how do I find it?"

"It's like this," said Risch the glazier. "First you go along the embankment until you come to Malchinstrasse, and then you turn to the right and into the lane at Susemin's corner, and then you again go to the right around the mayor's garden, and then you'll find a path . . ."

"No, no," said Otto Bold, "the gentleman doesn't have to go that far. From my house you just have to cross the street diagonally and then you go through Christopher Schult's yard and garden and then you are in the open field."

"Yes, but . . ." the Prussian officer started to say.

"Pardon me," I said, "I have nothing to do just now; I would like to take a walk myself; I'll show you the right path."

He accepted my offer very politely, said good-by in a very friendly way to the young girl, and we left.

"Did you notice that shy young girl standing in the post office?" he asked me as we came to the outskirts of the town.

I said that I had and added that she seemed to me to be very young.

"She is seventeen years old, has never before been away from home, understands less of the world than a seven-year-old child, and is on her way to Surinam without any money or anyone to take care of her. The couriers have been instructed to provide for her needs en route. The transportation by post coach has been paid for as far as Hamburg, and there she will be met by a ship's captain whom she has never seen. He will be in command of the ship which will take her across the sea."

"How did all this come about?" I asked.

"She is a member of the Moravian sect from Gnadenfrei in Silesia, and she is traveling to Surinam to marry a man who is a complete stranger to her. — That really takes courage," he added. "I tried to be of help to her in whatever way I could on the journey from Silesia, but seldom have I met such a shy and trusting person."

"From Gnadenfrei," I said to myself. "Why, that's remarkable! In that case I have often seen the girl. To be sure, I don't remember her specifically, but she must have been one of the small group of schoolgirls who came to Silberberg with their teacher once every year. The girls, each with a bunch of wild flowers, were dressed in gray and made the trip to Silberberg in order to enjoy the broad panoramic view over the whole countryside from that vantage point."

"Silberberg? Pardon me, but what were you doing in Silberberg? A Mecklenburg farmer in Silberberg?" he remarked looking at my top boots.

I was about to answer, but he interrupted me and laughed, "To be sure, your postmaster has already taken care of the introduction, but for the sake of formality, I am General von Schuckmann from Glogau."

"The owner of the Mölln estate here in the vicinity?" I asked. "Then it's easy for me to introduce myself, since I am the son of your district judge."[13]

"Is that so?" he said. "I am very pleased to meet you! But what were you doing in Silberberg?"

I told him that I had once spent six weeks in his garrison town and briefly related the circumstances. I told how the good provost marshal had treated me to a dish of lentils, I told him about old Kähler and about Sergeant Altmann and about Schnabel and above all about Colonel B., the second commandant. — In good times it's not so difficult to talk about the bad times that lie in the far distant past, especially if one can recall those times with a feeling of gratitude for the acts of kindness which were shown him!

After a little while we came to that spot in the Stavenhagen woods where the path divides. I told him which way he should go and then I stopped, as I was going to turn back.

"But, General," I asked, "how are all my acquaintances in Glogau?"

"Your old friend Kähler must be dead," he answered. Another noncommissioned officer, whom I don't know, has been taken on as a guard. Sergeant Altmann probably belonged to the garrison company, and so I don't know him, but the provost marshal is hale and hearty. He still performs his many duties, which are often very unpleasant, with the same friendly easygoing manner and the same conscientiousness as when you were there."

"And Colonel B.?" I asked very sincerely.

"Colonel B.? Do you know about the experience he once had on a Christmas Eve?" he asked.

I told him that I knew about it.

"Then you probably also know that Colonel B. was a widower and had no close relatives except one very lovely daughter."

I said that I had seen her and that she was indeed a splendid and beautiful girl.

The general said nothing for a moment. Then he lowered his glance and it seemed as though a slight shudder came over him. "And this one very lovely daughter," he said — and the words came out slowly and with much difficulty — "this only daughter of a most outstanding man died on a Christmas Eve, at the same hour at which he had stabbed the convict to death — and the father is in an insane asylum."

I stood there as though thunderstruck. A man full of strength and love and sound health — and insane! — insane because of a single hasty impetuous act which had fallen like a heavy stone upon a noble and honorable life!

The general took my hand in his: "I'm sorry that I have to thank you for your company with such sad news." He then continued on his way along the footpath.

I turned around to go home, and as I went along in deep sadness, I recalled a sermon of an old Catholic priest. He was what we called a "Water-Polack" from Upper Silesia, who by governmental order had to preach in German. I had often laughed about that. In his sermon he said, "What is human life? — Human life is like straw roof; comes wind, bang! all fall down."

I had often made fun of those words, but now as I walked home through the beautiful green meadows and the lovely familiar countryside, I was of no mind to ridicule anyone. I translated the words of the truehearted old priest: "What is human reason? Human reason is like a thatched roof; if our Lord sends a whirlwind, then it ceases to be."

II *The Fortress of Magdeburg*[1]

T HE trip to Magdeburg began. Again barren fields and horrible weather. We always had to report at the office of one district magistrate after another, or sometimes just to the office of the mayor. At times I had a gendarme with rifle and sword accompanying me *inside* the van, at other times a mounted gendarme with saber and pistol *outside* the van. In the latter case it was quite a spectacle to see my gendarme prancing around to the right or to the left of the covered van, in which I was being driven through the country and placed on exhibition as a horrible example to all. The driver of the van continued at a funeral pace through the towns and villages until he finally came to a stop at a hostel. Then everyone crowded around us and looked at me, so that I seemed dangerous even to myself, and as gruesome as though while still alive I were walking around among the people carrying my head under my arm. — Yes, it was truly a very solemn procession, and even the young boys on the street must have thought so too, because they accompanied us as an escort and greeted me with all kinds of honorary titles which sounded exactly like "scoundrel."

I was thus the recipient of much attention before I reached my lodgings in the evening. The first thing I then had to do was to pay a visit to the district magistrate or the mayor, who assigned a couple of old, venerable, pensioned-off citizens to accompany me back to the hostel and stay with me overnight. They fumigated me with their tobacco smoke and incidentally saw to it that I did not escape and set the royal Prussian state on fire at all corners.

For the most part they were fine, decent old gentlemen, but after they had almost tormented me to death with questions, and then wished me good night, they never failed to express their own opinion as they took their leave: "Yes, but you did want to kill our king."

Down below in the public room of the inn sat the town's elite, who invited the gendarme to join them at their table. He then had to drink and talk, and the more he drank, the more he talked, and everything he said was at the expense of my good name.

On Easter Sunday, 1837, we arrived at the small town of Belzig. After the honor of meeting the district secretary I had the pleasure of being escorted back to the inn by a noisy crowd of friendly little urchins. Here I was again subjected to further close questioning by the two guards who, as was always the case, were assigned to keep me under surveillance.

On this evening, however, things were to turn out better for me, for the innkeeper, a tall man with a friendly face — his name was Stier[2] — came up to my room and invited me to spend the evening with his family.

"Well?" I said, looking at my two old guards.

"Oh," the innkeeper answered, "don't worry about them; I know them. — Meyer, go downstairs and tell them to give you a bottle of beer."

Meyer went, and I went too.

There for the first time in many years I again sat at a round table with the members of a family and drank tea and listened to piano music. I had heard plenty of music in Silberberg where I had been imprisoned at first. Every evening my good friend Bohl[3] used to play me to sleep with the overture from "The Lady in White," so that to this day I can whistle the whole thing from memory. As misfortune would have it, "frère" Braun[4] had managed to lay hands on a fiddle which he belabored horribly for three hours every day, but when "the clod"[5] below me started to play the horn, then I had to take matters into my own hands: I reached for the water jug and poured its contents — splash — on the defective flooring, so that the water ran through and arrived below as a veritable gutter spout and at least soaked his damned sheet of music.

Therefore, it was not the music which warmed my heart on this occasion, nor was it the warm stove, because I had always had a warm stove, at least in the winter. Then what was it? — I didn't know then what it was, but I know now. It was the comfortable feeling one has when sitting with a group of people at a round table like this. It brought back memories of the happy times, when the old government official Weber[6] used to sit at such a round table drinking tea with my mother. It also brought back memories of Parchim, where I used to sit at a round table beside the wife of the privy councillor as Adelheid,[7] her daughter, poured tea for me. What impressed me most on this evening was the sincere compassion felt by all, but expressed without any obtrusiveness which might have hurt me. — I felt like a soldier sleeping in an eiderdown bed for the first time after camping in bivouacs for years.

God bless those people for what they did for me! For the first time in a turbulent and storm-tossed life they offered me a quiet place of refuge. The future, to be sure, still lay far away! — God bless the young girl who peeled my potatoes for me that evening!

Many a person might laugh about this, and I suppose I might laugh about it myself. After all, I had always polished my own boots, made my own bed and swept out my own room, and so I could have peeled my own potatoes. What was so unusual about that? — Better people than I had to do all these things, but that this kindness was shown me by a friendly young girl, that's what made the difference. For the first time after all those years! — My dear wife always peels my potatoes for me now, and I am very grateful to her for that, but now I am used to it.

And how did I act in such company? — Of course, as awkwardly as might be expected. — For human society a Jena student[8] is a very indigestible mouthful, and if in addition he has been pickled for three and half years in Prussian fortresses, he will probably be a little tough, especially for the ladies. — That's the way it was in this case too. I couldn't have been very good company for the ladies, but they were all the better company for me, and as I returned upstairs to my two old gentlemen about eleven o'clock, I said to myself with a feeling of great joy, "The good Lord is still in His heaven!" — With this thought I must have fallen asleep.

The next day we had to make a big detour, because straight ahead there lay a different German state,[9] one in which the office of district magistrate was not in fashion. And we couldn't carry on without district magistrates; we simply had to have them.

On this day — Easter Monday — we came to Z.[10] Here there was no district magistrate and the mayor was not at home, since he had taken the only glass-enclosed carriage in town and had driven out to visit his father-in-law. So the gendarme had to arrange everything on his own. This was easily done, for at the inn where we were staying about fifty old gentlemen were sitting and drinking their beer. The gendarme selected two of them at random and they sat down at my table, continued to drink their beer and then began with the usual questions. The innkeeper, a rather young man, stood close by and listened, and when he heard that I was a Mecklenburger, he came up and greeted me as a fellow countryman.

"Good Lord!" I said, "what are you doing here in Prussia?"

"Oh," he said, "Mecklenburg is not that far away. From here to the border it's not more than ten or twelve miles."

One word led to another; he was from Grabow and knew some of my friends, and I knew some of his friends. He made special inquiry about Klappenbach, who had also been arrested and imprisoned. Klappenbach later became mayor in Anklam, but is now in America.

What thoughts were going through my mind! So close to the border! If I were once over the border, the Prussians would never catch me again. It's possible that the innkeeper might have been willing to help me; he might even have loaned me some money, because money was what I needed. There was no district magistrate here nor any mayor. The gendarme had driven back with the van, and the other gendarme who was supposed to take me into his custody was probably not at home either, because he had not as yet put in an appearance. I was in the care of my two worthy old gentlemen, but they seemed to be concerned only with their beer, and ever since my Jena student days beer had always been a good friend of mine.[11] Beer would help me out; I knew that. While on the journey I had eighteen pennies a day to spend. Today I hadn't spent anything, and so I had a good supply of pennies to my credit with the innkeeper. I was therefore very generous in treating my two old gentlemen to beer.

The innkeeper smelled a rat, which was all right with me. He said nothing, but made a face as though to say, "What business is that of mine?" After a while I casually inquired about the road. Everything was going fine except for two things: I had no money in my pocket and outside the snow was two feet high and still falling. It would be next to impossible to follow any path or road. However, if the snow made it difficult for me, it also made it difficult for those who would have to catch me.

When it became dark, I went up to my room and put on my best boots and two shirts, one over the other, to protect me against the

cold, because I hadn't been able to scrape together enough money to
buy an overcoat. There! Now I was ready to go, but what about the
money? — Then came another consideration which upset the entire
plan.

In almost every letter my old father had begged me not to enter-
tain any thought of escaping. He said that he was an old man, and if
I were to become a fugitive, we would never be able to see each
other again. He was convinced that I would soon be released. Of
course we would be released soon; that was our morning and evening prayer. That's what our parents wrote us and that's what the
courts of justice told us. Our defense counsels told us that we should
by no means appeal, because that would then take too much time;
we should merely trust in the mercy of the king. — Yes, mercy! —
After he was dead, then we got mercy.[12] But I had promised my old
father that I would not think of escaping.[13] That, to be sure, was at a
time when I did not know that I might have such a good opportunity. But I had to be released soon!

That was the worst part about the entire proceedings. On all sides
our hopes were constantly raised and then later these hopes were
shamefully destroyed by ministers[14] and councillors of state.

That night I didn't sleep a wink. I thought about it over and over
again. Should I do it? Did I have the right to do it? I was sure that I
would be able to make my escape. My two old gentlemen in the corners of their sofa were sleeping the sleep of the just with the help of
my beer. Fully dressed I lay straight across the bed. There were still
people down below in the public room, and the outside door had to
be open, because it was Easter Monday. — No, I wouldn't do it. I
would surely be released soon! So I undressed and lay down, but I
wasn't able to sleep; there were too many thoughts going through
my mind.

Was it right or not that I stayed? — Who can tell? — Some of the
students were able to escape: Von Massow from Kolberg, Bönninger
from Silberberg, and Wagner and Reinhardt from Magdeburg,[15] but
I never learned that they were any the happier for it. What can any
fugitive do abroad as a half-trained German law student or as a
theology student or, for that matter, as a medical student? — At any
rate, it was good for me that I gave up the plan, because the next
morning the temperature was down to 16—17 degrees below zero.[16]
I would certainly have frozen to death.

Early in the morning the gendarme came rattling up to the door in the covered van. I hadn't slept at all that night. That in itself is enough to make one feel the cold, but in addition the thermometer read minus 16 degrees and I was without suitable clothing. It was about as much as anyone can bear. However, to the credit of the gendarme I must say he took care of me as well as he could. He gave me a horse blanket to wrap around my legs, but how much could that help? The wind blew into the covered van right into our teeth, so that I was chilled to the bone.

Half-way to Lehnin we were met by the mayor in his glass-enclosed carriage, and when he saw the gendarme, he stopped and asked what was going on. — He wore a nice warm overcoat, sat in a windproof glass carriage, rode with the wind at his back, and beside him peering through the window there sat a young, warm, and beautiful little wife with rosy cheeks. Oh, how I wished I could have changed places with him and sat in the glass carriage with his little warm wife at my side and the wind at my back. But that was not to be; very well, "giddap!"

In the evening we arrived at the monastery in Lehnin. Sitting in the public room of the inn were about eight or ten young boys who, I soon learned, were pupils in the highest class of the Wienbarg high school. I went into the darkest corner of the room and sat down by the stove. They were very pleasant and lively young fellows; I've always had a warm spot in my heart for that type and still do even to-day, but on this evening I had to thaw out first of all.

They were drinking punch, and when I came in they kept looking at me and whispering to one another, because they probably realized what sort of a character I was. The gendarme must have told the inn-keeper, and he in turn must have informed them. As soon as they were convinced that they were dealing with a real regicide, one of them, probably the leader, came up to me and offered me a glass of their punch, and asked whether I would like to join them at their table. I had to decline, because I was really dead tired, but that didn't prevent him from telling me in all brevity that they had organized a little German Students' Association at the Wienbarg high school and that he was its speaker.

How nice! The royal Prussian state had set us up as horrible examples for all the world to see, and now the high school students were taking up where we had left off. — No, nothing can be gained through capital punishment, and certainly nothing by using fear as a deterrent!

As an honest man I advised him to let Germany continue on its same old crooked course; otherwise his lot might be the same as mine. But he knew better — the younger the people, the more they think they know. — They had already organized everything on a grand scale with secret conspiracy, nicknames, and slogans.

There was nothing I could do about that, so I went to bed.

CHAPTER 7

T HE next day we came to Magdeburg, and it was just in the
nick of time; otherwise we wouldn't have made it at all for the
time being, because it was during the first days of April, 1837, that
terrible snowstorms blocked off all roads and highways in North Germany.

We drove up to the quarters of the provost marshal[1] who was living at the citadel. Formerly he had been provost marshal at
Silberberg, where I had just been, and so I had to tell him how
things were there, and at the same time I looked out the window to
see how things were here. When he noticed that, he shook his head
and said, "You're not going to stay here; you're going into a detention cell."

That was outrageous! As bad as a fortress might be, one still has
room to move about a little in the old casemates and to see someone
once in a while, for the building wasn't constructed for the express
purpose of harassing a prisoner in every possible way. A detention
cell, on the other hand, set off by itself, deprives a prisoner of even a
little light and air and the opportunity of moving about and seeing
something, to all of which he is entitled according to the law. We
had been sentenced to a fortress imprisonment, but what did the
Prussian state care, if it suited its purpose to put us in a detention
cell!

We went to the detention cell area and then through several
courtyards to the last wing, where the windows faced north. It was a
three-storied building and it had about twenty cells and three long
corridors which ran the length of the building, and in each corridor
there was a sentry.

The provost marshal brought me to my new quarters and then
left. I was then taken to the warden's room, and this man[2] and his
flunkey, the turnkey Dahlmann, stood in front of me and looked at
me, and because there was no law against it, I looked back at them.

"Now I must request you . . . ." said the warden and then he
paused.

"What?" I asked.

"It is the rule of the commandant . . . ." he continued to stammer.

I didn't know what he was trying to say, and so I looked at him and Dahlmann.

"That you strip naked," said the turnkey.

I looked at him, because never, not even when I was imprisoned on remand at the preliminary examination,[3] had that been requested of me. Then the scoundrel's face broke into a surly grin as though his mouth were smeared with greasy goose fat. There's always something greasy and surly about people of this type, but this fellow was also impertinent, because he was conscious of the fact that he used to clean the uniforms of the first commandant, General and Count von Hacke,[4] and wore the general Order of Merit in his buttonhole for services rendered to the Prussian state and to the boots of the first commandant.

What could I do? — I had to show them how I was built, and after they had examined God's handiwork, they also inspected my tailor's by turning all my pockets inside out and searching the seams to see whether I had any pistols or knives or dangerous weapons or possibly even money.

When the search was completed, I was allowed to put on my clothes again, and then they went to work on my trunk. — The first thing they laid hands on was an old silver single-case pocket watch, which had been out of order as long as I had been in prison, because I had never been able to raise the money to have it repaired and also because the time of day was of no great concern to me. Then he found an old pipe lid, the kind with clasp attached.

"Is that silver?" the warden asked.

"Yes," I answered, because it occurred to me that a silver pipe lid might cast an aura of affluence upon me. I wasn't lying, because it really was of silver, but only silver plated.

Then they discovered a little gold scarf pin, which I had received from my sister for Christmas, and my writing and drawing materials. After they had added all these things to my personal documents, I was permitted to return to my cell with the turnkey.

My cell was located on the first floor and had a certain reputation in the building due to the fact that the sun and the moon, try as they might, were never able to throw even a fleeting glance into its interior. That was not surprising, because the small hole which served as a window was one and a half feet long and one and a half feet wide and was located right under the ceiling. To the right and to the left of the window broad blinds were attached, so that the two heavenly constellations and I hadn't even the slightest chance of looking at one another by peeking around the corner. When the days were longest in summer, and the sun moved around so far that it almost succeeded in peering in, then the high wall of the courtyard and the rampart of the fortress loomed up in front of its lovely countenance, and God's most beautiful creation blushing with shame had to surrender to cheap products made by man's hand. If I placed my stool on the table and climbed up on top, I had a good view of a little rectangular courtyard, a nice white wall and a black and white painted sentry box. The only variation in the monotony of this scene was that in bad weather a soldier stood inside the sentry box and in good weather he walked up and down in front of it.

My cell, and they were all the same, was about twelve feet long and six feet wide. There was no stove, because we were supplied with a controlled heating system which had warm air coming in through a hole at the top of the wall and cold air through another hole from below. The result was that we always had cold feet and very warm heads, which is not supposed to be very good for the health. But we couldn't do anything about that. That was a recent discovery of a very learned architect who was specializing in prison construction. In order to find out whether this was conducive to good health, they couldn't have selected more appropriate subjects than us. We had a good number of years ahead of us, and if we survived, then the system was excellent.

In the door there was a little square hole with a cover. While I was there the hole was never opened, thank God, but my comrades told me that the former second commandant, Colonel von Bieberstein,[5] who was later to be imprisoned for shameful behavior — to be sure, not for thirty years — enjoyed the private pleasure of looking at them through the peephole and bringing along friends to share this fun with him. This amusement of looking through the peephole continued until His Excellency, the Minister von Rochow,[6] a man with the limited intelligence of the common herd, while on a visit to the fortress, decided to observe the results of his strict administration. When he looked at his beautiful artistic creations through the peephole and saw how in the course of four years he had transformed healthy red-cheeked young men into colorless stone statues, he was ashamed of his own bungling workmanship and forbade any further prying through the peephole. Colonel von Bieberstein was not ashamed, but he did desist on orders from above.

Yes, these once robust and healthy people, through whose veins blood had flowed so merrily, had all become faded, colorless, and gaunt images of stone. Their young limbs had become as stiff as those of very old men, and their minds were burdened with the torment of imprisonment, human depravity, and the hopelessness of their future.

As I was returning to my cell with the turnkey after the search of my person by the warden, I saw a dear old friend of mine standing in the corridor before his door. His cell was just being swept out. I had seen him and known him when he was in the full bloom of his youth, blessed with the beauty and purity given to a young man in the springtime of life, and what was he now? The burned-out embers, the ashes of his former self! — What did he say to me as we met? — "Unfortunate creature! What are you doing here?"

That was the greeting that I received from my best friend. I was relatively fortunate, because I had been treated fairly well where I had been, but my friends here! — They had been imprisoned here for more than three years, and their lot had not improved in the least in all that time.

When I returned to my cell, I looked about: four bare walls, a table, a stool, a bedstead with a mattress of sea-grass, and far up at the top of the wall the little window. With the exception of whatever was to be seen from the little window there was nothing here with which I was not already well acquainted. So I placed the stool upon the table and climbed up to my lookout. There was nothing to be seen but a courtyard under four feet of snow, and in the courtyard a sentry box, and in the sentry box a woebegone and sad-looking sentry, who was standing as still as my pocket watch. And for a prisoner sentries are really pocket watches, which give the time by day and night and which have to be wound up every two hours. In the daytime they are pleasant enough, but at night they are somewhat disagreeable, when they shout "Who's there?" and slam their rifle butts on the floor to dispel their own fears.

"Well, my friend, just stand there!" I said. "In two hours you will be relieved; I think you'll be able to hold out until then." As I was

standing there pondering over his lot and mine, the door was unlocked and the turnkey came in with my trunk.

"Well," he said, "I call that pretty brazen to be climbing up there
in the first fifteen minutes."

"Why?" I asked. "Is it forbidden?"

He replied that he hadn't said exactly that, but he added that I
seemed to be one of those people who take great liberties. He again
had that surly and greasy sneer on his face.

Did I come down from my throne in a hurry! I stood in front of
him and said I was taking no orders from him. If I was doing
something I wasn't supposed to, he could report it. Otherwise, he
was to mind his own business.

He remarked that I was a damned quick-tempered fellow, but
they had known many like me, and they had been able to make
them all tractable, and they would make me tractable too.

I was just about to lash out at such impudence, when the warden
came in and asked what was going on. — I told him what had
happened and asked whether the turnkey had the right to speak to
me in such an insolent way without cause. — His answer was that it
was none of the turnkey's business what I did, as long as I did not
speak to anyone through the window. Then he turned to the turnkey
and reproved him sharply for his impertinence. — The scoundrel's
face was twisted into a sneer full of spite and venom, and as he left
the cell he mumbled something about "general" and "get to know."

The warden had three pounds of tobacco under his arm. It was
part of the half-case which my father had sent to me at Magdeburg
before my arrival. The warden said that he would let me have the
rest of the tobacco as I had need of it. — That was very good, but it
was just as good to find out about the relationship between the
warden and the turnkey. If there is dissension in the devil's realm,
the poor souls have a picnic.

I lit my pipe and lay down on my mattress, and because I was
tired from the trip I fell asleep, and as punishment for claiming that
my pipe lid was made of silver, I burned a hole in my dressing gown.
It had already been singed, but this time it was burned through all
its nine layers, because in the course of time I had mended it again
and again by sewing one layer of cloth over another, so that in this
respect it resembled the shield of Achilles with its nine ox hides. [7]

It was smoldering very nicely, when the turnkey, who was supposed to mind his own business, came in again.

"Holy smoke!" he cried out, "you're on fire!"

He helped me put out the fire. — I thanked him for that, and then he seemed to think that he had the upper hand, so that he became over-friendly and as fawning as a dog that has been whipped. He began by telling me that I should have nothing to do with the warden, because he was friendly to people to their faces, but very deceitful behind their backs. He himself would do what he could to help me. Then he said that he had only been joking before and hoped that I could take a joke.

In short, he was a worthless scoundrel, and I already knew many of his type. He was a scheming wiseacre, who felt malicious joy in another's misfortune, and who was prepared to render any service for his superiors, even though it might be of the most degrading nature. At the same time such people are always cowardly, if one shows them his teeth.

He got a whiff of my tobacco. "Is that good tobacco?" he asked.

"Yes, it is," I answered. "Do you want to try it?"

"Oh, no! How can you say that?" he replied. "Do you think I would let myself get involved in any irregularity like that?"

"Very well," I said, "think no more about it."

Shortly after, Herr Dahlmann came in again, although he had no business in my cell: "Well, how are things?" he asked.

"Very good."

"Do you like the tobacco?"

"Very much so."

"Well, as long as you were so friendly . . . I will try it after all."

Herr Dahlmann filled his pipe: "It's good! It's really very good!"

"Well, then take along a pound," I said.

No, he couldn't do that. A pipeful he could accept, but a pound! What kind of an opinion would I have of him? — However, when Herr Dahlmann went out the door, he had a pound of my tobacco in his hand, and I had a certain opinion of him.

The next day some of the convicts were ordered down to the little rectangular courtyard to shovel snow, so that my comrades might again have a place to walk. All those from the same corridor were permitted to go out into the fresh air for one hour a day.

The men from my corridor had their turn first. I, of course, was not included, because I hadn't received permission as yet; so I climbed on my table and stood and looked at them from above.

Right below the pigeonhole which served as my window there stood a couple of men, one of whom I knew very well, for he was an old friend from Jena. They had short narrow sticks in their hands and they were dueling, just as we used to duel with real sabers in the marketplace of Jena. With every thrust and parry a few whispered words reached my ear: "We two are in the cell to your right, Grashof[8] is at your left" — he was the one who had greeted me in the courtyard upon my arrival. — "The first commandant, Count Hacke, is the worst slave driver. The second commandant, Colonel von Busse,[9] means well, but he can't do anything, because Count Hacke, an old friend of the king from their school days, considers it his duty to harass us as much as possible. For the same reason the provost marshal can't do anything either. The warden is a decent man, but he lives in mortal fear of the first commandant on the one hand and of the turnkey Dahlmann on the other. Dahlmann is a sneaky informer and the meanest of all put together. We have caught the jail attendant K. stealing from us, and so he has to do what we wish. However, he can't do too much, because Dahlmann watches him like a hawk. So keep your eye on Dahlmann. He's a real rotten character and hates us all. He could certainly be bribed, if we were able to pay him a good price.[10] As it is, we have nothing, and so we can't get to him."

These bits of information came up to me piecemeal. My old friend Grashof walked past my window: "I have a knife you can use."

That was something — if only I had it! — Here just as during our imprisonment on remand, knives and forks were taken away right after dinner, and so I had found it necessary to have recourse to an old expedient. I had ground down one side of my old tin spoon, so that I could at least cut myself a piece of bread.

But what was this about Dahlmann? — "Keep your eye on Dahlmann! He won't accept anything from us." — The man had accepted a pound of tobacco from me. — Well, time would tell.

In the afternoon the warden came in and announced that I would be permitted to go out for a walk for one hour. To be sure, the permission had not yet come down from the commandant's headquarters, but he was assuming full responsibility for his action, because I had to have some fresh air. — I accepted gladly, and as I went down into the courtyard, I noticed that a thaw had set in and that the snow was sticking. In order to get a little exercise, I rolled some big snowballs together and placed one on top of the other until I had made a pedestal. Then I took a nice white lump of snow and began to work on it and shape it until I had fashioned a sort of bust. When I looked at my work of art more closely, I was struck by its resemblance to good old Dr. Martin Luther. I filled out his cheeks a little and also flattened his nose a little, and there he stood true to life. It really wasn't such a great work of art, but the jail attendant K., in order to say something nice about it, later remarked that anyone could see that it was a man and not a woman.

I wouldn't have told this story, if something good had not come of it. Right after this recess of one hour the provost marshal had come and seen Dr. Martin standing there. He had the turnkey unlock the door and asked me whether I would like to have my writing and drawing materials. I, of course, answered that I would, and he promised to take care of the matter for me, and he did.

CHAPTER 8

TOWARD evening a few days later I heard my neighbor Grashof's cell being unlocked. That always happened at the same time of day, for the cells were then cleaned up and fresh water brought in. I knocked on the door and Dahlmann unlocked it, although the jail attendant had not yet finished his work in Grashof's cell. I left my cell and walked over to Grashof and was able to exchange a few words with him. When his cell was ready, Dahlmann called out "Herr Grashof!" and Grashof went back into his cell. However, I also went in and without further ado sat down on Grashof's bed. Dahlmann ordered me out, but I didn't budge. I thought he might very well let me sit there with my friend until 9 o'clock, at which time he would come back again to lock the cells for the night.

No, he couldn't do that; that was against regulations. The warden might come, and then there would be hell to pay, because the warden kept a very close check on him.

I told him that the warden would certainly not come and that I might do him another favor some time. Not unintentionally I made very clear reference to the tobacco. And what was the result? — Herr Dahlmann locked us both up in Grashof's cell.

We sat there and talked about old times and also about the present. Grashof gave me a knife and all sorts of small articles, of which he had no need, and we decided that I should make application at headquarters for permission for the two of us to room together. Almost all the other prisoners were living two to a cell, and we thought we might be that fortunate too.

But why do I tell about such petty matters? — Simply because I want to demonstrate how my pound of tobacco knocked into a cocked hat the strict and otherwise rigidly enforced prison regulations. — The jail attendant K. had seen that Dahlmann had broken the rules established by Count Hacke and reported this immediately to the warden. The warden now had the turnkey caught in a trap, so that he couldn't go behind his back and report him to the commandant. In short, Count Hacke's harsh code of rules and regulations, the observance of which was based on mutual fear and vilification among the prison officials, came to naught just because of one pound of tobacco.

Gradually things went so far that before the end of one year I was able to take the keys from the warden's room and unlock all the cells. However, I don't mean to say that we did anything wrong in all this, but I can truthfully say that in the course of four years there were no complaints lodged at headquarters against twenty or thirty young men. This was much to the vexation of the first commandant, who at dress parade was said to have raged at the warden: "Again you have nothing to report? — Report something, and I'll show these people how we deal with prisoners guilty of high treason!" — And will anyone say it was not worth a pound of tobacco to be spared all this harassment and oppression?

At this point someone might ask whether it was right on my part, and whether it was in keeping with Christian morality, that I diverted an official from his duty. To this I must answer: I have often read and heard it spoken from the mouths of very pious people that the behavior of those who represent the highest echelons of human society is not to be evaluated according to any Christian morality. Why then should anyone from the lowest ranks — and we prisoners are from the lowest ranks — be measured by any other standard? The whole world was against us, and if we were not to succumb, we had to defend ourselves — and against whom? Against such a scoundrel whose Christian morality wasn't even worth a pound of tobacco, and whom we later caught stealing cigars from us!

How could one defend himself with Christian morality against a person who almost exploded with wrath because he couldn't inflict even greater punishment on young people who for years had borne all oppression with superhuman patience and who in that time had never given any cause for complaint! The printed regulations issued during our imprisonment at the time of the investigation were severe enough, but he discovered new and more severe regulations and had them posted in our cells! — How could one defend himself with Christian morality against such a beast, who in his abject baseness hatched plans to make our poor miserable lives even more miserable!

And what did the Prussian state do for our Christian morality? — It is a rule and it was a rule then that every prisoner be allowed to go to church on Sunday, and in Silberberg, where I had been, we had always received permission to do so — but here? — That which is granted thieves, robbers, and murderers, was denied us. In four years not a single prisoner had attended a Protestant church service or even seen a pastor. The Catholic prisoners were somewhat more fortunate, but only because of the persistent efforts of the priest Ernst.[1] It must be said to his credit that he surmounted all obstacles placed in his path by general headquarters and made it a point to visit the fortress once a week to hear confession. But the Protestant pastors! Nothing of the kind! They didn't even dream of coming!

Finally we appealed to the commandant with an urgent request for a church service. That produced results, for one day there appeared in the courtyard — it was just during our leisure hour — a doleful-looking creature, who reported that he had been sent to us by the commandant for the purpose of conducting a church service. However, he was quick to add that he had no time just then because he had too many other matters to attend to, but that he would preach a sermon for us the following week in the loft — that was the laundry, where the shirts and trousers and stockings of the prisoners were hung to dry. We told him we were very sorry that he didn't have the time, and if there was any relationship between the quality of his sermon and the laundry as a place of worship, we were also very sorry that we couldn't make use of his soggy commodity. He was apparently very happy to hear that, and he left.

As we had agreed, I then applied at headquarters for permission to room with my friend Grashof. Permission was granted, and so I moved over to his cell. There we sat together and had comfort from each other. Questions were asked and answers given in such haste as though there would be no time for it the next day. We asked questions and received answers, but every answer was a sad one. His information, however, was much more depressing than mine, because conditions had been at their worst here in Magdeburg. At the moment about eight of our comrades were in the military hospital. All the others were sick too, but there wasn't sufficient room in the hospital, and so all had to wait and take their turn. One of the prisoners had tuberculosis, another had a spinal infection; one had lost his hearing, and another had become paralyzed. One prisoner had been set free because he was wasting away, and another because of insanity. Still another had given indications of a mental derangement just about the time I arrived in Magdeburg.

Those were the most serious cases; others had eye infections, liver infections, or high blood pressure, and when I finally came out of this hell, I was practically the only one of all the 24 to 25-year-old men who didn't have at least traces of gray hair.

During my first months in Magdeburg some of my comrades were released. They were for the most part students from Bonn and Halle, who had been sentenced to lesser terms. That was cause for great joy for those who were fortunate enough to be set free, but also for the others who had to remain behind. I must add, however, that the joy in the latter case was not without personal hopes and wishes, for we reasoned that if they were freed, we would also have to be freed soon. We were not any more guilty than they.

The release of these prisoners had additional significance for Grashof and myself, because it worked to our advantage that we were thus able to move up to the second floor and into a corner cell, which was separated from the other cells by the warden's quarters. That was very convenient, for whenever the warden had a letter or anything else to deliver to us, we pulled up a stool and he sat down with us for a while — for time hung heavy on his hands too, and furthermore, the other prisoners couldn't hear anything from this location.

One word led to another, and although newspapers were prohibited, some of the news trickled through to us, and we thus found out what was going on in the outside world. — Grashof was Catholic and occasionally received visits from the priest Ernst, an intelligent and vivacious man, who brightened up our lives with his cheerfulness and often turned our minds to more pleasant thoughts. I also received occasional visits — whether with or without permission of the general I don't know — from a Herr Kämpf,[2] the manager of the well-known commercial house of Müller and Weichsel,[3] and that gentleman always thought of some suitable way to make me happy. Every Sunday the reliable old porter of his store came and brought me something special for my dinner. It wasn't just one of those little covered dishes that the pious rich in their good moments send to the poor and sick. I should say not! It was a real substantial roast, big enough to take the wrinkles out of a couple of shriveled-up young stomachs for a few days. Until my last hour in Magdeburg the man treated me like a brother, and for that reason I

was under the impression that he had been commissioned by my
father. But that was not the case at all! My father knew nothing
about it; the man had acted out of the goodness of his heart. But why
all that kindness for me? — I don't know. — He has passed away
now; I never asked him about it and never even thanked him for it.

When he had noticed that I had some talent for drawing, this
generous and esteemed man brought me a box with pastel crayons.
Now I was all prepared to make some sketches, but the sad fact of
the matter was that the color wouldn't stick to the paper. I tried
everything, but nothing would help. I struggled for some solution
for almost a year before the warden came up with the very simple information that the color had to be rubbed into the paper with one's
little finger.

From that one can see how difficult it was for a prisoner to help
himself and to learn something. Usually people say, "You had plenty
of time to learn something; no one disturbed you at your work." —
Oh, how wise these people are! The only prisoners to continue in
their field of specialization were those who had already finished
their study at the university and who had a good comprehensive
knowledge of their subject. The rest of us simply gave up and resumed
our studies later, but in other fields. Much time was spent in cooking
and the darning of stockings and mending of clothes and shoes. All
these little tasks had to be taken care of, and that was our good fortune, for it was an easy and beneficial way to pass the time and to
divert our thoughts to other things.

For that reason I can very well understand that a man may
succeed in acquiring manual skills in prison, but a prison has never
produced an artist or a scholar who can be of any real benefit to the
world. Music may possibly be an exception, although that didn't
apply in our case either, for all singing and whistling was forbidden.
One of the prisoners who knew something about music had constructed a kind of accordion, but this instrument was taken from him
on orders of the commandant.

I took up portrait painting; my old friend Grashof was my first
subject. I painted him from the right and from the left, from the
front and from the back, with pencil, with black crayon, and with
colored crayon, once with an azure background, once with a
background of clouds, and once even with a rosy glow just as when
the sun sets in the evening. With this last picture I took particular

pains, but one could never tell by looking at it.

When Grashof had been fully exploited, it was then the warden's turn. The picture was to be given to his fiancée, and therefore I had to make him look handsome and give him a friendly expression. It was difficult, but I think I produced a very good likeness. Fortunately, he had a rather large nose — that's always good for a beginner. I started with the nose, and once I had the nose, the rest had to follow, whether it wished or not. But the handsome look and the friendly expression? I managed to catch that too. I made his eyes squint a little, puffed up his cheeks a little, raised the corners of his mouth by a half-inch, and added a couple of real lines, so that it looked like a buttonhole that a skilled tailor had reinforced at both ends.

Much honor accrued to me from this picture. The warden in his great joy showed it to all his comrades, and now everyone wanted me to paint his picture. With all kinds of tricks the warden was induced to let my friends take turns in coming into my cell. My atelier was as good as any other. I had a very good lighting from above; it was the best lighting from the north that any painter might wish. In addition, I had one great advantage over my other artist colleagues: the people who sat for me were used to sitting; they had great endurance. If I pushed up my table so tight that I had them in close quarters on one side, and Grashof moved up his chair to within a half-foot to block off the other side, they were then caught as in a vise. They couldn't escape; they had to sit there, for the door was locked.

I must now confess that during this time I was guilty of many grave sins against God's image on earth. I made paintings of faces the likes of which had never before been seen nor will they ever be seen again, and I painted them in colors which otherwise have never existed in this world. — I did fairly well with the brunets, but I had my difficulties whenever I had to paint a towhead. Unfortunately, I was accustomed to shade the yellow hair with green, and I also had the stupid habit of adding too much red coloring to the face. As a result my towheads from a distance looked for all the world like pineapples, especially when there was a green coat underneath.

My pictures were sent for the most part to parents and sisters and brothers for Christmas and for birthdays, and if any of them are still alive, I wish to take this opportunity to ask their pardon if they were ever thrown into a fright on such a festive occasion at the sight of their beloved kinsmen. — In any case, when I sent my father my self-portrait, which I thought was an excellent likeness, he wrote that it had given him a terrible shock and that I must have changed in appearance very much.

Be that as it may, from that time on we were able to pay visits to one another, and even though Dahlmann looked askance at that and put many obstacles in our way, he was nevertheless placated with an occasional pound of tobacco. When I later caught him stealing some cigars which a good friend had sent to Grashof from Lübeck, and when the provost marshal himself honored me by having me paint his portrait, Dahlmann's authority was completely broken. He then walked up and down the long corridor like a cherubim who has put his flaming sword in his sheath, because he has had his wings singed.

As far as painting is concerned, the portrait of the provost marshal was really the highlight of my stay in Magdeburg. — I had to leave my hole and go over to the warden's room, for the big event was to take place there. — I brought all my drawing and painting materials with me; I spread out a sheet of paper, which had a very beautiful greenish hue, and all my crayons were sharpened. However, as I came in, I was quite taken aback, because the room had a large window of the usual type, but none of that beautiful light from above to which I was now accustomed.

I began by moving the provost marshal around the room from one corner to another in order to find the best light, but nothing seemed to help until the warden attached his bedspread to the lower part of the window. — As bad luck would have it, the provost marshal was a towhead and furthermore, he had no eyebrows — and I, poor wretch, had the bad habit of always beginning with the eyebrows. — What to do now? — Usually I would first make a rough sketch of a couple of eyebrows and then let the nose, just as it was, short or long, dangle down from there. But what was I to do now? He had no eyebrows and I had nothing to begin with. From the artist's point of view his nose was also just barely adequate. I had taken too much upon myself; I was completely bewildered. However, I had to start somewhere and I had to start with some hair — that was simply my habit — and so I started with the mustache.

That caused me no regrets, and if any of my artist colleagues should find themselves in a similar predicament, they can take heart and follow my example. Before long the warden, who always used to look over my shoulder, said it was a good likeness. The man was expressing his considered opinion and he knew what he was talking about, for he had observed me at my work often enough and had developed his art appreciation from a study of my paintings.

Before long the face was completed; it was very beautiful except that it had a rather greenish tinge, for which the green paper was to blame. Then, however, came the uniform, blue with a red collar, and then the gold epaulets and the shiny buttons. — Whoever attempts to paint a Prussian uniform for the first time will find that he is faced with serious difficulties. That was my experience too. I had some Prussian blue and vermilion and chrome yellow in my box, and so I went to work with enthusiasm. I had once read that "in a portrait incidentals are to be treated with a certain casual originality," and therefore I followed that advice. It was casual enough, but the originality left something to be desired, because when I had finished painting the uniform, the warden and the provost marshal both said that it wouldn't do! They thought that the Prussian blue coat was adequate at the best, but the epaulets and the buttons looked as though they hadn't been polished in seven years, and the collar was no provost marshal's collar at all, but just a plain ordinary Prussian postmaster's collar. — I was very annoyed at that, but what they said was true. It did look somewhat yellowish, because I had apparently been taken in with the vermilion, which was nothing but plain red minium. Furthermore, I had again shaded too much with that confounded red coloring.

I had already learned enough about the art of painting not to let myself get flabbergasted. I said I would take the picture with me and we could discuss it again in a few days. In my cell I kept moving around trying to get the best possible light on the painting. I polished the provost marshal's epaulets and buttons until Grashof took pity on me and told me they were now shiny enough. But, my goodness, that collar! Even today, whenever I see the collar on the uniform of a Prussian infantryman, my sins come back to haunt me again. I couldn't get it right; I simply couldn't get it the way I wished! Finally, pure chance came to my rescue; Grashof's canary bespattered the collar with a drop of water, so that it became a beautiful scarlet at that one spot. — I thought of giving it a coat of varnish. No, that wouldn't do! Varnish is too oily; it might make it look like a real grease spot. Gum arabic might have helped, but I had none at hand. I thought and thought and finally I hit upon sugar. That would do it! I dissolved a few pieces of sugar in water and then began to test my theory by touching up the edges very carefully with a paint brush. It was beautiful! I took courage and touched up the entire collar, and before long I succeeded in painting what anyone would have taken for a real Prussian military collar.

To be sure, Grashof said that the collar was too shiny compared to the rest of the painting, but what did Grashof know about art? I placed my provost marshal upon the table, lay down on my bed, and admired him until nine o'clock in the evening, when the sentry called "Lights out." — It is possible that Raphael looked with admiration at his Madonna for a long time too, but I don't believe he was so much in love with her as I with the provost marshal. I lay there for a long time, but I couldn't fall asleep for joy. — A Prussian officer in full uniform! That really means something! Finally, I did fall asleep, but then I didn't wake up until the sun was already high in the heavens.

And as I awoke — good Lord in heaven! — this time Grashof had not acted like a friend; he could have prevented it — there were a thousand flies nibbling away at the provost marshal's collar. Furthermore, they had made their own contribution to the painting by adding little black pinpoints to my most beautiful highlight halftones.

That was what I call bad luck. — And what now? — The only thing I could do was to varnish it over again and keep the flies away until the picture was out of my hands. That's what I did; I got rid of my work of art, but I never found out what the provost marshal's dear wife had to say about the likeness, or whether the provost marshal had the picture hung in his official residence as a keepsake from me. So much is certain: I was now in favor with him and the warden, and this worked to the advantage not only of me but also of the other prisoners as well.

CHAPTER 9

ONE occurrence which had great significance for all of us was still to take place. It was to indicate very clearly how successful we had become in the abolition of the commandant's prison regulations. — My father had written me that I should have a coat made for myself. One day the warden came to my cell and told me that I should go to his room, because the tailor was there and he wished to take my measurements for a coat. I went over in my dressing gown. However, there were two people standing in the warden's room; one didn't look like a tailor at all, but the other looked all the more so. Therefore I asked the latter whether he wished to take my measurements, but before the tailor could answer, the other man came up and asked if I were one of the political prisoners.

I couldn't very well deny that.

"Then you certainly know my brother:[1] my name is Heinzmann and I'm from the Rhineland."

"Of course," I said, "I know your brother very well. He's up on the third floor in the same cell as Messerich."[2]

He was about to reply to that, but at that moment the warden came in. The tailor then went about his business.

The tailor had not quite finished with that when the door was opened again and the porter from the "City of Prague" came in with a basket full of bottles. The warden opened his eyes in surprise, but the Rhinelander didn't give him much time to stand there gaping. With the most polite expression in the world and in a friendly and spontaneous manner so characteristic of the jovial Rhinelanders he said that he had taken the liberty of presenting the warden with a dozen bottles of vintage '34 wine. — The warden was now a sight to behold! — The tailor was present, I was present — He said he couldn't accept it and that it was too much, and all the while he was nodding his head and shrugging his shoulders, as though he were a puppet operated by strings in the hands of someone in the planks of the ceiling.

Then I learned how resolute and determined a real Rhinelander can be. Without further ado he pulled out a corkscrew, opened a bottle, took a water glass which stood upon the table, filled it with wine, and had the warden smell its fragrance. That helped! He liked the aroma, and now had a distinct desire to taste it too. Persuasion helps and he was persuaded; he emptied the entire glass.

"I'll fetch your brother now," he said, "but . . . ." and he looked at me and the tailor.

The tailor was a man of culture; he understood the hint and left. I didn't want to do any less and was about to go too.

The Rhinelander, however, stood right in front of the door and said, "You stay here! He'll stay here, won't he, warden?"

Now that confounded fellow in the planks of the ceiling began to pull at the strings again, and the warden shrugged his shoulders, moved his hands up and down and shuffled his feet, but the upshot of it all was that I stayed there.

Heinzmann's brother came and the two Rhinelanders fell into an embrace. It was a great joy with many questions and answers, and because the brothers in their happiness couldn't be expected to sit down, the warden and I took our places upon the sofa and drank Rhine wine. Thus we shared in their joy and found pleasure for ourselves, and so we were all happy.

After the first expression of emotion had passed, the brothers sat down and helped us with the business at hand. The warden complimented the Rhinelander on the excellent quality of the wine.

"Then do it justice," said the stranger as he refilled the warden's beer glass, for it was the only glass we had.

Now anyone can understand that under these circumstances one beer glass is not enough, and so I had the bright idea of getting two additional glasses from my cell. Since the warden could not very conveniently get out from behind the table, I took my key from the board on which the keys were hanging and was about to go.

Turning around at the door, I said, "Warden, I'm going to bring Grashof along too."

"Yes," said Heinzmann," and I'll get some glasses and bring Messerich along too."

The warden began to shrug his shoulders again, but it wasn't as emphatically as before, and finally he merely nodded.

Just as I came out, Dahlmann was walking up and down in front

of the warden's room. He had been eavesdropping in order to hear
what was going on, and when he saw that I, an unqualified apprentice, was taking over his position as turnkey, he asked me what right
I had to do that.

"Herr Dahlmann," I said, "you can see that I have just come out
of the warden's room with this key, and as you know, he is in his
room. Now if he raises no objections, I don't believe you can raise
any objections either. Furthermore, I want to advise you not to make
any trouble for me; you know how we stand. On the other hand, if
you are sensible about this, I'll see to it that you'll have your share of
the fun too."

He replied that he really had no objections.

I unlocked my cell door and fetched Grashof and the beer glasses.
Heinzmann also came back with his cell mate, and now the company
was all present. We got "organized," as they say, not only inside
around the table, but also outside, so that no one might take us by
surprise. Dahlmann had to patrol the lower corridor, and to keep
him company in his loneliness he was given a bottle of wine. We had
the prison attendant K. stand on a table in our corridor, and he was
to keep an eye on the front courtyard in case the provost marshal
should come. He didn't get a bottle of wine, but merely the suggestion that he should cough if he became thirsty. On that afternoon he
did his share of coughing, and it didn't hurt him in the least, except
that toward evening he coughed himself right off the table.

We sat in the room and completely forgot everything that had
taken place during the last five years of our life. Here we were again
at a drinking bout and it was just as though we were picking up
again where we had left off the last time in Bonn and Jena. The
warden was looked upon as the freshman of the group, and
Messerich, because he was the oldest, was given the task of teaching
him at short notice the basic rules of the "Komment."[3] Above all he
made it clear to the warden that a dashing young freshman was
always supposed to drink "bottoms up." In this respect the warden
proved to be a very good student, and because we wanted to set a
good example for him, we were all soon in that condition where singing usually begins.

At one time Messerich had been a Catholic priest and had taken
the first three vows. He could sing very well, because in his former
calling singing was quite important for the performance of his

ecclesistical duties. In his highest pitch and most beautiful voice he therefore struck up the tune to "Freedom which I love; freedom which fills my heart," and we others joined in with great feeling.

Suddenly the sentry interrupted our "Freedom which we love" by banging against the door with the butt of his gun and shouting, "Quiet in there!"

The warden jumped up; he had completely forgotten that the sentries had orders to forbid all singing and whistling. — That was very unfortunate for my comrades who for five years had not been allowed to sing and who now had such a wonderful opportunity to do so. Here it was Heinzmann who saved the situation. He tore open the door, invited the musketeer to take a look into the room, and then he asked whether this looked like a prison to him.

Well, the sentry agreed that he had never seen a prison such as this with so many bottles and glasses on the table. Then he asked us not to take it amiss, because he was new on the job.

Everything was now in order again, but our dashing freshman was quite upset. "For heaven's sake, no more singing!"

That was easy to say, but difficult to carry out. — After a lengthy discussion with the warden it was agreed that we had to sing, but we would have to sing softly, very softly.

That was just as if one were to say: wash my fur, but don't get me wet; or as if during the most explosive time of the French Revolution people had said: heads must fall, but gently, very gently!

The first one to break this new agreement was the warden himself. He had a musical instrument which looked somewhat like a guitar and he had the voice to go with it, but the only songs he knew were old, faded and time-worn love songs, which had to be dusted off and polished up before they were halfway appropriate. And he did just that and sang them with great feeling. Each of us also wanted to hear how his voice sounded after so many years or whether it had been completely corroded through inactivity. Before long therefore the singing was again in full swing.

Who knows what finally would have happened if, as I have said, the prison attendant because of all his coughing had not fallen from the table just at that moment. He landed on his back with a very loud crash right against the warden's door. Upon hearing the racket we all rushed out, and there he lay on the floor with the table on top of him, as though he had taken the table top for a bedspread and had covered himself with it to keep warm. — He told us later that because of our singing he had been unable to get results from his coughing, and so he had tried knocking, but he had leaned too far over the edge of the table and had lost his balance.

At that moment, however, he said nothing; he was very quiet, and as we pulled him out from under the table and had him sit up straight, he was very dizzy either from the fall or from all that coughing. However, when the warden reproved him sharply and started to say that he should be ashamed of himself . . . ., he had enough presence of mind to quickly interrupt him and say, "I think the provost marshal is coming."

Well, now we were in real trouble! Grashof and I rushed into our cell, Heinzmann and Messerich raced up the stairs, the warden and the Rhinelander threw all the full and empty bottles together with the glasses into the basket, and the prison attendant locked us in our cells. Now for all we cared, the provost marshal could come, but he didn't come after all.

The next day, as we thought about it, it seemed to us very much as though it had been a trumped-up game just to disrupt our party. However, we didn't mind; we had spent a happy afternoon and had thrown the lovely prison regulations into utter confusion, for after that we went visiting almost every evening in one cell or other. We talked and drank a glass of beer together, we played chess and sometimes cards, and we read to one another. We also exchanged books, which was forbidden.

Books and newspapers were the two things we missed most of all. Newspapers were completely forbidden, as were almost all books except those of a technical nature. One incident, which took place before I arrived in Magdeburg, may serve as an example of how strictly this rule was enforced. One prisoner wished to acquire a copy of the *Brockhaus Encyclopedia* and another wanted to have an atlas of the ancient world. Both requests were denied, because the encyclopedia, according to Count von Hacke, contained "revolutionary articles" and "maps are never permitted, because they might abet an attempt to escape." — That was a very amusing conclusion on his part, but a very severe one for us.

Occasionally, however, we did get to learn a little of what was going on in the outside world from the priest Ernst or from the medical officer Reiche or from the warden and sometimes even from an old newspaper in which cheese or herring had been wrapped. Toward autumn of that year (1837) we were told that our case was to come before the Federal Council, and that there was a possibility that we might be granted amnesty at the fortieth anniversary of the accession of King Frederick William III to the throne. That stirred up much discussion and hope; some of us were optimistic, but others were very dubious as to what would actually happen. One of the latter group even used the disrepectful term "the old clod" instead of "the old king." My old Captain,[4] who was later imprisoned with me at the fortress of Graudenz, considered that a case of lese-majesty, and was so infuriated that he immediately challenged the guilty party to a duel with scimitars to be fought on the first day after their release. — That's the kind of regicides we were!

Thus we continued to hope; we were certain we would be released! However, it didn't turn out as we had expected. Duke Karl of Mecklenburg,[5] as president of the Federal Council, had spoken out against us and had cast the deciding vote; we had to remain in prison. That didn't exactly net him many pious wishes from us.

One time shortly after that the medical officer came to us and told us that Duke Karl of Mecklenburg was dead.

"We already know that," we said.

He replied that was impossible, because he had just come from the general, Count Hacke, and the general in his very presence had opened a telegram containing this information. Nothing of this was as yet to be found in any newspaper.

We said that might be, but nevertheless we already knew it.

"From whom?" he asked.

"From Z . . .,"[6] we answered. "He told us this morning."

"From Z . . .? From Z . . .?" he asked shaking his head, "From Z . . . because of whom I came here today? Remarkable! Remarkable!"

With that he went out the door.

Z . . . was a splendid and powerfully built fellow whom I had first met when he was passing through Jena. Here in Magdeburg just as at that time he was the tallest and strongest of all of us. He was a true and loyal friend to me. That I know, because later in Graudenz we were placed in the same cell, but his mind had suffered. They said it had happened at that moment when his death sentence was pronounced. I don't know about that, but at this time he imagined that he could make predictions and foretell the future from the movement of crows, sparrows, and canaries. He said that a beautiful lady in a black silk dress came to him every evening, sat down beside his bed, and told him what was going to happen. — He had prophesied many things, but nothing of what he said had ever come true. But he did foretell the death of Duke Karl of Mecklenburg. That is the truth! There was one other thing which he predicted in most minute detail — but I'll tell about that in proper time.

In his opinion the crows were the bad birds, and the canaries, some of which were kept by almost each prisoner, were the good ones. Once it happened, very strange to say, that almost all the canaries in the entire prison became sick within one week. Although they were fed differently, they all suffered from the same type of cramp and toppled over in their cages, and some of them even died.

This had disturbed Z . . . greatly and the medical officer had to put him in the hospital and later he was taken to the charité[7] in Berlin where he remained for three quarters of a year in order to be cured. Presumably sound again, he was discharged, but when he joined us later at the fortress of Graudenz he was just as sick as he had been. It didn't occur to the Prussian government to free this poor creature whom it had all but destroyed in such an atrocious way.

To my great joy I have since learned that freedom has again returned to him what servitude had taken from him, and that my old "Frenchy" is alive and well.

As I mentioned before, we all took our turn in the hospital, and in due time it was my turn too. The medical officer had a compassionate heart and, furthermore, we were all in such poor physical condition that he could in all good conscience accept the responsibility of admitting us to the hospital. It was there that I experienced an incident which threw the commandant's office into complete disorder, and which in time would be of the greatest significance to us.

CHAPTER 10

IN order to tell this properly, I must first tell of the nature of our living quarters and the conditions under which we lived. — We lived in two rooms; in one room which lay to the front three of us slept, and in a large room to the rear the number of prisoners varied from six to eight. We received good food, were allowed to go out for a walk for four hours every day and to associate with our friends without having any difficulties placed in our way. Of course, here too the cells were locked, but in time the guards began to ignore all kinds of little and great liberties that we took. Those of my comrades who had been here for a long time knew this sergeant and that surgeon; they knew which ones they could trust and which ones they had to be wary of. They sent off and received letters surreptitiously. They were able to procure cash money and they found ways of acquiring other clothing than their blue and white-striped hospital garb. Yes, before my time at Magdeburg two or three of them had even stolen out of the hospital at night and had not reappeared until morning.

How they had accomplished this I don't know, and if I knew, I wouldn't tell! — In any case, they had become acquainted with various people in town, had money, and didn't live badly. Many a piece of roast meat and many a bottle of Moselle or Rhine wine were smuggled in, and even though we made every effort to get the full bottles in, getting rid of the empty ones was too troublesome. Therefore, we piled them up very skillfully behind the screen of our large old fireplace, and Heinzmann was appointed architect of this tower of Babel.

Now it happened that cholera broke out in town and in the hospital. The medical officer, therefore, often came to see us, because he had many things to attend to in our cells. Two of our friends, who were medical students, once asked if they might be permitted to accompany him on his visits to the sick. He granted them this permission, because he was firmly convinced that this disease was noncontagious. He even took along with him his only two little sons.

Whether he was correct in this belief or not, I don't know; I merely know that Wagner and Reinhardt had no fear, nor did the rest of
us either. Finally, however, when these two fellows came back with
some pieces of lungs and liver and intestines and started to cut them
up on a wooden cutting-board and munch them, they were escorted out
of the large room into the small front room. And that's exactly what the
rascals wanted, as one can see from the later course of events.

One day I was out walking when I passed a man in the uniform of
an army doctor. As he walked by, he looked at me with a grin on his
face. I wanted to get a closer look at him, but he turned his back and
went straight to our room. — Directly opposite us in the same corridor there lived another army doctor, and so I thought this man was
paying a visit to a colleague of his. I continued my walk until it was
time to be locked up again.

When I returned to my cell, I found someone sitting there with his
back turned toward me. He wore a hospital jacket, to be sure, but he
had a bald head. Among our friends there were only two with bald
heads. One of them, Piter, had lubricated and smeared his head with
so much grease that he had already produced a short growth of
lamb's wool, and the other, Breyer,[1] had been given his freedom
three months ago. Who could this be? — I went closer — it was
Breyer, good-natured, light-hearted old Breyer, who had given
"Uncle" Dambach so much trouble, and who always had a new joke
ready for every bad situation. Once when his father was visiting him,
he came running up to us and said, "Just think, my old man has a
bald head too!"

And out of friendship this brave fellow had dared to put his
faithful old bald head into the lion's jaw. However, it wasn't so entirely thoughtless; his friendship had something else in mind.

That night he stayed with us, and he had a great deal to talk
about. The next morning as an army doctor he walked straight out
the hospital door.

After he had gone, Wagner came up to me and asked, "Charles
douze,"[2] — that was my nickname, but the men from Pomerania
and Mecklenburg always said "Korl Dusz" — "Charles douze,
would you like to escape from here?"

"Why not?" I replied. "Very much so, my dear sir!"

"Can you get hold of some money?"

"From no one except possibly my father."

"Will he send you some?"

"I don't know," I answered. "Until now he wouldn't listen to any talk of escape."

"We'll have to try," he said. "Sit down and write a letter; I'll see to it that the letter is delivered, and your father can trust the person who will help me with this."

I sat down and wrote a "written" letter to my father.[3] I told him that an escape would be very beneficial to me, that I would arrange everything very ingeniously, that I had a couple of real good associates, and that there wouldn't be the slightest chance of being caught again. I would go to Sweden, become a farmer, buy myself an estate in Scania,[4] or possibly even a small earldom, and then I would steal over to Mecklenburg once in a while to visit him. For all this glory all I needed was a couple of hundred talers. He should supply that much; I myself would procure the rest later.

Wagner took my letter, and a week later he brought me the answer. — My father wouldn't do it. He said I would most certainly have to be released soon. — I received no money, and so I had to remain in prison.

I don't know the name of the man who delivered the letter, but he came within a hair's-breadth of being caught. The whole affair would have come to light, if my sister, the quick-thinking little imp, had not shown the cleverest ingenuity. — I must tell about that incident now.

At this time Bönninger also escaped from Silberberg, and the provost marshal there, who was a Mecklenburger and sometimes corresponded with my father, was bewailing all his troubles in one of his letters.[5] He wrote that they wanted to charge him and General von Langen with dereliction of duty because of Bönninger's escape. My father replied to the provost marshal's letter and informed him that he had received a letter from a man who was a complete stranger to him and who had offered to help me escape. My father added that he had rejected the offer. The commandant of Silberberg then took the letter and sent it to the "blessed" Prussian ministry with the comment that if things continued in this way, and if people from outside the fortress were actively engaged in an attempt to free the prisoners, then as far as he was concerned, the devil should guard the prisoners; he would prefer to accept any other most difficult task.

The Prussian ministry appealed to the Mecklenburg government — at that time there was no ministry in Mecklenburg — with the request that it be on the alert and try to find out who had written the letter to my father. Sure enough, one day, as my father was eating his dinner, a grand ducal police commissioner arrived to inquire about the letter. Now my father became frightened, because he realized that he had been guilty of a big stupidity. But this time luck was with him! — My sister, the wily little imp, saw that my father was in a jam. She knew where the stupid letter was, and she left the room immediately to get it. Then she went into the kitchen where a fire was still burning and held the letter to the flame. When it was completely burned up, she placed the ashes on a clean plate, went to the police commissioner and said, "Here's the letter!"

And then what? — My father pretended that he could not recall the name, and my sister, the little rascal, had saved a good man from a long sentence of fortress imprisonment. — I always liked this story.

But what was going on in the hospital at Magdeburg? — I knew which way the wind was blowing, and I also knew that I was not involved in the affair at all. The wisest thing for me to do was to pretend ignorance of everything, and that is what I did.

In the meantime fresh replacements had come into the hospital, including a couple of our comrades who were seriously ill. The place became so crowded, that one day the medical officer ordered four of us — myself included — to be transferred to a small room on the second floor. That same evening, when everything was locked up, the provost marshal came, had the door on the first floor unlocked, and delivered a letter to one of our men. In his presence the door was again locked by the sergeant on guard duty, in his presence the key was delivered to the hospital warden, and the next morning Wagner and Reinhardt were gone.

How they accomplished this, I don't know from personal observation, nor did any of the other prisoners either, but little by little we learned something by asking questions of one another. One prisoner knew this and another knew something else; and finally we even got to read the letter they had written to Count Hacke, the first commandant, in which they told him in detail how they had done it. — It was a mean and sarcastic letter and I'll speak about it later. For the time being I'll just say this.

Out of pure friendship for Wagner, little Breyer, little old light-hearted Breyer, in order to set his friend free, had run the risk of losing his own recently obtained freedom. Anyone can understand what that means, but only a man who has been freed after many years of imprisonment and knows how sweet freedom is, can truly appraise the courage required for such a deed. — Breyer had to leave family and fatherland. He became a refugee far from home and jeopardized his whole future, but he accomplished his purpose; he set his friend free. I understand that he has fared very well; he is said to be one of the most popular writers in Vienna, and I am happy from the bottom of my heart that he has received a good reward for his brave deed.

Earlier in the guise of an army doctor he had come to the fortress and made wax impressions of the locks. He became acquainted with a washerwoman, who did the laundry for a medical officer, and induced her to smuggle in under the laundry a couple of uniforms and whatever else his two friends inside needed. Then on this day about which I am speaking he had come from Berlin and was just about to open the door with a skeleton key, when, as I have said, the provost marshal came in to deliver the letter. — Breyer had just enough time to beat a hasty retreat to the toilet, and there he sat until the air was cleared — that is, outside.

After the provost marshal had left and everything had been locked up very securely, Breyer unlocked the door again, and the other two quickly threw themselves into the uniforms, and then all three very casually walked out the door, one as an artillery lieutenant and the other two as army doctors. With a post chaise, which was waiting for them in the marketplace, they rode to Hamburg, and from there sailed to Helgoland. — I'm just telling this from hearsay, and the facts of the matter may have been slightly different, but what happened after that I saw with my own eyes.

Very early the next morning there was a big commotion in the room below us. One of our friends, the bookseller Cornelius[6] from Stralsund, who was a know-it-all and who could never keep his mouth shut, opened the window and called up to us.

We looked out the window: "What is it?"

"They're gone!" he shouted.

"Who's gone?"

"Wagner and Reinhardt," he said.

"Well, let them be gone, you jackass! What's the idea of shouting like that?" we said and slammed the window shut again.

However, some other people undoubtedly heard all this noise too, because the warden soon came running with the keys long before the regular time to unlock the doors. Shortly after that there was great tumult and confusion and a running back and forth of sentries, attendants, warden, and noncommissioned officers. Finally, the president of the hospital commission, old Lieutenant Colonel Heidenreich, came tottering in. He was the oldest officer in the entire Prussian army, for he had served as a lieutenant under "Old Fritz." Now it became very noisy down below, because in spite of his age the old man didn't rant and rage badly at all. When he was finished downstairs, he came up to us.

"Gentlemen," he said, "two of your comrades have gone to the devil."

"Very good," we said.

"The devil it's good!" he replied. "If I tell this to General Count von Hacke, he'll give me a good dressing down."

We told him we couldn't do anything about it.

He answered by saying that he knew what kind of people we were, and that we were just as guilty as those who had escaped.

We said that was not true. It wasn't our job to keep them under arrest, and we hadn't escaped with them either. The matter was none of our concern.

Then the old man became enraged. "I'll see to it that you will not escape. I'll place a guard here in this room to watch over you day and night."

Now it was my turn to become angry. I told him he could do anything he had a right to do; he could station guards in front or in back, but we would not tolerate having them in the room.

Now the old man was furious! He started to rage at me! Who knows what would have happened if the medical officer had not come in — also out of breath.

He called to him, "Lieutenant Colonel, Lieutenant Colonel, don't be over-hasty! Everything is in order; I have just informed the general of the escape. All prisoners with the exception of three, for whom any movement might be extremely dangerous because of their physical condition, will be returned to their cells this evening."

Now the old man calmed down; now he wouldn't have to go to

the general and receive the dressing down he feared.

In the meantime the provost marshal and the judge advocate had also arrived, and all our comrades were brought up to us on the second floor, so that the gentlemen might have a clear field down below in order to ascertain on the spot how the prisoners had made their escape. We could listen to all their conversation and we could also see their frantic activity, because the floor was not one which was reinforced with beams and straw, so that there were wide gaps in the planks.

At this point I wish to mention that our very sick friends remained in this second-floor room, even when the room below was later set up as a hospital ward for the cholera patients. Thus by day and night they had to listen to the moaning and groaning and the spasmodic fits of the poor dying creatures below. This was just another little example of human kindness!

The first conclusion drawn by the gentlemen downstairs was also the most simple: namely, the prisoners had made their escape through the door. However, the provost marshal disputed this, because he himself had been present the previous evening when the door was locked for the night. The second possibility was that they had escaped through the windows, but the old iron bars were still intact, and no one could possibly have squeezed through. The third possiblity was, of course, the chimney. On his own initiative the judge advocate opened the fireplace, but he was not nearly as skillful as my friend Heinzmann, because as soon as the fireplace was opened the entire tower of bottles crashed down on him. That evoked great laughter from all below except from the lieutenant colonel, who reprimanded the hospital overseer for permitting such an irregularity. Once again, however, the army doctor interceded and made it clear to the old gentleman that the bottles were after all empty, and that an empty bottle can do no harm to a sick prisoner. The old gentleman had to acknowledge that, and when they parted, once again reconciled to one another, they knew exactly as much as they had known in the first place.

Toward evening those of us who were able to walk were brought back to our cells, and — oh, good God, how things had changed there! All our "acquisitions," as they are called nowadays, were lost. The warden's ears were hanging like those of a drenched poodle, and Dahlmann was exultant. His Excellency, General Count Hacke,

came in person to the detention cell area, and after huffing and puff-
ing like a locomotive that has gone off the track, he ordered the im-
mediate dismissal of the jail attendant K. as a warning to all others.
— Now everyone was going around on tiptoes.

Two days after the escape of Wagner and Reinhardt an amusing
incident took place between the judge advocate and the provost
marshal. We found out all the details later, when conditions had
again improved.

The two men met in the warden's room, and the judge advocate
said, "We'll certainly recapture them," and by that he meant
Wagner and Reinhardt.

"No question about it," answered the provost marshal. "Where
can they possibly go? The warrants for their arrest . . . ."

"Yes," the judge advocate interrupted, "I've been meaning to ask
what you have done about the warrants."

"I?" asked the provost marshal.

"Yes, you," answered the judge advocate.

"You are supposed to take care of that," said the provost marshal.

"The devil I am," answered the judge advocate, "that's your
responsibility."

Well, to make a long story short, the warrants had not yet been
issued.

After six or seven days we received the comforting news that our
good friends had arrived safely in Helgoland. They reported this
happy circumstance to the general in a very amusing, but sarcastic
letter, and the following day we were able to read this letter in a very
neat copy. — How this was made possible, I don't know, and if I
knew, I wouldn't tell. — But it's true! His Excellency was furious,
and what annoyed him most of all was the fact that the escaped
prisoners informed him that the guards, due to the presence of the
"artillery officer," had saluted them with all dignity, and that they
had walked out of the hospital with the usual military honors.

For His Excellence, or His "Pestilence," as the farmers say in our
part of the country, that was a rather bitter pill to swallow, and annoying also were the reprimands which he received from Berlin. It
occurred to him, therefore, to put the entire blame on our good army
doctor for admitting healthy prisoners to the hospital. However, the
army doctor was too smart for him; he was not the man to let anyone
take the butter from his bread. He demanded that an investigation

committee be brought to the fortress to examine the state of our health. One day, as a result of this request, three men appeared: Major General Büttner of the medical corps, Privy Councillor André, and Major von Lamprecht of the engineering corps.

Grashof and I were the first to be visited, because our cell was located right at the staircase. Major von Lamprecht recorded the dimensions of the cell and also of the window and the distance of the window from the floor. The other two gentlemen asked us whether we had any complaints to make about our health.

Grashof answered that he was suffering from a liver ailment.

The major general asked what he was doing about it.

Grashof answered that he drank quassia tea.

The privy councillor asked me what my trouble was, and I told him that I had been transferred from Silberberg to Magdeburg because of my weak eyes.

He looked about, shook his head, and said, "To this place where you never have any direct sunlight, where you have nothing but a weakly reflected light?"

He examined my eyes and advised me when washing not to wet my hair so much as was my custom. Otherwise, I would run the risk of getting glaucoma.

The three also sampled our drinking water and then left.

In other cells they inspected our marvelous controlled ventilation, and then they went out into the courtyard where we were permitted to take our walks. There they smelled something very unpleasant. In the courtyard there were two cesspools into which ran the human waste from approximately five hundred men living in the cells. To our left in a westerly direction there was a large iron foundry, from which we got the full benefit of coal-gas fumes.

This fresh air was not to their liking, as one can well understand, and as honest men, which they really were, they pronounced the following opinion: "The political prisoners in the detention cells of Magdeburg lack the three most vital factors necessary for the preservation of human life — fresh air, light, and warmth. Furthermore, their drinking water, since it is river water from below the town, is unfit to drink."

There! After four years of wretched misery that was the judgment of three honest experts! Ministers, generals, colonels, overseers, and cruel slave drivers had been here, but it had not occurred to a single one that if we were to spend thirty years in prison, we would also have to live thirty years.

I won't say any more about it, because even today after twenty-five years I still get gooseflesh when I think of it. And then people wonder how a man can become a democrat! We were not democrats when they locked us up, but all of us were when we came out.

CHAPTER 11

THE report on the conditions under which we lived and the state of our health was sent to the distinguished Ministerial Commission in Berlin. One of the three men who served on this commission had an eye affliction, the second suffered from chest pains, and the third from cold feet. They actually considered the most severe punishment to be altogether too lenient for us, but in their good moments they must have realized that one can hardly exist without light, air, and warmth, and that tepid, cloudy, and impure river water is not as conducive to good health as the drink from which they derived the strength to carry on their business.

> The ministers of the goverment
> are drinking Burgundy wine.[1]

In short, they decided to find other lodgings for us. However, I believe nothing would have come of this for a long time except for another circumstance. Just at this time the first commandant, General Count Hacke, died, and with him a good part of our hatred was buried too. The second commandant, Colonel Bock, marched in the funeral procession, caught cold, and three days later went the same way as his superior officer. Before he died, however, he summoned the provost marshal to his bedside and enjoined upon him the responsibility of carrying out that for which he no longer had time. He was told to write to the gentlemen in Berlin and inform them that if an improvement in our living conditions did not take place soon, we would all perish. The provost marshal carried out the colonel's wish and the ministers of the government had to come to the realization that we were after all human beings too, even though our colors were black, red, and gold.[2] The gentlemen, therefore slowly began to make arrangements for our transfer.

These arrangements, however, dragged on for a long time, since one must not be overhasty in acting upon such matters. As a result of the delay, the interim commandant, Lieutenant General von Thile,[3] who was commander of the army corps, had sufficient time to become acquainted with us. The man paid us a personal visit — the late Count Hacke never set foot in our cells; he didn't have the courage to look at the misery, for which his slogan "With God, for King and Fatherland" had been responsible.

This man, however, did visit us, and because Grashof and I lived in the cell directly beside the staircase, we were the first ones he called on. He asked us all kinds of questions: how we felt, in what frame of mind we were, and how we were being treated, and to all these questions he received one and the same answer: "Terrible!"

Once the stopper was removed from the bunghole, all the hatred and vitriol, which the deceased count had stored up within us, just poured out. Lieutenant General von Thile didn't say much, but he was visibly moved when we told him that we were not even allowed to attend a church service. He said that we should most certainly be allowed to do so, and that he would grant us this permission on his own responsibility. Otherwise, however, there could be no changes until the new commandant was appointed.

At that time people said that he was one of those religious fanatics, but I didn't despise the man, even though his treatment of us was motivated more by godly piety than by humaneness. In any case, it was far better for us to have him as commandant than the deceased count, who was a notorious hedonist. The count knew the value of material things, because he would eat a whole roast goose for breakfast and then say to his dear wife, "My dear child, a goose is a strange bird; one for breakfast is not enough, but if one eats two of them, he spoils his appetite for dinner." — At least, that's what people said about him.

The next day each of us received a hymnal from the lieutenant general, and what was more important, a visit from the divisional pastor Leist.[4] He was quite a different man from the pastor who couldn't spare us the time, but promised to preach a sermon for us some day in the laundry. This man could spare the time, and he made arrangements for us to go to church. To be sure, we went only once, and then in the company of many gendarmes, but this one visit was worth more than a hundred visits at any other time. I can still hear the sound of his words in my ears, and I hope the echo will remain in my heart as long as I live.

I had been living in this cursed detention cell for appoximately one year, and because of the miserable treatment given us I had lost whatever little zest for life I had had before. One evening in February, 1838,[5] when the snow was piled high before both doors and it was cold enough outside to freeze sticks and stones, the provost marshal came to visit us. In one cell after another he asked whether any of us were willing to get up at four o'clock the next morning, and in freezing cold and darkness be taken in a van to another fortress. — Where to, he didn't say, and probably wasn't allowed to say.

No one wanted to go. Most of us were sick, and the others didn't have the proper clothing for such cold weather. Nothing would have come of the Council of Ministers' promise to have us transferred to another fortress, if it hadn't been for the coat for which the tailor had taken my measurements on the day of our merry wine-drinking party. I thought about it for a moment. I had a nice warm coat, my health was fairly good, and furthermore, I thought to myself, "What can be worse than this? One has to give an ox with a load of hay the right of way. You've already been in four or five places, some good and some bad; possibly it's your turn to find a good one now, and furthermore, nothing can be as bad as it is here."

Therefore I told the provost marshal that I was prepared to leave. He said that if we could find a second prisoner who was willing to go, everything would be in order — and we did find this second one. My old friend, the Captain,[6] was of the same mind as I. He was also fortunate enough to have a coat, which was made of seven layers of cloth, one over another. The coat was gray, and even this color was somewhat faded, but anyone could see that it was a valuable piece of clothing in spite of its shabby appearance, and that in its long lifetime it had afforded its many owners much warmth and protection. The Captain had faith in this old friend of his, and at four o'clock the next morning the two of us were sitting in the van and together with two gendarmes we were on our way in the cold winter morning. Where to? Only the good Lord and the all powerful Ministerial Commission knew that.

If I have just now described the coat, I must also say a few words about the fellow in the coat. — We called him "Captain," although he wasn't a captain at all. However, he was richly deserving of this rank, and as far as his military appearance was concerned, he should really have been called "Colonel." However, because of the poor food which was given us, he lacked the required corpulence around the ribs to qualify as a regimental commander. He was quite thin, but it made no difference, for despite his slight build there was so much of a military nature in his whole bearing that the sentries, seeing him out for a walk in his old gray coat and army cap, never knew whether they should present arms or not. They would have done it, they undoubtedly would have done it, if he had still had his blond mustache hanging down beneath his nose, just as in those good days at Halle, when he was a fusilier fulfilling his military commitment of one year. However, the late General Count Hacke had had this mustache shaved off, and as was the case with all of us, it was not done at the state's expense, but at our own. The late count probably reasoned to himself, "If I can't get the heads and necks of these damned fellows, I'll have to be satisfied with their mustaches."

Thus it happened that in addition to all the other shearings we also had our mustaches shaved off twice a week. On the other five days of the week we had to walk around looking like porcupines. No one was more annoyed at this harassment than my Captain. The rest of us lost merely a little insignificant growth of hair on our upper lips, and we even had to pay to have that shaved off, but he lost a very impressive military mustache, which he had trained and cultivated for the entire year he had spent in the army as a volunteer — and that was really too bad. As prisoners it was only natural that all of us hated the general, but the Captain as an army man felt a very intense aversion for him. He said that in 1813 many far better people than the general had lain in the trenches, and he made many other indiscreet insinuations.

Once when the Captain received a letter from the commandant addressed to "the demagogue Schulze," he took the bull by the horns and answered the commandant. He said that "demagogue" was a term of abuse, and he would not tolerate it. The general wrote back that he was a demagogue and he would continue to call him that. Once again the Captain wrote that he was not a demagogue, and once again the general answered that he certainly was a demagogue, and thus they wrote a whole series of letters back and forth. In his letters the Captain included intimations and innuendoes, and the general responded with coarse insults before finally putting a stop to all this correspondence.

Then my good old Captain went to his trunk, took out something that was wrapped in a paper and placed it upon the table in front of him. He unfolded the paper and continued to look at its contents until big tears started to roll down his cheeks and fall into his mustache, for it was indeed nothing but the remains of his army mustache that he had kept wrapped up in this paper.

Despite his military service the Captain was a warm-hearted person, and he felt very deeply the loss of this hairy friend, which in good times he had held, if not close to his heart, at least right under his nose. Now he broke out in rage at the meanness of the general, who had first deprived him of his mustache and had then committed the outrage of calling him a "demagogue." He swore a sacred oath that he would make use of every opportunity and summon all his strength that he might again get something under his nose and the general something in the neck.

It wasn't possible to carry out the first part of this vow, because such a mustache needs time to grow, especially on newly cleared land. On the days after he had been shaved he managed to let his mustache grow into a tiny forest preserve, but then the barber would regularly shave it off again, so that he was never able to raise a real military mustache beneath his nose. Thus he had to be satisfied with the second part of his vow, namely, to see to it that the general got his just deserts. So he sat down and wrote a letter to the Supreme Court and told about his epistolary skirmish with the general, and demanded that he be given his rightful title instead of the disrespectful "demagogue."

Sure enough! He was successful. The general received a stern reprimand from his superiors in Berlin, and later the Captain holding up a letter came running out into the courtyard in great joy. The letter was from the general, who wrote that henceforth he would no longer address his letters to the "demagogue Schulze," but to the "political criminal Schulze." That, of course, made a big difference, because a political criminal is much better than an ordinary demagogue.

Yes, the Captain had accomplished something, not only for himself, but for all of us. We were very happy with this new title, and we thanked the Captain, and held a long meeting to discuss the possibility of applying for the even longer title: "secret political criminal," because it was a secret why we had already been imprisoned for years. However, nothing came of this, because shortly afterwards the general died.

The Captain had accomplished something, but he couldn't get his mustache back again, and that was the reason he was willing to be transferred. The climate in Magdeburg did not agree with his mustache.

From this little incident one can get a general idea of what kind of man my old Captain really was. In appearance he was an impressive figure with blond hair and a blond mustache — that is, he didn't have the mustache now, but he would have it later — with military bearing and in a gray coat with seven collars, but very thin. He was a splendid fellow, honest and sincere, but emotional and with a lively imagination which would carry him off to the other side of the fortress walls in search of "the one" whom he wanted to have for life. Sometimes it was a blonde, somtimes a brunette, and sometimes a redhead. — Well, we shall soon see.

III   Berlin and the Magistrate's Jail[1]
(Not for the first time, but for the second time)

CHAPTER 12

R EUNION! Reunion! Who is not familiar with this delightful
heart-warming word? Who has not known the thrill of seeing
loved ones again after years of separation? Who has not had a reunion with his young bride or with his old parents, and who has
never embraced a good friend from earlier years (Karl Krüger,[2] Fritz
Peters[3])? — One may think that he becomes less emotional as he
grows older, but nevertheless he always feels a lump in his throat
whenever our Lord again shows him these loyal old faces. God, who
holds them all by a string, stands close by and says, "There they are;
look at them and be happy!"

Who has not revisited those places where he once knew happiness
or where some sorrow befell him? — Yes, those places have added
significance, because in our mind's eye so many silent and beautiful
figures rise up from the past from bush and woods, from grass and
flowers, from arbors and graves. Some smile at us; others weep their
bitter tears, but we can't grasp them nor hold them, nor can they
give us any answers to our questions!

Yes, a reunion is beautiful, with places as well as with people, but
if one comes to a place where he was once brutalized, where he experienced nothing, absolutely nothing, of God's blessing or human
kindness, then his heart freezes, and then the reunion is poison. The
figures which rise up before him are pale gray specters, and in their
hands they hold the rack of torture and the gallows and a senseless
book: *Prussian State Law;* Chapter Heading: *Attempted High
Treason.*

Oh, I have seen you many times since then, you old gray building
on the Schinkenplatz in Berlin. The most recent time was last
summer[4] when young people in their gray jackets and loose-fitting
athletic trunks came there from all parts of Germany to take part in
the gymnastic festival. The black-red-gold banners were waving

117

from all windows and even real privy councillors were calling "welcome" from their windows.

On the first day one of my old friends called to me, "Come along, Fritz, we're going out to Spandau[5] today! The city of Spandau is spending some money; the magistrate has set aside 400 talers to pay for the welcome extended to the city's guests."

"No, thank you!" I said. "I'm very well acquainted with the black-red-gold road that leads to Spandau."

Then I went home, took my good wife by the arm and said, "We don't have to go to Spandau. I can show you the same thing right here." I took her to the Schinkenplatz, stood in front of that old gray building and said, "See, that's where they once played a game of chance with my own happiness at stake — and they won."

Across the street a black-red-gold banner was waving from a window. I held my wife in my arms and said, "I have paid the price; no one can do more than that, nor can he be expected to."

As she looked up to me with a kindly smile, I said, "My dear love, one should be thankful to God for everything. If I had not been imprisoned here, who knows whether I would have ever found you."

The next day we took the train and rode home.[6] The festival no longer held any interest for me; my spirit had been crushed at the reunion with that old gray building.

But to return to my story!

As I have said, the Captain and I were sitting in a van and we were riding along with two gendarmes, who were carrying chains and locks in their cartridge pouches as necessary "requirements" for us; we were on our way to — Berlin. — The following night at half past eleven we arrived once again at the magistrate's jail in that little unpretentious gray building at the Schinkenplatz. It was here that we had begun our new careers and where Criminal Councillor Dambach, our distinguished "Uncle,"[7] lived. To be sure, he had been rewarded with a higher title since our last meeting. He was now criminal director of the magistrate's jail, because through his wily investigation he had succeeded in making us stupid young fellows look like the most dangerous political criminals who had brought the Prussian state and the beloved Federal Diet to the very brink of destruction.

The gendarmes drove up to the door and rang the bell, and the warden appeared.[8] He still had the same bony skeleton-like face and the same greasy sheepskin coat he used to wear five years ago, when he did us the honor of coming to our cells every morning and every evening. He was very embarrassed because he didn't know what to do with us, since — as he said — we had not been properly announced, and he therefore had no cell ready for us. As a result we had to go from the bitter cold into the guard room and sit there in dense smoke and fumes and a heat of 22–24 degrees[9] (the temperature in a Prussian guard room never goes below that) until two o'clock in the morning. At that time the warden returned and announced, "Everything is ready now," and we were supposed to follow him.

As we walked over the old familiar courtyard, I stopped to think how often I had paced up and down on this ground during that earlier year when the prison had been the only world that existed for me.

Then and now! — Then we were torn from that beautiful, young, and happy student life and thrown behind bars, where we were kept under lock and key and deprived of any contact with our loved ones. Just like a street organ which plays the same tune over and over again, so too were we forced to repeat those statements which Criminal Councillor Dambach wanted the most esteemed Supreme Court to hear, and which would help him in his own professional career. He had gotten his wish. We paid the price, over a thousand young people had to pay the price that he might become the foremost criminal officer in Prussia. In our innocent uprightness we disclosed not only what we had done and what we had thought but even what we had felt, and from these statements he fashioned rungs on which he ascended to his present lofty position.

That was then! — If we were deprived of love, we at least had hope. He himself had said — the criminal director, that is: "Let them take you to the fortress; you will certainly be extradited to your own state."[10]

And now? I had been imprisoned for almost five years and my lot had not improved in the least in all that time!

I remembered the criminal director from that earlier time, and so I knew that he was a mean fellow, but I was to get to know him even better. He was more than mean; he was despicable! The few days we remained in Berlin this time were to give ample proof of that. Well, I'll tell about it. —

The warden escorted us to a cell. Amazing! It was the same cell where I had been before. There was the same window with metal reinforcement on the outside, the same cracks in the wall, which had so often held my attention, the same floor, which I had so often paced in my troubled anguish. There was the spot where I had secretly cut out a chip from the pine floor. From this chip I had made a pen — secretly, of course! At Christmas I had received a few walnuts; I had burned the walnut shells and made some kind of ink with which I had written — secretly, of course! I didn't write anything bad or anything that was against prison regulations; I wrote merely poems — poor poems, in which my rage broke out, and in which the bitterness of my fate cried out to heaven. I wanted to smash the world into pieces and later establish myself on the rubble as "God the Second." Fortunately for the world, all these poems were lost, and fortunately for me, they no longer find a responsive echo in my heart. Even the pen, the pine chip, with which I wrote everything, and which I kept as a souvenir for years, was used by Mariken Gramkows as an ordinary piece of kindling wood to start a fire in the stove.[11] — However, if anyone visits me, I can show him something I wrote at that time: Byron's "Daughter of Jephtha," which I wrote down from memory. — Byron was a writer I admired at that time.

We came into the cell on this bitterly cold night. Everything was as it used to be, but cold, cold, bitterly cold! Everything was the same, except that formerly there had been a bedstead with a straw mattress; this time they were missing.

"Well, Captain, there's nothing we can do about it!"

We lay down on the floor, put something under our heads and covered ourselves with our coats, but we couldn't sleep because of the intense cold. The cell had not been heated in a long time.

The next morning the warden unlocked the door and asked in a real friendly way how we had slept. We pretended not to notice his sarcastic words, and asked for a bed, or at least a straw mattress, in case we were to stay here a second night. He said he couldn't make any decisions on matters like that, but that he would report it to Director Dambach. Then he told us that we had five silver pennies a day to spend.

I answered that we were traveling from one fortress to another, and that under such conditions the regulations provided for an allocation of twenty pennies a day.

He said the director had decided on five pennies, and with that he left the cell.

After he had left, the turnkey came and asked us what we wanted to eat. We were frozen stiff and were running around in our lockup like wild animals just to keep warm. What was therefore more natural than to ask for a cup of hot coffee? So we ordered two pots of coffee!

We got the coffee, but a pot of coffee cost four silver pennies, so that we each had one penny left for the rest of the day. What should we buy with that? Bread, of course. So we ordered a penny's worth of bread for each, and that was the end of our five silver pennies.

Toward evening when we had finished eating our dry bread and were cowering in the darkness, the warden returned to wish us a good night. — That was nothing but the most despicable derision, but I wouldn't give him the satisfaction of letting him know how fierce my rage was. I asked whether we were again supposed to sleep without bed or straw mattress. If the prison administration could not give us a bed, I still had 26 talers of my own money and the Captain also had 21 talers, which the gendarmes had brought with them from Magdeburg and delivered to the director. With that money we could pay for the price of a bed.

The warden bowed politely and said that was all well and good, but the director had decided that we should save enough from our five silver pennies to rent a bed.

That was simply unconcealed meanness. If from our miserable allotment we were to save one penny each day, we would have to lie on the hard floor and in darkness from five o'clock in the evening until eight o'clock in the morning for thirty days, before we could scrape together the one taler which the bed would cost for one month. We would have to suffer hunger and grief, and why? Had we committed some new crime, for which they could take us to task in this way? — I demanded permission to speak personally to the director. — The answer was that I could not speak to him at this time, and with that the door was again locked, and we lay down on the floor and shivered in the cold.

The next morning the same thing: again we received warm coffee and a penny's worth of bread. — I now wanted to speak to the director; as magistrate of the prison it was his official responsibility to hear the complaints of the prisoners, and we had complaints to make.

The answer was: the director did not want to speak to us at all. Therefore I sat down and wrote to him, and I demanded a recording clerk, because I wanted to lodge a complaint with the Supreme Court against him. — I received no answer.

That evening we were again given the friendly good-night wish from the warden and the hard floor to sleep on.

The third morning came and it was no different from the others, but I shall always remember that day, because in addition to all the other hardships which had so broken our spirits, it brought with it a new fear and a new misery. My good Captain became sick. He was afflicted with an uneasiness and a nervous restlessness. He reached for one object after another. There was a Bible in our cell; he picked it up, read in it, and then threw it away. Again he read in it, and again he threw it away, and ran around in the cell. His face was as red as a beet and he threw himself on the hard cold floor. I feel certain that the ordeal of these few days in Berlin was the cause of a lung ailment which he suffered a year later at the new fortress.

A Bible in a prison cell is a beautiful, humane thing, and the man who first arranged to have it placed there belongs to those select people who have an understanding not only of the weak human heart but also of all the merciful intentions of our Lord. Many a heart has become mellowed through God's word; many a criminal has come to a true understanding of God through the Bible, but we were no criminals. To be sure, we were all sinners and poor wretches, no different from all those people who walk around enjoying their freedom, but we hadn't done anything wrong. We were innocent before God. However, it was not God who brought grief and sorrow upon us, but the baseness of human beings who wanted to wreak their cruel vengeance upon us. They knew nothing of God; on the contrary, they had traffic with the devil.

"Let that book lie there, Captain! Our Lord did not strike you; His base image here on earth has merely thrown a few stones in your path! Let that book lie there, Captain! Don't make yourself a party to those who blaspheme God, and who have their wanton pleasure in making people suffer and then offer them His word as a sop!"

I knocked on the door and was let out into the corridor. There I met an old court attendant whom I remembered from earlier times.

His name was Heubold. They say that he was later sentenced to a fortress imprisonment for embezzlement, but I can't vouch for that. However, if he was imprisoned, he deserved it, even if it was merely for the sarcastic grin on his face, when I asked, "Heubold, do you know how long we are going to have to stay here?"

There he stood before me with his weak, pale, and bloated face, with his broad mouth twisted into a malicious grin, and with his red wig, and slowly he answered, "You're going to stay here always. Do you think that the king wants to have all these buildings standing here empty? No, you're going to stay here, and your friends will all join you later."

The scoundrel knew that was not so. He knew damned well that we would soon be leaving; he knew damned well how cruelly we were being treated here and how despondent we were, but it pleased the blackguard to send us on our way with a kick. One could read in his face the execrable pleasure with which he said, "No, you're going to stay here."

I cannot and will not deny that I was completely unnerved by the meanness of this fellow. — A prisoner is always very apprehensive, and he is not likely to gain courage if he is given nothing but bread and water for three days and forced to sleep on the floor in intense cold. — I believed he was telling the truth, and I was terrified, much more so than at that time when I had heard my death sentence pronounced. That had been just a matter of seconds, but this was a long endless torture. There are very few people who have any conception of what it means to be slowly tortured to death at the state's expense. It could be done; they had already made a good beginning, and there was no reason why they might not continue. — Oh, how despondent I was! But the worst was yet to come. My faithful Captain had listened to the whole conversation, and what for me was woeful agony, could be a deathly poison for him.

When we were again locked up, we fell into each other's arms, and we probably stood there for a long time — how long I don't know — seeking mutual help and consolation. However, one thing I do remember as though it had happened just now, and that is that my brave Captain recovered from his illness and walked around in the cell with a firm step, and a mighty defiance surged up in me. One has to fight the devil with the devil.

I knocked on the door; I wanted to have a recording clerk! I

wanted to file a complaint with the Supreme Court! — After a few
hours a miserable-looking wretch came in. He looked like one of
those judge's assistants who never pass their bar examinations and
who are used as lackeys at the higher court.

"Did you want to file a complaint with the Supreme Court?"

"Yes!"

"It would be best if you would write down your complaint
yourself."

I told him that I didn't want to do that; that was his job. He would
have to do it, and he would have to testify that we had been forced
to sleep on the bare floor for three nights, and that we had had
nothing to eat but bread and water.

With great difficulty I got him to do it, but the language I used in
reference to the criminal director — it wasn't too refined — he refused to include in the record.

Of course, the Captain and I had to sleep on the floor again that
night. We tried to keep each other warm, for misfortune binds people together so closely.

The next morning, the fourth morning[12] in this cell, and the same
cruel treatment! My brave Captain lay motionless on the hard floor,
while I walked up and down in the cell and finally stopped before
the metal-reinforced window. The gray light of morning was just
beginning to shine through this small window which was located
about a foot below the ceiling. — Good God! Twenty-five more
years in this place!

The Captain had gotten up. He again started to reach for the Bible. "Let that book lie there, Captain! Our Lord helps only him who
helps himself. We'll fight it with all our might, Captain!"

Oh, good God! Here we stood by ourselves in this gloomy cell,
with no possessions we could call our own and with no food in our
stomachs, and we were going to fight against the whole world!

It is possible that one of those very pious people may despise me
because I so disregarded the Bible, but I can assure him that just at
that moment there came over me a warm and refreshing trust in
God, independent of Bible and prayer, and to the praise and glory of
our Lord I can say: "That faith has never failed me!"

The door was unlocked, and there stood the gendarme Rese, who
five years ago had often come to escort me to a hearing with the
criminal director. He was a tall, somber-looking old man with a face

scarred by pockmarks and covered with freckles. He had sparse gray hair, and like Frederick William III he also had hair that looked like a gray tallow candle hanging down from each nostril. — He was not handsome, and yet! — if our Lord ever wants to send me an angel of mercy in my last hours, he should send me the old gendarme Rese.

There he stood in the doorway in his royal Prussian angel's uniform and called into our cell, "Gentlemen, get ready; we're leaving in a half hour."

Oh, Captain!, Oh, Charles douze! What joy! — Away! — Away! — Where to? — We didn't know, but we just wanted to get away! — Away from that cruel beast, who had made us unhappy for the rest of our days, who had had his joy in tormenting us almost to death!

Someone might say that many other people, who were much better than we, had to suffer even more. — Just think of the militias of 1813!

Yes, it is true, but those people didn't suffer in silence; they were able to do something about it. That makes the difference! — We young people who with every breath we took wanted to achieve and accomplish something were just supposed to suffer and be patient? We were supposed to let ourselves be mistreated for the gratification of a Count Hacke or a Criminal Director Dambach?

Yes, gendarme Rese and our Lord delivered us from our misery on this occasion, and I am willing to cross off the record whatever harassment I suffered at the hands of Criminal Director Dambach either at this time or five years earlier during my imprisonment on remand. However, for one thing he must be called to account — he's dead now and on this earth he can no longer answer to the charge — but in the world to come he must explain to me why he would not let my father visit me. While I was imprisoned in Berlin my good father had come to find out whether he might do something to bring about my release. He was within twenty steps of my cell, but he was denied permission to see his only son, who longed to pour out his grief in tears in the arms of his beloved father. — For this I shall call you to account! —[13]

CHAPTER 13

"GENTLEMEN, get ready; we're leaving in half an hour."
Well, we didn't need much time to get ready. Our trunks
were packed; our coats, which we had used as blankets during the
night, were still lying on the floor and, thank God, we didn't have to
say good-by to anyone. The Captain merely took under his arm the
large bird cage with his flock of canaries, which he always took with
him on his travels. He had covered them with his old gray coat to
protect them from the cold, and thus he took better care of them
than of his own knees and legs. — How bedraggled his little flock
looked! All the time they hadn't emitted a single sound.

I collected our pipe supplies from all four corners of the cell, put
the partly used-up pound of tobacco into my pocket — and now we
were ready to go! But gendarme Rese didn't appear.

When one has to wait for a carriage, which is to take him *to*
another place where he longs to be, he becomes terribly impatient,
but he becomes even more impatient if he has to wait for a carriage
to take him *away* from a place he loathes.

Well, Rese had to come sometime, and indeed he did after a
while. He appeared with another gendarme — his name was Prütz,
and he was a lively and friendly little fellow — and the two came to
fetch us. Our belongings were loaded into the van, and so were we,
and then it was good-by forever to the magistrate's jail! I have seen
it again from the outside,[1] but I have never had any desire to see it
again from the inside!

In the meantime a thaw had set in; it had rained for two days and the
snow was gone. The lovely sun of early spring was shining brightly on
the dreary earth and it was also shining brightly into our troubled
hearts. Even though it did not radiate much warmth as yet, it promised
that it would do so later, and it kept its word. Our worst days were
behind us; from now on things should get better. The Captain pulled
back the edge of his gray coat from the top of the bird cage and let the
sun shine on his canaries. The poor bedraggled little creatures became
beautiful glossy little birds, merrily bouncing back and forth, and they
began to chirp, even though they did not exactly sing.

Oh, how things had changed during the last hour! My Captain was beginning to thaw out just as I. Old "Uncle" Rese was telling stories from the time of our imprisonment on remand, and they brought back memories of some of our old friends from those days. Little Prütz cared for us like a mother: "Look here, I have another blanket; let's put that over our legs. — Put your legs over here; then you'll be more comfortable."

And everything would have been fine, if it hadn't been for two things which weighed upon my mind and my stomach. The first was the uncertainty as to where we were being taken, and the second our terrible pangs of hunger. — However, for this there was to be a remedy too.

After we had traveled for some distance, the countryside began to look very familiar to me. I had traveled this road once before and I knew we were going in an easterly direction.

"Good God," I asked, "are we going to Müncheberg?"

"Yes, we are," said Rese, "and that's where we will have dinner."

"And after that?" I continued to ask.

"Oh, then we'll keep on going to Graudenz," answered "Uncle" Rese in his good-natured naiveté.

To this very day I think he was completely unaware of what he was revealing, for "Uncle" Rese was somewhat stupid.

That took care of the uncertainty as to our destination; we were over that hump, and for the time being we wouldn't worry any more about what would happen after that. — However, as for our hunger . . . Well, we would find an answer for that too.

After we had traveled about two miles, the little gendarme Prütz, who was sitting opposite me, took off his shako — they didn't wear helmets in those days — unlaced the lining and took out a blue checkered kerchief. — Well, I thought he was going to blow his nose, but that's where I was mistaken. — From the kerchief he took a piece of cold veal and from his pocket he took a good-sized chunk of bread and a knife, and with obvious relish he began to eat his breakfast. When "Uncle" Rese saw that, he also took his food box from his shako and unwrapped his provisions while assuming a reclining position. There they sat in front of us and ate like angels in heaven, and the Captain and I looked on with great reverence.

Our reverence, however, must have been so devout that it was reflected in our facial expressions. In short, Prütz got the message and said that his kerchief was quite clean, and if we were hungry . . ., and "Uncle" Rese said that his sausage was from the best butcher in Berlin. Both he and his wife thought very highly of it, and if we cared . . . With this the blue checkered kerchief was spread over all eight knees like a damask tablecloth, and the sausage made the rounds, and we took turns with the cold veal and the knives. Before long it was the Captain and I who were eating like angels in heaven and Prütz and Rese were looking on with great reverence.

Since that time I always feel very grateful whenever I see a Prussian gendarme and a blue checkered kerchief. I can't always find a gendarme, but I do have a couple of blue checkered kerchiefs which I purchased not for the usual use, but rather as tablecloths. These are spread on the table only when something special is being served, as, for example, a nice delicious roast of veal or an excellent Mecklenburg mettwurst. Then I always ask myself, "Does it taste as good as at that other time?" and the answer is always, "No, Prütz's cold veal and Rese's North German sausage, that was something altogether different."

However, the Captain and I were so famished that we could not satisfy our appetites, no matter how much we ate. At about two o'clock we reached Müncheberg, and there a large table was set for the guests arriving on the mail coach. This table had a white linen tablecloth, and not a blue checkered one. I hadn't eaten at a table with a white linen tablecloth for a year, and everything looked very appetizing to me. At Magdeburg we had also spread out a tablecoth at noon, but it was gray blotting paper, so that the bare table wouldn't get dirty. Here it was pure white linen!

"Four dinners," I said to a young girl who was standing there gawking at us, as though we were monkeys and bears on exhibition with a traveling circus.

"No," said "Uncle" Rese, "just two dinners! — Prütz and I are not having dinner; we have already eaten."

"No, that wouldn't be fair! The Captain and I want to return the invitation. We shared your breakfast, and now you must accept our invitation to dinner."

"Well, that's very nice, but we don't have enough money. The two of you have one taler and eight pennies to spend, and if we use it up here, then you'll have nothing for this evening. We are going to travel all night, and the night is long."

"But, Herr Rese, we still have our own private funds."

"But your private funds cannot . . ."

He got no further with his objections, because the four bowls of soup were already being served. Little Prütz sat down saying, "Well, there's not much we can do about it; what must be, must be!"

The Captain and I also sat down, and "Uncle" Rese, because he didn't want the soup to get cold, sat down too.

"And please bring us a bottle of wine!" I called.

"For heaven's sake, we're going to run into debt!" cried "Uncle" Rese.

"Don't worry; we still have our own money!"

"Good God, your money is all sealed up in an envelope, and I have to deliver it to the headquarters at Graudenz."

"Never mind, we'll make it stretch, as the tailor said of the new suit."

The wine came, we drank, and "Uncle" Rese drank with us.

"Oh, Fräulein, another bottle, please, but of a somewhat better brand!"

"Good heavens, we can't do this!"

" 'Uncle' Rese, we still have our own money."

So we drank another bottle, and still another, and when we were all a little tipsy, I said to the old fellow, "Now, 'Uncle' Rese, open up my treasure box and take out a ten-taler bill, and you, Fräulein, bring me a pen and some ink."

I sat down and wrote out a receipt for old Rese. I declared that he had spent ten talers of my personal funds for my needs. Then I paid the bill and put the change into my pocket, for why should I bother Rese with that? As long as I had the pen and ink, I also wrote a letter to my friend Grashof in Magdeburg, in which I informed him that I had forgotten my drawing board, and that he should keep it for me. — "Uncle" Rese was watching me like a hawk and he asked me what I had written.

"A letter," I told him.

He said he could not permit that.

I told him that I had forgotten something in Magdeburg.

It made no difference to him; he couldn't permit it.

I asked him to read the letter himself.

He replied that he was not interested and that he wouldn't permit me to send any letter.

Finally I requested him to sit down and address the letter to the office of the commandant in Magdeburg, and then the letter would certainly be delivered into the proper hands — and "Uncle" Rese complied.

"Uncle" Rese, "Uncle" Rese, I put one over on you that time!

I had previously told my friend Grashof that if I wrote that I had forgotten a pair of stockings, that meant we were going to Pillau. A book would indicate Glatz, a shirt, Kolberg, and a drawing board, Graudenz. In this way they would know where we were going and in all probability where they would be going too. And the plan worked.

After a short time we were again riding in the van as evening approached. I don't believe that any company of gendarmes and criminals ever went driving around so merrily in the Prussian state as we. The only disturbing note came from "Uncle" Rese, who called out at almost every milestone, "I hope you don't get us into trouble!"

We weren't thinking about that, for we were just as happy as we could be. We found the idea of writing receipts so intriguing that we continued with it until we came to Graudenz. Later when "Uncle" Rese was supposed to deliver our private funds to the commandant, he had nothing left but receipts.

Well, it made very little difference whether he had the money or we had it. "One egg is just like any other," said the sexton, as he reached for the largest one.

After two days and two nights we approached Graudenz, but a broad river[2] separated us from our new fortress. Ice still covered the middle of the river, but it had already melted-away at both shores. Here we were supposed to cross.

" 'Uncle' Rese," I said, "I'm not risking my life here. The Prussian state can't expect me, a foreigner, to have so much heroic courage that I should be in any great hurry to return to one of its fortresses. The situation is different with the Captain; he's a Prussian, and he wants to cross the river. I'll make a suggestion; you cross over the ice with the Captain, and I'll stay here with Prütz in the tavern on this side until the river is free of ice."

My suggestion wasn't that unreasonable, and Prütz seemed to like it. It might have been accepted, if instead of Prütz I had chosen Rese to stay with me in the tavern. As it was, he merely stood there and scratched his head. He said that it looked dangerous, and that even as a child he had had a terrible fear of water, but there was no alternative; we had to cross over now. Nothing could be done about it; they were all against me, and so we set out and I had to risk my young life, as though it were some worthless trifle.

At about eight o'clock in the morning we were loaded into a boat together with the two gendarmes and our belongings, and six Poles wrapped in six sheepskins rowed us through the open water, which had inundated the meadows for a quarter of a mile, until we came to the ice. There we had to disembark; the two gendarmes took their rifles, the Captain took his bird cage, and I took our smoking equipment. Then with the water up to our ankles we walked over the ice, and from above our good Lord sent down a fine drizzle. The six sheepskins pulling our belongings on a sled followed us. — It was a very impressive procession, but we all came within a whisker of drowning, gendarmes, bird cage, the treasured pipes and all, and nothing would have been left to tell the story except possibly the six sheepskins.

We had walked about three quarters of the way across the ice when all of a sudden some people on the further shore began to shout and wave handkerchiefs and other things. We stopped short, and only then did we realize that we were about to walk straight into the water, for how in the world can anyone see where he is going, when he is sloshing through water a foot deep and the rain is coming down in his face? "Uncle" Rese immediately gave the command: "About face!" After a while we were fortunate enough to find our way between the many holes, which the river had made in the ice, to a spot where planks had been laid down, and from there we came to a kind of gangway which led to the shore.

With that we had overcome one serious difficulty, but now we were to be faced with one even more serious, and that was a Polish tavern.

We had to go into the tavern at the ferry landing. There a fish-oil lamp had been burning all night, and in the thick haze, herring, old cheese, and cheap whiskey were competing to ascertain which one could stink the most. In the middle of the room there was a green-tiled stove as large as our baking ovens at home. It was circled by a bench on which there lay three boatmen sleeping like logs. On the top of the stove seven sheepskins were hung up to dry.

When the Captain and I opened the door, the smell almost knocked us over and we fell back. Rese was trained for something like this, because he had already had his nose in many a guard room. He said that even if it didn't smell like woodruff, it was at least warm, and it was also drier than outside in the rain. There was therefore nothing to do but to go in and wait until Prütz had secured a van. — However, before long everything inside me was turning topsy-turvy; I had to go out, and the Captain followed me, and old Rese had to follow both of us. Whether Rese wanted to have something to eat, or whether he was really cold, I don't know, but in any case, he finally ordered us to reenter the tavern and content ourselves with cheese and herring and cheap whiskey instead of fresh air. After many requests and entreaties he finally yielded to the extent that he allowed us to stay in the vestibule until Prütz returned.

Well, he eventually came, and we got into the van and rode to the fortress.

IV *The Fortress of Graudenz*[1]

CHAPTER 14

I F a person's trust is in our Lord and all that He decrees, then he must be satisfied with whatever befalls him, and if he is a devout man, he will have to say, "I accept God's will, for it is good."

It is altogether different, however, if a man's happiness or misfortune is placed in the hands of another human being. In such a case he has an anxious feeling, for everyone knows from his own experience and conscience how fallible human judgments and human kindness can be. — Now our whole future was again placed in the hands of one single man, the commandant of Graudenz, and what that can lead to we had already seen in the person of a Count Hacke in Magdeburg.

The fortress was situated along one shore of the river at a short distance from the town. From the outside its walls and parapets looked just as disconsolate and dreary as all other fortresses, at least to the eye of a prisoner. Its gateways were just as somber, and its drawbridges, as one rode over them, produced the same hollow rumbling sound. From the inside, however, the fortress presented a somewhat different appearance. To be sure, here too there were casemates all around, and I was familiar with them from Silberberg, but these were clean and neat, and from the outside they looked quite pleasant. Furthermore, a row of houses stretched out through the entire fortress area, so that one could see that some other people besides soldiers and prisoners lived here. There were also lanes lined with linden and poplar trees. In short, the first look was not bad, as Adam said, when he saw Eve for the first time.

We drove to the largest of the houses, which was the commandant's headquarters. When we got out of the van, "Uncle" Rese went in to deliver our papers to General von Toll,[2] while we waited in the vestibule.

After a while the door was opened and the general came out. He was a tall and stately man with a snow-white mustache and snow-white hair. Later some people said that he wore a wig, but in any case it was very becoming. He spoke to us with a distinct Westphalian accent, "I can see from your papers that you are decent people. You will be well treated here, because it is not my business to inflict further hardship upon unfortunate people. Of your friends who have been assigned to Graudenz you are the first to arrive, and therefore I shall give you the first choice of the casemates which have been set aside for your group. You may choose the one you like best, but once you have made your choice, you will have to abide by it, because I don't stand for any tomfoolery."

I remember very well that these were his exact words.

We thanked him and were about to leave when he called us back and said, "I should like to tell you that one of your comrades has already been here for some time. His name is Schramm;[3] you probably know him. He has been foolish enough to become engaged — formally engaged to a very respectable girl. I have given him permission to have his fiancée and her brother visit him three times a week, but you must not in any way look upon this as a precedent, because I would not give you this same permission."

We told him that we didn't plan to get involved in anything like that, and as far as we were concerned, Schramm could pay court as much as he wished, if the general had no objection.

"That's the answer I expected from you," he said, and we left.

He assigned a clerk to escort us to the casemates. This was done, and we now had to make our choice. Fortunately, I knew something about casemates, because I had lived in them for years.[4]

"Captain," I said, "we'll take a cell on the second floor. It's true that it looks frightful up there, and because of the vaulted roof one has the feeling that he is enclosed in a large steamer trunk. However, it is always better to trample on other people's heads than to be trampled on by them, because between the two floors there are no reinforced ceilings, but just boards. In the spring at the first thaw these old ceilings begin to leak, water seeps down the walls, and the poor fellow down below gets the worst of it."

We therefore selected a cell on the second floor. The clerk provided us with a cleaning woman and she secured a bed for us. Our belongings were brought up and "Uncle" Rese and Prütz came to say good-by. I wondered what explanation "Uncle" Rese had given the general for all those lovely receipts.

I asked the clerk about it and he said, "The general doesn't concern himself with such matters. That is the provost marshal's business, and he'll probably come to discuss it with you tomorrow."

The man was somewhat inquisitive; I could tell, because he stayed with us a long time, although he had no further business. I was inquisitive too, and so I asked him how Schramm was; I knew him from Jena and also from the time when we were imprisoned on remand.

The answer was, "Very well!"

One word led to another, and eventually he told me that upon Schramm's arrival the general had read his name and had asked him who his father was. — Schramm told him that his father was the regimental officer Schramm from Gleiwitz.

Then the splendid old general had thrown up his arms and called out, "And I should treat harshly the son of the man who saved my life at Waterloo!" — The general saw to it that he was well treated, but nevertheless Schramm did many stupid things.

Yes, that's the way things go in this world! This fellow had been treated well, whereas other people much better than he had suffered bitterly, and the lives of some had been completely ruined. He had been a member of our students' association, and he was a big windbag who always wanted to play first fiddle.[5] However, when the crucial time came and "Uncle" Dambach put pressure on him and flattered him by telling him he had "a philosophic mind which was able to grasp and comprehend the scope of the investigation in its absolute totality," then his miserable vanity and deplorable weakness came to the fore. He not only confessed — the rest of us did that too — but he also began to denunciate.[6] He wanted to court the favor of the criminal councillor and asked permission to speak to him at any time of day or night, whenever he called to mind some poor pastor in Saxony or some poor doctor in Silesia, who at one time had been a member of the students' association, but who was now at home with wife and children. This he did just so that they might have the pleasure of seeing his surly countenance, when they were brought face to face with him at the investigation trial.

Yes, this fellow had been treated well! — Criminal Councillor Dambach was grateful to him for the information, and for that reason he had him transferred to another fortress, where he would be alone and where we couldn't make things difficult for him. And at this fortress the commanding officer was none other than the man whose life had been saved by Schramm's father! We were hardly allowed to talk to one another, but he was permitted to associate with educated and cultured people. He could hold his fiancée in his arms and embrace her and kiss her, while the poor wives and children of the men whom he had informed on grieved and stretched out their arms for their husbands and fathers. — That's the way things go in this world!

The Captain and I talked about this after the clerk had left. I was particularly angry at Schramm, because he had unnecessarily implicated me in his gratuitous confessions. He had betrayed me the very first day of the trial and declared that I had been politically involved. But that was all long ago. Everywhere we had been until now we had lived in harmony with one another; so why should we stir up old troubles now? The Captain and I made up our minds to stay on good terms with Schramm. We didn't think that should be too difficult, since he lived in another section of the fortress, and it would be only during our free time that we would have any contact with him. Nevertheless, he made things so difficult for us that nothing came of our good intentions.

That evening the general's attendant was admitted to our cell by the guard commander, and he brought us a basket. He said he was bringing best wishes from the general and also a little something for supper, since we were probably not completely settled as yet. — That suited us perfectly and we looked upon the brown fried potatoes and the warm egg beer as indications of better things to come.

The Captain said, "Charles, I think we're better off here than with the deceased count."

"I think so too, Captain, but now we have to go to bed because I'm dog tired. But one more thing! When you get into bed, don't go in with your head straight up; you have to sit on the edge of the bed and then duck as you crawl in. Otherwise you'll crash your head against the arched vault. That's the way one has to do it in casemates."

I crept into bed, but he rummaged and fumbled around for a while, and just as I was about to fall asleep — bang — I heard something crash against the boards above me. The Captain had forgotten my warning, had crashed his head against the flying buttress and fallen backwards out of his bed. Yes, the casemates have their inconveniences too. —

The next morning the provost marshal[7] came to us. He was a good-natured, but long-winded old bore, who told us about all kinds of things, but of gendarme Rese and his receipts he said nothing. As he counted out on the table our munificent royal Prussian per diem of five silver pennies in cash, we realized that henceforth we would be well-to-do people who, when occasion arose, would have money jingling in their pockets.

Now we had to report to the general, but first we had to be shaved, because we had beards that looked like flax combs. It didn't pay to keep a regular barber at the fortress, and so it was a soldier who took care of the haircuts and shaves, whenever he didn't have any other wood-chopping to do. Everyone said that he had a very heavy hand, and that was my opinion too. Furthermore, he had only a very cheap razor. He had once had the misfortune of mistaking the general's beautiful wig for real hair, and since he wanted to do a good job in cutting off a few curls, he had inadvertently shaved off the entire back part of the wig. As a result he stood in very ill repute with one and all, and no one wanted to be shaved or have his hair cut by him except in a case of necessity.

Well, this was a case of necessity, and so I sat down, but never before or after did it take such a long time to be shaved. It's an experience to be shaved by a Prussian fusilier with a cheap razor. — After me it was the Captain's turn and he held out very bravely, but when this fellow was about to lather only part of the face at a time — the Captain said, "Stop!"

He explained that the mustache was his pride and joy. He had been fortunate enough to nurture this little forest preserve through a whole week, and if the work had been his, the pleasure should be his too.

And ever since that time he did have great pleasure in it, and I have never again seen a mustache such as the Captain raised. He didn't curl it or paste it or grease it; he simply trained his blond mustache to grow downward, never upward, so that it looked like a trellis falling down harmlessly over his two lips or like a newly thatched roof over the two half-doors of a cottage in which peace and contentment reign. — Later I tried to raise a mustache too, but it didn't amount to much.

We went to the general and he introduced us to a man who was to be our overseer. He was supposed to guard us and watch over us, so that we would not leave the path of our prescribed walk. His name was Sergeant Bartels.

Bartels left with us, and when we came to the linden lane, he said, "Gentlemen, for two hours every morning and again for two hours every afternoon you may walk back and forth in the fresh air from this little linden tree to the lower gate. You will not be allowed to speak to anyone except to one another and to me."

We were thus informed of the regulations, and since our lot had improved to such an extent that we were now better off then ever before, we accepted the conditions without complaint.

CHAPTER 15

NOW it would have been no more than right if we had been grateful and satisfied with what the general and good fortune had so kindly placed in our laps. However, man is by nature a restless spirit; he tries to effect a change in a good situation just as in a bad one. He always wants to change and improve things, and if he is not able to do so, as in our case, then he begins to overburden his heart with wishes and hopes and designs, even though the fulfillment of his dreams is completely hopeless.

Now I have always been such a restless spirit, but this time it was not I, but the Captain who threw the sourdough into the kneading trough.

We had already been at this fortress for two weeks and every morning and every afternoon we regularly went for a walk as far as the little linden tree. We walked one behind the other just like ducks on parade, because the path was muddy and we were not allowed to leave the lane. Herr Bartels sat on a pile of cannon balls at the carriage house halfway between the linden tree and the lower gate, and when the weather was good, he sat out in the sunshine. He watched our legs and played with the tassel on his sword.

On the second day we saw Schramm; he walked with us and talked a great deal. The "philosopher" from the time when we were committed for trial had turned into a "poet" here at the fortress. He had written a long heroic epic, *Paulus*,[1] and unfortunately, he knew it by heart and declaimed the most beautiful passages from the epic to us. The poem was supposed to have the metrical structure of Homer, but it sounded more like Johann Heinrich Voss[2] trying to add a little lacquer to Goethe and Schiller.

For the Captain and me Schramm's *Paulus* was very annoying, because we had nothing comparable to offer in return with which we might have silenced him. However, it was still more annoying when he started to tell us about his fiancée, because in that category we really had nothing to offer. He seemed to enjoy making us envious, because he described her from head to foot. He pointed her out to us in the distance, and finally we saw her at close range, and she was certainly very attractive. Schramm made it sound so wonderful when he told us that she came to see him three times a week and that he then imparted to her some book learning, for — as he said — "she had not as yet reached the level of his culture." In short, he currycombed us with thorns and nettles and was thus a cause of continual irritation to us.

The Captain and I were angry, and we shared equally in this anger; I was angry because of *Paulus*, and he was angry because of the fiancée.

One day we happened to meet an older lady and a slender young girl, and since the footpath was so narrow and the road so deep in mud, we walked in single file and edged our way past the two ladies. It was easy enough to pass the young girl, but more difficult to pass the older woman, because she was somewhat corpulent. The Captain, ever the gentleman, was wearing his boots, of which the soles were pretty well worn through. In military fashion he raised his hand to his cap, spoke a few courteous words, and then stepped into the deep mud with his inadequate footgear. With difficulty I managed to squeeze past the ladies, because in those days they didn't wear crinoline petticoats.

After we had gone a few steps Sergeant Bartels came straight up to the Captain and said, "You have just spoken to the ladies; you're not allowed to do that."

The Captain replied that he had merely spoken a few polite words.

"Polite or impolite, it makes no difference," said Bartels. "You're not supposed to speak to anyone, and if some people pass by, you're not allowed to greet them, because they don't know you."

I then asked who the ladies were.

"I can't tell you that," said Bartels.

"Well, then I'll tell you," said Schramm. "That's the wife of Quartermaster Lucke,³ and the young lady is her daughter by her first marriage, and her name is Aurelia Schönborn.⁴ They live in that casemate which they are just now entering."

"Herr Schramm," said Bartels, "I am well aware that you know everybody at the fortress, but I must report to the general that you are imparting information to these two newcomers."

The casemate which the two ladies had entered was located directly opposite the little linden tree, and that was as far as we were allowed to walk. When we arrived at that point, the Captain took his stand at the tree, drew his gray coat with the seven collars more closely about him, and looked over toward the casemate.

Schramm and I retraced our steps, and now for the first time Herr Bartels was in a dilemma; should he remain standing there with the Captain, or should he continue walking with us? Finally he chose a middle course; he sat down again on the pile of cannon balls and toyed with the tassel on his sword, but he observed the Captain more closely than us.

We came back again and the Captain was still standing at the linden tree. We left and returned once again, and the Captain was still standing there, except that he had now made himself more comfortable by leaning against the pole which supported the little tree.

"Come along now, Captain!" I said.

"Let me be!" he answered.

He stroked the yellow stubble which was now thriving very well under his nose and leaned against the pole with even more determination.

Our free time was now over, we were locked up again, and with long strides the Captain was pacing up and down in the cell.

"Such a stupid fellow!" he said. "Such a very stupid fellow!"

"Bartels?" I asked.

"No, Schramm," he answered; "that clown is a downright braggart who boasts that he has a fiancée. Is that such a clever feat to have a fiancée if one is at liberty to associate with the whole world?"

All the time the Captain continued to pace up and down even more resolutely.

"Captain," I said, "for the most part he was quite friendly today. He even let me have a copy of *Paulus*. Just look here, he has also drawn pictures for it."

"Is that so? He can do that too? — Yes, he knows everything, he can do everything, he has everything. His bragging is simply unbearable! — What decent person brags about his fiancée like that? Charles, I consider such a relationship as something most tender and sacred, which must be kept as a secret even from one's most intimate friends. And yesterday as we were taking our walk that simpleton even brought along one of his fiancée's shoes just to show us what a small foot she has."

What the Captain said was true, but why did it make him so

angry? I thought it was all very amusing and laughed about it. —
Now I began to read in *Paulus*, and gradually I became angry too.
Every sentence began so grandiloquently, as though it were a
pronouncement of Schramm's infinite wisdom, but when the important point was to be made he missed the mark, just as when one
misses a fly with a swatter. And then the meter!

"Captain, listen to this! Dum de dum de dum de dum . . . ."

"Oh, never mind! I've already heard him declaim that same
passage twice, because it's supposed to be something very
special."

"Then look at the picture that goes with it."

It was a picture of Paulus pursued by Satan. Paulus is running as
swiftly as he can, but Satan doesn't let up at all and follows him on
the wings of a bat. From his long tail he keeps shooting infernal
flashes of lightning at Paulus.

The Captain looked at me over his shoulder with an expression as
sour as though he had been marinated in vinegar. The devil only
knew what was wrong with him today. He was as angry as I had ever
seen him. "A miserable wretch!" he said.

"Schramm?" I asked.

"No, Paulus," he answered, "Schramm's Paulus. He runs away
when the going gets rough, just like Schramm himself. I'll wager
that Schramm in his vanity stood in front of the mirror and thought
he was Paulus."

It was impossible to talk to the Captain on this evening. He was
very upset, and his face was as flushed as it had been in the Berlin
prison.

"I got my feet wet," he said as he pulled off his boots.

"Oh, that explains it," I thought to myself, and aloud I added that
he should have used his common sense. If he knew the condition of
his boots, he should not have waded through the puddles because of
the old lady and then stood for a whole hour with his wet feet at the
little linden tree.

"Charles," he asked and his eyes really lit up, "did you see the
young lady?"

"Yes," I answered, "and she is a very slender and willowy young
maid."

"Did you see her hair?"

"Yes," I answered, "it's red."

"Red? — You call that red? — I call it blond! I'll even say it is light blond! And that is a color which has always been praised by poets and artists. It is not the sunbeam that gilds the hair, but the hair that gilds the sunbeam."

"What in the devil's name is the meaning of all this?"

"Did you see the complexion of the young lady?"

"Yes," I said, "as far as it was possible through her green veil and in passing."

"As white as alabaster!" he called out.

"Yes," I replied, "but she has freckles."

The Captain looked at me, shrugged his shoulders, and walked up and down. After a while he stood in front of me and asked, "Charles, are you trying to annoy me?"

"No," I answered, "that wasn't my intention at all."

"Then why do you specifically mention that feature which is always considered an indication of a delicate complexion?"

I told him that I was not trying to annoy him. I hadn't said anything against the girl except that her face was spotted like a turkey's egg.

"I object to such comparisons," he said irritably and started to walk up and down again.

The situation was getting more and more difficult, but finally I understood what it was all about, and so I told him to disregard what I had said, because she was really a very beautiful girl. That pleased him and he was once again my good old Captain, full of spirit and enthusiasm, when his imagination was given full rein.

"Charles," he called out, "did you see her eyes?"

"Yes," I said, "they are blue."

That was not good enough for him, because many girls have blue eyes; hers had to be something special.

"Blue?" he cried. "Yes, blue, but what a blue! A blue so warm that it actually takes on a greenish luster. Not only the clear blue heavens, but also the warm green of the earth are reflected in these eyes!"

Then I had to laugh in spite of myself, and I told him that it was probably because of the green veil that he had mistakenly taken them to be green.

Now I had really said the wrong thing. He had always had great respect for women's eyes, just like modern poets who always write only of the eyes and let the rest of the human body fit in where it will.

That evening it was impossible to talk to the Captain; we could no longer come to any understanding. Nevertheless, as I started to read aloud the sublime passages in *Paulus*, which Schramm in his infinite wisdom had underlined in red, the Captain walked about in the cell, accompanying my reading with violent gesticulations.

If I had more understanding, or if as a child I had paid more attention to old wives' tales and their nostrums and magic formulae for curing all human illnesses, it would have been obvious to me immediately that something was wrong with my good Captain and that he was coming down with some sickness. As it was, I thought nothing of it and went to bed. The next morning, however, I was to become well aware of it.

I was awakened early by a loud noise, and as I sat up I saw my good Captain sitting upright in bed and shouting at the top of his voice, "Victoria! Victoria!"

"Captain, what's the matter?"

"Victoria, I am your Albert!"

"In heaven's name, calm down!"

I jumped out of bed and saw in what a bad state the Captain was. His face had a brownish-red color and he was throwing his arms around without knowing what he was doing. — "Victoria, I am your Albert!" he kept repeating again and again. "Charles, damned turkey's egg! Throw that clown Schramm out! There he stands and shows me his fiancée's shoe. — Her hair isn't red — it's blond — just blond!"

And that went on and on.

I gave him a glass of cold water, because I didn't know what else to do, and then I ran downstairs to call the sentry and ask him to fetch the surgeon major.

He came after a while and had the Captain bled until he became calmer. However, he didn't forget his "Victoria"; he kept on mumbling that to himself.

"What's all this talk about Victoria?" asked the surgeon major.

I told him that I didn't know myself, but I might venture a guess. He had read in the newspapers that Queen Victoria of England was going to marry Prince Albert, and since the Captain's name was also Albert, he might have thought that he was the real Albert, and that on the whole it would be more beneficial to him to be a prince regent of England than to sit any longer in a Prussian fortress.

The surgeon major saw the point and arranged to have him sent to the army hospital.

And so my Captain left me and I had to take my walks with Schramm and *Paulus*, and in the evening I had to sit alone in my cell.

CHAPTER 16

THROUGH God's mercy my good old friend soon recovered from his pneumonia. I was very happy when he came back from the hospital, because the "Philosopher," who was served up to me every day as the only course on the menu, finally became too tough and leathery for my taste. Furthermore, he annoyed me and wore me out with his conceit, because he considered himself an important person and acted as though he had been sent to Graudenz by the highly esteemed Supreme Court for the express purpose of serving as an object of our admiration.

Who was therefore happier than I that my old Captain was now back again in circulation? But strange to say, he was very quiet; he always walked around absorbed in his own thoughts, and when we had our free time outdoors, he again took his position at the pole supporting the linden tree and looked over at the casemate under the dark vault of which his star had once set. I could now see very clearly that he had given up all thoughts of Victoria and the English throne. Such fantasy lay merely in the blood, and that had been drawn off by the surgeon, but thoughts of Aurelia were still in full swing, because they lay deeper, possibly even in his heart.

Schramm must have noticed something too, for he made all sorts of nasty insinuations, naturally with subtle references to the cleverness with which he had arranged his own betrothal. Even in the narrow-minded head of Sergeant Bartels a light flashed on. His thoughts may have gone back to earlier days, when in the dark hour of midnight he had stood all alone on sentry duty thinking of the woman who was later to become his wife. After making his rounds he had leaned on a pole with his chin on his gun barrel and dozed off, until the pole had given way and he had had to pick himself up from the ground with gun and all.

However, that was long ago, and in such matters he now had little sympathy either for himself or for others. He therefore barked at the Captain, "Are you going to start leaning against that damned pole again? I'll have to report that."

"Go, report it to the devil!" the Captain shouted at him in anger.

"No, I'll report it to the general," answered Herr Bartels.

"You can report it if you wish. — I'm allowed to walk this far and to stand wherever I want to."

"Yes, you may, but you are not allowed to lean against the pole. You keep on bending it crooked, and then I have to borrow an ax from the tax collector and straighten it up again, and the tax collector doesn't want to lend me the ax any more."

From this one can see that love at a fortress is connected with all kinds of vexing circumstances; the Captain's love was connected with the pole supporting the little linden tree.

In the midst of these vexing circumstances it was very fortunate that some of our comrades from Magdeburg were likewise transferred to Graudenz. This reunion revived our spirits, and for a while even the Captain forgot his longing for Aurelia, when little Copernicus,[1] his best friend from Halle, and Don Juan[2] moved in.

Now these were a couple of delightful fellows. Don Juan, who was from Stralsund, was an unprincipled rascal and somewhat of a reprobate. Love, which for the Captain was a sublime relationship transcending all time and space, was for Don Juan something which belonged to this world. He was not actually one of our group, because by vocation he was a book dealer who had once delivered a long speech at the Hambacher Fest,[3] but he had been imprisoned with us for a long time, both during the trial in Berlin and in Magdeburg. He was a tall strapping fellow, and what was more important to me, he was a poet of sorts. I was happy about that, because we now had someone on our side with whom we could overtrump Schramm and his *Paulus*. Don Juan was prepared at any hour to fall in love; not one time for always, but always for one time. I don't know whether they ever put the real Don Juan in chains, or if they did, how he reacted to that, but this Don Juan always rattled his chains whenever he saw a pretty girl and acted like a greyhound catching sight of a rabbit in the distance.

Little Copernicus, on the other hand, was a fellow of altogether different size. Don Juan was almost six feet tall, but Copernicus measured hardly five feet. Nevertheless, with the fusiliers at Halle he had been left-wing commander in the second file. Don Juan weighed over two hundred pounds, but Copernicus weighed precisely ninety-six pounds. Don Juan had a handsome red and white complexion, but Copernicus had a brownish-yellow coloring because his face was covered with freckles. They both had crooked noses, but Don Juan's was large, whereas Copernicus's was so pointed that one could have threaded the eye of a darning needle with it. This pert little nose looked out into the world as though it were about to say, "Here I am; have a good look," and it belonged to a fellow who was lithe and sturdy. Copernicus couldn't reach up to the tall fellows, but when he stood on tiptoe, he looked and acted just as tall as a six-footer.

Some people keep busy with their arms and hands, some with their heads, still others with their stomachs, but Copernicus was kept busy with his bile. For three quarters of the year that I spent together with him at Graudenz he had yellow jaundice, and half the time we were allowed for our walks he spent diligently looking into blacksmith Grunwaldt's tar barrel, because this faith cure was supposed to help him. Once when he came before the general, the old gentleman was so frightened at his appearance that he gave him permission to look into blacksmith Grunwaldt's tar barrel any time he wished, and blacksmith Grunwaldt, who lived opposite us, had no objection to that.

There was great joy when the two arrived, especially because of Copernicus, and especially for the Captain, since the newcomer was his best friend from Halle. They had both studied pandects and Prussian jurisdiction together, had taken their first bar examination at the same time, and later in Magdeburg they had lived together in the same cell. Copernicus was assigned to our wing of the fortress and was given the cell beneath us. Now we three could get together as often as we pleased, because our cells were not locked. We talked at length about this and that; Copernicus told us about our old friends, and that Witte[4] would soon join us. He added that the Frenchman[5] might be brought to Graudenz too, but for the time being he had been sent to the charité[6] in Berlin because of a mental illness. We told Copernicus about the old general, and also about Bartels and Schramm and *Paulus*. The Captain had brought along a cage containing canaries, and now little Copernicus brought along a cage full of white mice. He was raising them and he kept them in a neat glass palace. "Well, every bit helps," said the fly as it spit into the Rhine, and although I derived no great pleasure from the mice, I could at least look at them occasionally, and one should thank God for everything, even for mice, that is, as long as they are kept secure in their glass container.

A few days later there was a rumor going around at the fortress that Dunin, the archbishop of Posen,[7] was being brought to Graudenz to be imprisoned with us. It was just at that time that the Catholics on the Rhine and in Posen and Silesia were making considerable trouble for the Prussian state. We had learned of this from Schramm, and he had heard it from his fiancée. Herr Bartels had also mentioned it inadvertently once when his royal Prussian army regulations came into conflict with his Catholic faith.

Well, one day everything was astir. All those at the fortress who were Catholic — and most of them were — came out of houses and casemates and lined up along the street. "He's coming, he's coming! He's already here!"

We others also went as far as we were allowed to go, that is, as far as our little linden tree with Herr Bartels right at our heels. From there we could look over to the commandant's headquarters, and in front of the headquarters there stood a carriage around which the people were milling. After we had stood there for a while, a man came out and the people genuflected reverently and asked for his blessing. He had taken off his hat and was waving to the people, and as he came closer, we could see that he was a small dignified gentleman, rather corpulent and with a bald head. As he came closer, Herr Bartels also genuflected and asked to be blessed, but then all of a sudden we started to laugh. Little Copernicus pushed Herr Bartels aside and rushed up to the archbishop and cried, "Holy smoke! Where did you come from, my fat friend?"

We all crowded around him, and Herr Bartels kept calling, "I must report this! I must report this!" and "Men, you must not talk to the most reverend gentleman!"

Finally the clerk from the commandant's headquarters came and said very forcibly, "Are you crazy, Bartels? That's not the archbishop; he's a friend of these men."

With that things were back to normal again, and we left with our "archbishop." We couldn't stop laughing when he described with what great respect he had been received by everyone on the entire trip, and how the postmasters especially had paid their homage with food and drink.

As a result of such good treatment the Archbishop arrived at Graudenz in excellent condition. None of us others could have been so completely mistaken for an archbishop as he, because in ecclesiastical appearance he was superior to all. His face had a natural unctuous effusion which broke out at the slightest provocation. It would have been much better if he had used this as ointment on his head. It might have produced some hair, because his head was as bald as a billiard ball on the lower part of which someone had added a fringe. In addition, to keep himself warm he wore a long brown overcoat, which he had inherited from his father. Unfortunately, his father had been six feet tall, whereas the Archbishop was only half an inch taller than Copernicus. He also had a violet-red cap, which Don Juan had once given to him in Magdeburg as a Christmas present. Don Juan had accompanied the gift with a poem entitled: "This pumpkin needs a cover." On the trip to Graudenz it was this coat and cap that had first started the rumor of his sanctity, and the drivers of the mail coaches had spread it from town to town, until he finally arrived as an "archbishop."

But what were they going to do with him now? He was a typesetter and had committed such a horrible crime that even we others, who were listed as regicides, were horrified at the thought of living with him. The fact was that he had been in Switzerland earning his bread very honestly as a typesetter with Orelli[8] in Zürich. However — and this was the most terrible thing about the fellow — he didn't want to give up this good livelihood, when the King of Prussia suddenly got the idea of forbidding his subjects to live in Switzerland. Nevertheless, he later returned, whereupon he was imprisoned in Prussian fortresses for a number of years, so that he might again get used to eating Prussian bread instead of Swiss bread.

We could not possibly live together with such a hardened criminal. This time the old general fortunately decided the matter for us. The typesetter was to live with the book dealer, because they were related by vocation anyway, and so the most saintly Archbishop had to move in with Don Juan. — This was an unusual pairing, to be sure, but it couldn't be helped. In a way a fortress is very similar to the state of marriage: people who belong together will always get together, even if the devil has to bring them together with a wheelbarrow.

This was the beginning of a merry time for us, as things began to get more lively at the fortress. That is, there was fun and merriment for us, but for Herr Bartels it was a period of vexation and annoyance. He no longer had any time to play with the tassels on his sword or to sit on the pile of cannon balls. He now had to run from one to another to keep his eye on all of us, because sometimes while we were out walking we became separated from one another just like troops skirmishing with the enemy. Each one then tried to hide from Herr Bartels behind a tree or a building. Schramm walked with his future brother-in-law and talked about his fiancée, and Herr Bartels had to see to it that the brother-in-law did not talk to us. Copernicus stood in blacksmith Grunwaldt's gateway and looked into the tar barrel, and if Herr Bartels tried to keep him in sight, Don Juan would sneak away and begin a little romance with the tavern maid in the next house, or the Archbishop would stop an old woman, who was selling herring on the street, and ask her what they were selling for — because he had considerable business acumen. Sometimes I would walk past the limit of the little linden tree and look down at the floodgate on the river, and the Captain would always stand by his little linden tree and lean against the supporting pole, so that it was very much aslant. These were difficult times for Herr Bartels, and every day he had something to report to the general, but nothing ever came of it.

In the meantime Aurelia always sat at the window diligently occupied with her embroidery and sewing, for with such poor lighting in the old casemates where else should she sit except at the window? Sometimes she came out of the house, and then the Captain would march up as though in military parade and come to attention facing her. He would stroke his blond mustache — which he had let grow again — and talk to me or someone else in a loud voice about the beautiful weather. Sometimes Aurelia also went walking, and as she passed him on the narrow path she would graze him just as she had on that earlier occasion. The Captain would bow to her just as he had planned to bow to Queen Victoria in asking for her hand.

One time after the slim and graceful Aurelia had passed the Captain, he turned and followed her, staying about five paces to the rear and treading as far as possible in her footsteps. His heart was torn between love and anger, because Bartels wouldn't let him get out of sight and therefore followed five paces behind him. Another five paces back came Schramm merely out of friendly curiosity to see whether the Captain would be just as lucky as he. Behind Schramm came Don Juan on the lookout for a pretty girl, and behind Don Juan came the Archbishop hoping to deter him from any immoral act. When the Captain turned around and saw the entire procession behind him, he rushed into his cell in a fit of anger and carried on in a very agitated manner.

When I came in I heard some disconnected expressions such as: "The most sacred thing is trampled into the dust" and "Don't these people know what love means?" He didn't hesitate to call Don Juan a disreputable reprobate, Schramm a clown, the loyal Archbishop a jackass, and the worthy Bartels a complete fool. "Copernicus," he said, "is the only one of the newcomers with an ounce of tact and honor."

Poor Captain! — He didn't suspect that it was precisely this little Copernicus who was to cause him all possible heartache.

A few days after this incident Copernicus asked, "Charles, why does the Captain keep standing there as though he were nailed to the linden tree?"

That was a difficult question for me to answer; it was a matter which could not be kept secret, and yet at the same time I didn't want to reveal in what toils of love the Captain was ensnared, and that because of Aurelia he had renounced all his claims to the throne of England and to Queen Victoria. I therefore merely said, "Oh, he's just looking; there's a pretty girl living across the street."

"The same one he was following a couple of days ago?" he asked, and with that the impulsive little creature came at me as though he were going to stick his nose through my necktie.

"What's the matter with you?" I replied. "Can't he look at a girl and follow her, if he wishes?"

"Charles, is it the same one with the beautiful blond hair?"

"What the devil!" I answered. "You say it's blond, and he says it's blond, but I think it's red. Don't I have any eyes in my head?"

He abruptly changed the subject and started to ask me about her family, and since he was a good friend of the Captain, I, stupid fool, suspected nothing and told him everything.

The next day as we were standing there at the linden tree during our free time, there was the scoundrel standing there at the linden tree with the Captain. I thought to myself, "The little fellow has a feeling of sympathy for the Captain; he doesn't want him to stand there by himself, and probably wants to cheer him up a little, even though he himself has one of his jaundice spells, for which wet feet might be very harmful."

I was really pleased with Copernicus. — Serpent!

CHAPTER 17

A few days later Bartels came up to me and said, "Now there are always two of them standing there."

"Where?"

"Over there, at the little linden tree."

"Let them stand there!"

"No, I shall have to report that."

"Then report it!"

"Well, that's just the trouble. If I report it to the general, he always agrees with what I have to say, but then he does nothing about it. I wouldn't mind if the two would lean against the pole with their backs to each other, or if they would both face the coach house."

"Why shouldn't they look in the other direction?"

"Well, because of the young girl; girls stand at the very top of my list of instructions."

"Why is that?"

Herr Bartels came closer to me and whispered softly, "It's because of Herr Schramm; the general has enough with that one courtship, and he doesn't want any other affairs like that to worry about."

What Herr Bartels had noticed, the rest of us were certain to notice in due time too. The two friends from Halle had become rivals in love: the Captain in the secure feeling of original ownership, and the conniver Copernicus as an interloper contesting the Captain's rights of legal ownership.

We never found out whether or not Aurelia ever noticed the Captain's constant presence at the pole. She continued to sit there and sew and act as unconcerned as though the Captain were wooing her dear mother. Day after day for hours at a time the Captain appeared in her heaven like a planet radiating its soft light, but now that Copernicus was shooting back and forth on the horizon like a sulphur-yellow comet — with the difference that the comet stuck out its tail and Copernicus his nose — she must have become aware of something going on. However, as is usually the case in such matters, the Captain, who should have been the first, was the last one to notice that something was wrong. While Copernicus had his inquisitive nose sticking in other people's business and was directing all kinds of pointed questions at Aurelia, the Captain stood quietly at his pole. His face was as calm and peaceful as the evening star, and he hardly noticed the ardent machinations which Halle's wing-commander of the second file was carrying on before his very eyes. Well, finally, finally, he began to smell a rat, but before I continue, I must make a short digression.

Close by our casemates there was a school for young girls. At noontime when we were again being returned to our cells, we were met by the little girls who skipped about in the beautiful spring sunshine like a swarm of butterflies flitting from flower to flower. In the fresh springtime breezes the musty schoolroom was forgotten as the young children came dancing merrily down the linden lane. They tossed their bothersome old dog-eared textbooks high into the air, so that they too might share in the warm rays of the sun. Above this joyful scene the linden trees spread their fresh young leaves and so blended light with shadow that the red and white and blue and green dresses looked even more brilliant in color. From these varicolored dresses there peered delicate little faces with blue or brown eyes radiating the happiness and freshness of youth. However, when the children saw us in Bartels's company, they became quiet and observed us with a wary glance, as though we were something strange and a deterrent to their merriment. One of the older girls made a forced curtsey, as she had been taught by her mother for just such a frightening situation.

However, it didn't take too long before we became friendlier with the girls. They knew from their own schoolroom what it meant to be confined, and it is also possible that Herr Bartels did not look upon the young children as young ladies as yet, and therefore paid no attention when we exchanged a few words with them.

There was one girl in the group who was the crown jewel of all. She was a child so lovely that not even Bartels had the heart to object whenever I spoke more than just a few words to her. There was a roguish gaiety shining in her large brown eyes, and on her bright face there lay a blend of light and shade, as though she had been born beneath a sunbeam and in the soft shadow of the green linden tree, and as though she had spent her short life in a land where it was always spring. — She is dead now — and I have become an old fellow, but she still stands before my mind's eye in all her loveliness. Whenever I see a beautiful child, I subconsciously measure its beauty against that of my little Ida, and even today I still thank God that He allowed me to experience such pure joy in the person of this lovely child.

She was a half-sister of Aurelia, and although Herr Bartels had a profound hatred of the older sister because of all the trouble she caused him, he could never be angry with this little girl. He permitted me to speak to her, and to show his own affection he always added a double ending of endearment to her name and called her "Idachechen."

Every afternoon at two o'clock Idachechen went by Copernicus's window, and since he lived on the ground floor and the weather was pleasant enough to keep the window open, it naturally followed that he began to pass the time by chatting with her.

All in all, Copernicus was a decent fellow, but he had nothing of the Captain's good nature, which extended as far as the sky is high. Copernicus, on the other hand, was earthbound, and there he knew how to work out everything to his own advantage. What was therefore more natural than that he should make a talebearer of my sweet little Idachechen? She had to tell him what Aurelia had said on that day, and what she had said the day before, and where she had gone walking the day before that. Then he mentioned casually in his confounded sly way what he had said about Aurelia, and what Idachechen should tell Aurelia that he had said. — In short, this telegraphic system was in full operation and the conniver was making a fool of the Captain, who was naive enough not to realize what was going on down below. I could have laughed aloud if I had not been so concerned about the Captain.

Whenever the Captain had the good fortune to greet his beloved on his walk, he would always return to the casemate and carve a notch in the doorpost as a sign and souvenir of his fleeting happiness. Then he sometimes stood for hours before the notch recalling the special circumstances of the meeting, and he drank so deeply from the beaker of hope that his eyes shone brightly with courage. Then he took from his bird cage his most beautiful young yellow male canary and stroked it and comforted it and told it how well it would be treated some day and how much it pained him that they would have to part.

"Are you going to sell it?" I asked.

"For no money in the world!" was his answer. "But . . ."

I understood the meaning of this "but" and thought to myself, "Who can tell? He might find happiness with the help of this canary!"

The Captain, however, was thinking only of the canary's happiness and ignoring his own, because Copernicus was stealing a march on him.

One noon the deceitful little conniver came upstairs to our cell.

"Charles, do you have a box or a carton?"

"Yes," I said, "I have one, but I need it myself."

That was true, because in the box I kept my black crayons and the pine soot, which I always used in large quantities, because for the most part I had to draw people in black clothes.

He said I should loan it to him for a few days; then he would return it to me.

Well, I gave it to him because I had no idea what he was going to do with it. He took the box, went downstairs, took a couple of white mice from his mouse palace and put them into the box. I followed him with the intention of telling him about the inside of the box, but just as I came downstairs I saw him pass the box through the iron bars and I heard him say to little Idachechen, "And give Aurelia my kindest regards!"

Now I had clearcut proof that he had betrayed the Captain. — "What did you put into the box?" I asked.

"Oh, I merely gave little Ida a couple of white mice," he answered, and with that the blue blood rose in his yellow face, so that he began to look green.

"Aha!" I thought. "He's trying to put one over on me!" I was angry that he was taking advantage of the innocent little child in this way and cutting in on the Captain, who after all had a prior right to Aurelia. On the other hand, I was also delighted to think of what the white mice in the pine soot box must look like.

I'm not exactly inquisitive, but nevertheless I like to know everything. Shortly before two o'clock, when the cells were unlocked and the little girls were going home from school, I went down to Copernicus, lit my pipe, and in a very affable way stood next to him at the window. Before long my little Ida came by with eyes red from weeping. She had been thoroughly scolded by her mother, and Aurelia had received a terrible fright when she had opened the box. Her mother told her to tell Herr Copernicus that if he ever again had something he didn't want, he should keep it, because in her house she already had enough mice that nibbled on her bacon.

Copernicus again became green with anger, and as he opened the box he found two ordinary gray mice, just like those that run around free everywhere.

I'll never forget the look he gave me, as he put back into the mouse palace the two little creatures covered with pine soot.

"I can thank you and that stupid box for that!" he shouted angrily.

Well, I defended myself, because I was in the right, but as bad luck would have it, the Captain came in just at that moment, and from our quarrel he learned that Copernicus had given Aurelia a couple of white mice as an everlasting keepsake.

At first, when the Captain unexpectedly stood behind us, I was terribly frightened, and Copernicus, the miscreant, was even more so, but then the Captain roared with laughter, "What can one say to that? This crazy little fellow gives a young lady a couple of white mice! I must say, Copernicus, a bouquet of roses would have been more fragrant."

"Thank God!" I thought to myself. "He's taking it all as a joke." To keep him in this jovial mood I said, "Take a look at the little beasts and see what happened to them in my pine soot box."

I showed him the mice, which had been intended as a present for Aurelia and which were now running around like crazy in the mouse palace frightening all the other mice with their gray coats. The Captain almost died laughing, but Copernicus had become as green as grass. He turned from the box containing his mice, ran out the door, which had been unlocked, and called, "If I want to give a lady something, it's nobody's business!"

"Nobody's business?" said the Captain, now also very angry, "Nobody's business?" He ran after Copernicus and shouted, "It's my business, and you know it's my business. I'll not tolerate having anyone make this lady an object of ridicule."

Thus they both rushed past Don Juan and the Archbishop, who had also just come back from their period of exercise. Copernicus went straightway for blacksmith Grunwaldt's tar barrel, because he felt that his bile had again been aroused, and also because he didn't want to be seen by Aurelia on account of the ill-chosen present. The Captain made his way directly to the little linden tree, where he began to pace back and forth looking for all the world like a blue lion, because in this beautiful weather he had discarded his gray overcoat with the seven collars and was now wearing a blue jacket. However, today he lacked the proper feeling of reverence to be standing quietly at the pole.

Don Juan and the Archbishop asked me what had happened, and I told them the whole story about the mice and the altercation between the two friends. That was oil for the Archbishop's spiritual lamp; it was his calling to make peace, and so he went immediately to the Captain and he ingeniously set to work by making use of some common figures of speech. He said that there are two kinds of people in the world: men and women. Our Lord has placed both on earth because they belong together. Sometimes they are perfectly suited to each other just like a lid on a pot, but sometimes they are not suited to each other, and sometimes the pot has its eye on some other lid, to which no one has been paying any attention.

At this point the Archbishop paused and looked at the Captain with an expression of deep sympathy in his eyes, and his bald head began to look more venerable than usual. The Captain looked at him too, but — as I have said — like a blue lion. The Archbishop, without showing the least bit of fear, continued with his speech and his metaphor. If pot and lid do not fit together, or if someone tries to force them together, it will surely result in breaks and cracks. Against this danger everyone must be on guard, and he, the Archbishop, gave him, the Captain, the good advice that he should let the pot which he has chosen just be a pot, and if the pot selects another lid, then he should let the lid go to the devil.

While the Archbishop was talking, more and more surprise was evident in the Captain's eyes, and when the Archbishop had put the last lid on his pot-and-lid speech, the Captain flew at the venerable gentleman, and — by God — if the Archbishop had had any hair on his head, the Captain would have gotten his hands in it. As it was, he grabbed him by his long overcoat, the heirloom from his father, and shook up the spiritual gentleman in the most secular manner saying, "What are you talking about? What are you talking about?"

Well, what else could the Archbishop say? He was caught in a jam and so he had to come out with the truth. He said it seemed to him, as it did to the rest of us as well, that Copernicus had also been observing Aurelia, and according to all indications he would have to say that she returned Copernicus's glances more than his, the Captain's, although Copernicus was smaller and not nearly as impressive as he.

It was the Archbishop's good fortune that he said this point-blank to the Captain's face, for the Captain suddenly stiffened, released his grip on the brown overcoat, stared blankly into the Archbishop's friendly eyes, and then said very emphatically, "You stupid fool!"

Then he cast a long and angry look at Aurelia's window and rushed past Don Juan and me into his casemate. I said to myself, "This is coming to no good end."

The Archbishop came up to me, twiddling his thumbs and with his hands folded over his brown overcoat. He looked as pious as God's holy word when it is bound in calfskin.

"He knows now," he said. "I told him."

"What did he say?" I asked.

"He really didn't say anything. Generally speaking he was quite calm and finally he merely said, 'You stupid fool!' "

"Yes," I said to myself, "you stupid fool!"

Then I ran into our casemate to look after the Captain. There he sat with his head propped in his hands and a clean sheet of paper before him. On it he had drawn all kinds of letters with beautiful strokes and flourishes. He always did that when he was very excited. I went up close to him: "Captain!"

He paid no attention. I looked over his shoulder and saw that he had written in German script: "friend"; beneath it in beautiful Roman script: "my best friend!" and beneath that in Gothic script: "my best friend has betrayed me!"

"Captain!" I again called.

He didn't hear me, and as I turned around in despair and looked about in all corners, I saw everywhere nothing but white mice! — "What goes on here?" I thought.

CHAPTER 18

COPERNICUS, the conniver, was so confused because of the severe dressing down which he had received from the Captain that he had forgotten to close the door of the mouse palace, and his entire hatch of three years — and everyone knows what that means — had disembarked with wives and children from their Noah's ark and now occupied every place that was stationary, and especially our casemate.

"Captain!" I shouted. "In heaven's name, all Copernicus's white mice are here!"

As soon as I had said that, I knew I had said the wrong thing, but who can think of everything? With these words I was rubbing salt into the Captain's wounds, because all the trouble had come from these damned mice. He jumped up and looked at Copernicus's harmless little white creatures with such anger as though a herd of wild animals had broken into the cell. He called them "miserable vermin" and threw everything he could lay his hands on at the poor things. Then he chuckled sarcastically when he remembered that Copernicus had wanted to present some of this trash to Aurelia, his Aurelia. Finally, he sat down again and ignored the whole mess.

I began to chase after the confounded mice. — They had come in through the door and they would have to go out the same way. — Scat! Scat! As soon as I got rid of one, a half dozen fresh reserves came in. — I could never get the job done all alone, and so I called in the Archbishop and Don Juan. We took off our coats and the chase was on! — "Here they are!" — "Grab 'em! Grab 'em!" — "Hurrah! I have one!"

We soon began to derive some fun from the chase, and with the fun came also the laughter, so that the vault of the old casemate resounded with our joyous hilarity. His Grace the Archbishop was spinning around in his shirt sleeves like a top and rolling about in all corners, Don Juan's long legs were kicking and wriggling under the bed, and my broad back was jammed under the high-legged stove.

However, fun is not permitted at fortresses, and hunting is definitely forbidden. Just as our chase was in full swing, Bartels

came in shouting, "I must report this. The sentry has already called
out twice 'Quiet up there!' and has reported it to the sergeant, and
he has reported it to the officer of the day, and I must report it to the
general."

Well, when one is in the midst of such hilarious activity, it is just
the same as when a thatched roof is on fire: it can't be extinguished
with *one* bucket of water. I was therefore bold enough to say that he
should go and report it.

When he ordered Don Juan and the Archbishop to leave our
casemate, Don Juan laughed in his face and tried to amuse him with
all kinds of nonsensical talk, and the Archbishop explained with his
innate pomposity that the exercise period was not yet over, and until
it was, they were allowed to stay with us.

Herr Bartels left in anger, as one can well understand, and went
down to Copernicus, who by this time had returned to his cell. He
too was chasing mice, but he was doing it in a furious wrath, and not
with any pleasure. When Herr Bartels told him that he would have
to report him for filling the casemates with vermin, Copernicus
replied with some insolent remark.

Herr Bartels went and made his report. — And we? — As soon as
we had finished with our hunting upstairs, we went down to Copernicus to continue the chase on his hunting preserve. The
Archbishop, who was very practical-minded, had a brilliant idea;
each one of us should take off one of his boots and place it in a dark
corner, and then chase the mice into the boots. — This is an excellent method for hunting mice, and even today I still catch them in
this way.

We were all excited from chasing the mice and hopping around on
one boot and one sock, when the door was opened and the provost
marshal entered. He wanted to know what was going on; a report of
this uproar had already been made at the guard house.

I was about to explain everything in all brevity, but the
Archbishop pushed his way forward. I didn't object, because I knew
that he stood in well with the provost marshal. The Archbishop and
the provost marshal were both long-winded bores, and bores are
very similar to drinking pals; they never desert each other, but stick
together as closely as pitch and leather. After one long-winded bore,
the Archbishop, had explained to the last detail everything that had
happened, the other bore, the provost marshal, cooperated by con-

tributing his share to the dull conversation. When Don Juan remarked that Bartels should not have made any report, the provost marshal agreed and said that Bartels had indeed done wrong in doing so.

Just at that moment Copernicus and I were closing in on a couple of mice, which managed to escape us, but which then ran up against the provost marshal's legs. I am sure that the words of the Archbishop had so convinced the provost marshal of the justice of our cause, that he would have joined us in chasing the mice, if he had not had his sword buckled to his side and his plumed helmet on his head.

Now we were ready for Bartels. Just let him come! We had the provost marshal on our side, and we could use him in our game as a beautiful pawn to our advantage. The next day he came: Copernicus and I were to appear before the general. — We went. — The provost marshal was with the general, and Herr Bartels entered with us. — The old gentleman looked very serious, and the white wig on his head seemed somewhat ruffled, as though the thoughts beneath it were not exactly calm.

"You made such a racket in your casemates yesterday," he began.

"Yes," I said, "we were chasing mice."

"The sentry ordered you to be quiet, and you didn't obey him!"

"We were so wrapped up in our chase that we didn't hear him because of the noise we were making."

"But you are not supposed to make any noise."

"Herr General," I said, "it was a regular hunt, and as you know, it is impossible to do any hunting without much noise."

There was a suggestion of a smile on the old gentleman's face, because he was a hunter, although he had probably never taken part in a mouse hunt. I thought I would strike while the iron was hot, and so I said, "The provost marshal was there and he saw that we were not doing anything wrong."

The old gentleman looked at the provost marshal, who shook his head and said, "No, they did nothing wrong; it was just this little matter of the mice."

The old gentleman discontinued this questioning and turned to Copernicus. He said that Bartels had reported that he and the Captain were constantly standing by the little linden tree. He had observed that from his own window too, and would like to know why they were standing there all the time.

That was a very embarrassing question for Copernicus. He stuttered and stammered and finally came out with the answer, "Because of the beautiful view."

The general looked at Bartels, and Bartels said very spitefully, "Yes, the beautiful view of the quartermaster's daughter."

"Now listen here!" the old gentleman said very emphatically to Copernicus.

At this point something had to happen if the game was not to be lost, and so I played my trump card against Bartels. I agreed with Copernicus that the view from the little linden tree was in fact the best one we had on our entire walk, and I added that Bartels was always looking for something to report, but that he could find nothing but meaningless little things. The provost marshal himself had acknowledged that the mouse hunt was a harmless incident. In addition, Bartels had reported that one of us had inquired about the price of herring, and that we had spoken to the little school children.

Now the old gentleman thundered at me, "He's supposed to report that; that's his duty. He's supposed to report everything that is in violation of regulations!"

If Bartels had now kept his mouth shut, we would have been sent back to our cells with a reprimand, and the whole incident would have been forgotten. However, he also wanted to strike while the iron was hot, and by this time it was evident that the general was hot under the collar. Turning toward me, Bartels said, "And you are always talking to little Idachechen, and if I were to tell everything . . ."

"Damn it, tell everything!" the old gentleman broke in.

"Well, there is another side to the story about the mice. That man put a couple of mice in a box and wanted to give them to the daughter of the quartermaster as a present."

"What's that?" asked the old gentleman, turning toward Copernicus.

Copernicus, Copernicus, this looks bad! — However, at the same time the general turned toward Bartels and asked, "How do you know that?"

Malicious joy shone in Bartels's eyes. A self-satisfied look came over his face because he was so pleased with his own cleverness. He answered, "I asked little Idachechen about that."

Herr Bartels, Herr Bartels, this looks bad!

"Children's talk!" the general shouted at him. "Did I give you orders to interrogate children? Does your manual of instructions tell you that you are supposed to spy? You are supposed to report just what you see. — Now go back," he said to us, "but let me tell you this: when the sentry calls out, you must obey orders."

That evening the clerk from the commandant's headquarters came over to Copernicus's window and with great pleasure informed us that Bartels had been dismissed. It is contemptible for anyone to derive pleasure from another's misfortune, but it is doubly despicable when a subaltern at a fortress or in a prison does so.

With this the general and all of us could be well satisfied; in place of the sneaky Bartels, who was forever reporting us, we had a good-natured old man who wasn't interested in seeing or hearing anything, and the general had a man who never had anything to report. — Lewandowsky was the name of the new sergeant, who on the side carried on his business as a tailor.

I ran upstairs to the Captain to cheer him up in his sorrow and to tell him that Herr Bartels had been dismissed, but I got a fine reception from him! — He said that as far as he was concerned Bartels could have stayed for any length of time, because he was by no means the worst person; there were many people in this world who were far worse than Bartels. He also said that if he himself had been smarter, he would have been aware of the difficulty Bartels was making for him at the little linden tree.

"But," he added with great emotion, "everything shall be torn from my heart, even the memory!"

With that he jumped up, took a knife, ran to the door and cut out all the romantic notches from the doorpost.

After that he became more composed and sat down on his chair. Before him he had a book on Prussian civil law, because he had had the sensible idea of dispelling all thoughts of love with the help of this legal volume.

"Charles," he said, "there is no longer any need for secrets. Yes, I loved her, I loved her with all my heart. However, I didn't love her for my own sake; I loved her for her sake, and woe!" — with that he shifted his glance from the paragraphs in the civil law which deal with unlawful possession, and gave me a piercing look — "Woe betide Copernicus, if he pursues selfish aims! — Woe betide him! I say, woe to him!"

And so it continued until we went to bed. However, if Copernicus had only half the aches and pains in his stomach which were wished on him from upstairs, he would have become aware of his great wickedness and found it necessary to seek recourse to some strong camomile tea.

For three days the Captain did not go out; for three days his mind was in a turmoil. For two days he was angry with Copernicus and on the third day he vented his wrath against Schramm. Whenever he caught sight of him in the distance, he said, "That clown thinks he's so important just because he has a fiancée. — Is it such a remarkable achievement to have a fiancée when one is permitted to go and move about as freely as he pleases?"

The very first day the Archbishop also came up and asked the Captain to go out for a walk, but he didn't want to go. The worthy churchman fervently beseeched him to join the others, because this was an emergency which concerned us all. We had to decide what tactics we should employ in our dealings with the new guard. However, the Captain still refused, and so the Archbishop had to be satisfied with the rest of us. The whole night the worthy gentleman had been preparing a speech, which he planned to deliver when Lewandowsky was invested with his new office. He had also reflected upon all measures which he prescribed for us in the future.

When all of us with the exception of the Captain were assembled about him, he commenced his well-considered speech. He began with a "Thank God" that we had been rescued from Bartels's leonine jaws, and then at the first opportune moment he made mention of Copernicus and his gift of mice, with the comment that through the obvious stupidity of one man things may turn out for the best for all others.

Copernicus was angered by this remark. When the Archbishop noticed this, he added in his kindly way that Copernicus through his intelligent behavior and daring words in the presence of the general had again saved the day.

With these words he was overlooking me, because I thought I should be given credit for anything intelligent or daring that had been spoken.

When the Archbishop noticed that I too was angry, he quickly added, "And Charles was of great help too!"

Thereupon he made the suggestion that henceforth no one should stand at the little linden tree.

Now Copernicus was about to explode, but the Archbishop added that even though it was unfair that one of us had been given more liberties than the others and could stroll about with a fiancée on his arm, nevertheless . . .

Now he was referring to Schramm, and as the Philosopher was about to raise an objection, the Archbishop silenced him with a wave of his hand, and continued his speech by saying that permission for that betrothal had been given by the general before our time at Graudenz, and the words and actions of the general were to be accepted as sacred law. "Therefore," he said, concluding his speech, "I beseech all of you, dear brothers, to stay within the limits that have been set for us; avoid all association with unauthorized people, and don't try to gain admission in any sly way to the houses of the local residents." — He was now looking at Don Juan. — "In short, let us show the newly appointed Herr Lewandowsky that we know how to obey orders, and he will forget about giving orders. Above all things, I warn you not to stand by the linden tree; you would not only be putting the tree, but also Lewandowsky in an awkward position!"

Then came the objections! The first one, of course, was that spiteful wretch Copernicus. He said he would stand at the linden tree if he cared to, and he would like to see anyone stop him from doing that! Schramm in his sarcastic and philosophic way asked whether there was any reason why he should give up his fiancée just for the sake of the Archbishop and Lewandowsky, and I asked the Archbishop whether he knew what he was saying. He himself had been the first one to violate the regulations by negotiating with an old woman about the price of herring.

However, that was nothing compared with the way Don Juan flared up. He said that he as well as the Archbishop had given considerable thought all night to the paths he planned to follow under Lewandowsky's regime, and for the most part these paths led behind stables and gateways into the houses. He had just heard a speech which was a "feeble performance resulting from the feebleness of a clerical frame of mind" — he always expressed himself very precisely, because he was a poet — but he himself was not pasted together with commands from headquarters or instructions from a sergeant.

He was made up of flesh and blood, and he was not there to make Lewandowsky's life comfortable and sweet; he wanted to sweeten his own life, and for that he needed association with people, especially with women.

Then he expanded upon the amenities of such association with examples from his own experience. He concluded his speech with the words: "Gentlemen, we must confuse Lewandowsky; 'confuse' is the proper word. The very first days we must take all kinds of liberties, but in a very casual manner, so that he will think we have a right to do so. Furthermore, I am of the opinion each one should do what he wishes."

On that we all agreed except the Archbishop, and our meeting ended as all meetings do: we left and we did what we wished. — Copernicus stood at the linden tree, Schramm went walking with his fiancée, I talked and joked with little Idachechen, and Don Juan was discovered with the tavern maid. Lewandowsky escorted him back to his cell, but he did not report him.

On the first day only our most reverend gentleman, the Archbishop, like a good law-abiding pumpkin went rolling down the prescribed walk. However, on the second day I saw him talking over the fence with the stout wife of the baker, and on the third day he was sitting beside her on the bench and she was telling him the story of her illness and the children with which she had been blessed, for, as I have said, he was interested in all practical and economic matters.

Only my good old friend the Captain still sat in his cell in sorrow and misery.

Finally, on the fourth day — it was a Sunday — I noticed that he was putting on his stand-up collar and dusting off his new blue coat. "Aha!" I thought. "He's going out today!"

But I was wrong; he was not going out, at least not that morning. However, after we had eaten dinner, he put on his blue coat, straightened his collar a bit before the mirror, and said, "Charles, I have to make a very important call; do you want to accompany me?"

I answered that I would go wherever he wished, and that I was always ready to assist him, but that the door below was still locked.

"We're just going down to Copernicus," he said as he left.

"Good God," I thought, "what's the meaning of this!" and I followed him.

As we arrived downstairs in Copernicus's cell, that mean wretch
was just preparing coffee. The Captain went straight up to him,
stretched out his hand and said, "Copernicus, for six years we have
been loyal friends; are we still friends?"

"Yes," answered Copernicus, and his face turned green as he held
out his hand in embarrassment.

"Copernicus," continued the Captain, as he shook his hand
warmly, "do you have any objection to Charles being a witness to
our conversation? Although we have not discussed the matter in any
detail, he knows what it is all about. He should be the judge between
you and me."

"You've got yourself a nice assignment here!" I thought to myself.
"I'd like to know how this will all end. I'll have to soften this fellow
up a little. The Captain is already softened up, and things always go
better between sentimental people."

And so I shook hands with Copernicus and looked into his
greenish face with all possible sympathy. Then the fellow tore
himself away, ran over to his coffee pot and shouted that the coffee
was boiling over! He said that he would add some more coffee, and
then on this afternoon we could enjoy a cup of coffee together, and
the Captain could smoke his long clay pipe.

Now in heaven's name, the Captain hadn't come here for a
pipeful of tobacco, and for a cup of coffee no one is going to give up
an Aurelia! — The Captain therefore said very dispassionately,
"Never mind that! I merely want to know whether you love
Aurelia."

Well, that conniver just sat there; he was supposed to answer, but
he wouldn't speak up. — However, the Captain was on the right
track; he had Copernicus where he wanted him. "I ask you: do you
love Aurelia?"

"Yes," Copernicus answered finally.

That was not enough for the Captain, nor could it be, because if
he had been satisfied with such an answer, the whole matter would
have been settled right then and there. However, such an un-
emotional answer is no answer at all. The Captain therefore asked
more forcefully, "Do you love Aurelia as intensely as I loved her?"

That was a stupid question on the part of the Captain. How could
Copernicus know how much the Captain loved Aurelia? As judge I
therefore said that the Captain couldn't ask that question, because

with it he was merely putting Copernicus in an embarrassing position. I thought to myself, "Well, you carried out your assignment
very well that time!"

But now that worm Copernicus jumped up and asked what
business that was of mine. He said they could settle their differences
by themselves. And the Captain said that he hadn't brought me
along merely to cause a split between them.

That annoyed me, and so I asked whether they wouldn't prefer to
replace me with the Archbishop, because he knew how to straighten
out everything, or with Don Juan, because he was most experienced
in matters of the heart. — Neither wanted that, and so I got stubborn too, sat down, drank coffee, smoked my pipe and thought, "Let
them settle it themselves."

During the three days that the Captain had been sitting by
himself in his cell he had devised a hard and fast plan, and he was
too good a military man to let his enemy slip away. Even though
Copernicus made feints to the right and to the left, the Captain kept
attacking very boldly with the question, "Do you love her as intensely as I loved her?"

Now Copernicus could no longer retreat; so he had to make a
stand. He said he did not know how much the Captain had been in
love, whether it was up to his ears or to the depths of his heart. He
merely knew that he liked the girl very much, and that he was just as
good as anyone else.

Then the Captain released his pressure on the wing commander of
the second file from Halle and let him escape. He walked up and
down with long strides and said, "You're in luck! That answer saved
you! If you had answered this question with a simple 'Yes,' I would
have considered you a liar, because you can't love her as much as I
have loved her."

"I can't?" cried Copernicus, picking up courage, as though he
were ready to move into battle again with banners and standards flying.

"Good Lord!" I interrupted. "Let's have some peace now! The
matter is all settled; now we can drink coffee!"

"You keep quiet, Charles!" said Copernicus. "You have nothing to
say in this matter!"

"Yes, keep quiet, Charles!" the Captain also said. "Now we shall
come to the main question."

"Well," I said to myself, "never again! What a way for them to treat their judge in this love quarrel!"

Then all of a sudden the Captain stood up straight in front of Copernicus and asked in a very calm and composed manner, "Copernicus, will you marry Aurelia?"

As this heavy artillery blast shot out unexpectedly from behind the entrenchment and caught Copernicus in the flank, he pulled in his banners and standards and was about to beat a hasty retreat, but the Captain kept firing at him with the same question, "Will you marry her?"

I was out of humor because of the treatment accorded me as judge, but when I heard this question, I had to burst out laughing. "Captain," I said, "as far as I know, that's the very last question, and it's the pastor who asks it at the altar."

"Is that so?" said the Captain, looking down at me. "Is that so? — Well, let me tell you, I am standing here as a pastor, so to speak. Before I came here to discuss this serious matter, I renounced my most precious possession. — And let me also tell you, that this question is in order, and Copernicus can answer it at any time; he is of age, his parents are dead, and he is capable of managing his own affairs. Furthermore, he is a man of means and has passed his first bar examination."

"And still has twenty-five years to serve," I added.

"That's none of your business," said Copernicus. 'Just worry about yourself! You have twenty-five years to serve too."

"Yes," said the Captain, "you can't get married, because you haven't passed the first bar examination. Anyone who has passed that examination in the Prussian state can get married, that is, if he has the financial means. I don't have the money, but Copernicus does, and therefore he must get married. I say he must get married, even if he has to wait twenty-five years before he does."

And now for the first time in all these negotiations something resembling enthusiasm seemed to move Copernicus, as green as he was, he shook the Captain's hand, and called out, "And I will get married!"

The Captain embraced him and kissed him on the top of his head; he couldn't reach his mouth because of Copernicus's short legs and crooked nose. He stretched out his arms and called out, "Herewith I renounce all my rights!"

Just at that moment it happened that Aurelia passed our casemate as she was going out for a walk. Quick as a flash the Captain turned about and went to the rear of the casemate, for he was a man of honor who kept his word. Copernicus stood at the window and looked at his new possession, and I sat there like the fifth wheel on a wagon and tried to help myself out of a difficult situation by drinking coffee. Both of my friends were angry with me, as though I were to blame for all their trouble, but that's probably what happens to all judges. — However, I didn't want to resign from my official position without saying anything, and so I said, "Wouldn't it be a good idea to let her know — and I pointed out the window — perhaps through little Ida, what decision we have made concerning her today, for you may say what you wish, she is involved in these negotiations?"

Then the Captain came back from the rear of the casemate and said that I didn't understand anything about matters like this. This was no time for children's talk or gossip mongers. On the following Sunday Copernicus would have to put on a black dress coat and white gloves and with appropriate words ask Aurelia's father for her hand in marriage.

Now Copernicus was on my side; he said he didn't have a black dress coat.

Then he would have to borrow one from the Archbishop; he had one.

Copernicus rejected the suggestion with thanks; he said it would make him look too much like a herring in a jacket.

"Yes," I said, "and what would the general say to that?"

The Captain was now baffled; evidently he didn't know what else to suggest. "Oh," he called out, "if you only knew what a great sacrifice I have made, and to think that it should be doomed to failure because of a dress coat and a general!"

Then he returned to the extreme rear of the casemate and paced back and forth. — After a while he came back to us and said to me very softly, "Charles, let us go!"

He wiped the cold beads of perspiration from his pale face. I knocked out the ashes from my pipe, and we went upstairs.

CHAPTER 19

T HAT was the end of one chapter, and now another was to begin. However, before it began the summer passed and the late autumn arrived. We did not live in peaceful harmony during this time, even though the rivalry between the Captain and Copernicus for Aurelia's love had ended. My Captain was an honorable man; not a single glance did he cast at Aurelia, with no step did he tread in her footsteps, and as far as he was concerned, the little linden tree might stand as straight as an arrow. — But — he hated Schramm intensely. He couldn't stand the sight of him, because Schramm had accomplished what he had been unable to do, namely, become engaged.

The Captain and Schramm soon had a disagreement about the meaning of "love." — The Philosopher, because he had a neat and plump little fiancée, had arrived at a concept of "love" which my upright Captain in his chivalry and mood of resignation could not possibly accept as the correct one. "Despite all his fine talk he is a sensuous egotist," said the Captain. — He avoided Schramm all the time.

Don Juan and the Philosopher were on bad terms from the very first days; they came into conflict as poets. When Schramm found out that Don Juan in his leisure hours was devoting himself to the muse of poetry, he played his highest trump; he bragged about *Paulus* in order to dumbfound Don Juan right at the start.

Now Don Juan had composed a beautiful song to the melody of "Aurora! Aurora!" However, instead of beginning with the dawn the song began with the evening: "Hesperus! Hesperus! Greet my beloved with this kiss!" etc. And because Don Juan had a beautiful bass voice and many sweethearts, to whom he had to send greetings and kisses, he broke out into song every evening, as soon as his messenger, the evening star, appeared in the heavens. We listened with great reverence, because in fortresses one rarely hears any singing. However, we never did hear the end of the song, because whenever he raised his voice and started to greet all his loved ones with kisses, the sentry always called out, "Quiet in there!"

Well, he tried to overtrump Schramm with this poem, and was thereby in my opinion guilty of a very great stupidity. How can a poem of three — I'll even say five — verses compete with a heroic poem of thirty pages, and one which includes pictures too? The Philosopher immediately realized how absure the comparison was, and he ridiculed "Hesperus," and in return Don Juan ridiculed *Paulus*. In short, here too a rivalry was in full swing, but a rivalry between two real poets is seven times worse than one between rivals in love. In the latter case generosity can sometimes bring about a reconciliation, as the Captain proved to us, but that can never happen with real poets. — Between Don Juan and the Philosopher any friendship was therefore out of the question.

All this time Schramm had remained on peaceful terms with the Archbishop. At the beginning of Lewandowsky's regime, however, when the Archbishop became acquainted with the stout wife of the baker, something happened which was to bring about a complete split between the two.

One day the Archbishop in his usual proper way was talking over the garden fence with the baker's wife. This time they were talking about her hens, because as I have said, the Archbishop had a good head for business. She was lamenting the fact that she had become so stout after her serious illness that she could no longer climb up into the chicken roost to fetch the eggs. Therefore, the baker's apprentice was assigned this chore, but he always sucked out the eggs and then said a marten had done it.

"You have no idea what a trial it is," she said, "when one spreads out like bread dough — and it's not normal either!" she added.

Now the Archbishop always felt compassion whenever he heard of any human tribulation. He therefore wanted to console the poor woman and said she shouldn't worry too much about that.

Just then the Philosopher passed by behind him. The Archbishop turned around and looked at him, and then he said to the baker's wife that he would prefer to walk around on a couple of legs as sturdy as poles rather than on a pair of match sticks hardly strong enough to support a person.

With obvious satisfaction he looked at his own underpinning, and he may very well have looked at the Philosopher's too. — In any case, the Philosopher turned around and said, "Such a clumsy clod!"

In the presence of the baker's stout wife he hurled this expression right into the Archbishop's face, just at the moment when the latter was trying to console her about her corpulence.

The Archbishop then put his two sturdy poles into motion and followed the Philosopher's match sticks, and as was bound to happen, the poles overtook the match sticks and they confronted each other. Just as the rest of us arrived the good-natured Archbishop said that he had enough Christian feeling so that he personally could forgive the Philosopher for using the expression "clumsy clod," although it was a despicable thing to say. However, Schramm had spoken it so loudly that it may very well have been heard on the other side of the fence, and the baker's good wife, who was even more corpulent than the Archbishop himself, may have been cut to the quick. As it was, the poor woman had a great burden to carry, and the Archbishop therefore demanded that the Philosopher beg her pardon!

Of course, the Philosopher refused to do so! — Thus the two sturdy poles and the two spindly match sticks never became reconciled.

Now the Philosopher had only Copernicus and me to talk to on our walks, and one could hardly count Copernicus, since he stood at the linden tree more than he walked, and had no time for any conversation. So I was the only one left for Schramm to talk to, and even that was not to be for very long.

One day he approached me and told me that he had now arranged to have his fiancée sent to his family in order to get more education.

"Why, you have been educating her for two years; doesn't she have enough culture yet?" I asked.

"No," he answered, "she still needs some training in the home."

"Well, then send her to your family," I said.

"But my family lives too far away, and I would like to have her with me occasionally," he replied.

"I don't blame you for that," I said.

"And for that reason," he continued, "I'd like to be transferred to Silberberg, because that is near my home."

"Don't do it!" I advised. "I know Silberberg; I know what would be in store for you there."

"It can't be any more boring than here," he said.

"Maybe not," I replied, "but it can be more disagreeable."

"What do you mean?" he asked.

"Can you stand to hear the truth?" I asked.

"Yes, I can."

"Well," I said, "then I'll tell you; you don't stand in very good repute among all our comrades because of what happened during our imprisonment on remand. When we came here, we all promised not to hold any grudges against you. However, you have made all kinds of trouble for us here, and you have quarreled with each and every one of us. In Silberberg there won't be any change in your disagreeable disposition. I know the men who are imprisoned there. With them you won't get very far with your *Paulus* nor will they be interested in your philosophy. Those fellows have a good recollection of Berlin and 'Uncle' Dambach, and they will confront you with all kinds of leading questions and insinuations, and you'll be as helpless there as a frog on ice."

I said this with the best of intentions and also because he had said that he could stand to hear the truth — but he couldn't.

He stepped back a few paces to get out of my reach, surveyed me from top to bottom, eyeing also my legs — just as he had eyed the Archbishop's legs — and then he looked me straight in the face and said, "Such a clumsy clod!" — just as he had spoken to the Archbishop.

He was really a very despicable fellow!

After he had broken with every one of us, one after another, he sent his fiancée to his parents and applied for a transfer to Silberberg. His request was granted, but before he left he played one more mean trick, which came close to depriving us of our main pleasure, our walk, and which was intended to set us at variance with the good old general. I don't know whether he did it simply out of revenge or because of the unpleasant feeling that he was now without any friends, but in any case, he went to the old gentleman and asked whether he could go walking on the other side of the carriage house. The old gentleman wanted to know the reason for this request. — Instead of telling the truth, that he was at odds with all of us, he said that there were too many people on our walk. Sometimes strangers looked at us inquisitively, and he didn't like being a spectacle for them.

The general gave his consent, but he added that from then on we would all have to walk on the same side. We were supposed to give up our beautiful walk, where the warm sun shone so brightly, where there were people to be seen, and where each one of us had made some friendly contact of his own. Instead of that we were supposed to walk behind a big box-like house among piles of cannon balls, where neither sun nor moon ever shone, and where we would never see anyone except Lewandowsky. And that was just because the Philosopher had spindly legs — that's what made him so angry.

We were all infuriated because of this new order. It was as though each of us had a kettle of water on the fire, and all the kettles were boiling over because the fire was so hot. The water in the Captain's kettle, however, didn't even begin to come to a boil, because beneath lay only the cold black coals of his charred love, and they didn't catch fire, for they were probably wet from many a tear.

The rest of us, on the other hand, were boiling with rage. Now Copernicus would no longer be able to see Aurelia, nor would I see little Idachechen. Don Juan would have to leave his tavern maid as well as all his other loves, and the Archbishop would not be able to talk to the baker's stout wife.

When the provost marshal came and gave notice of this new regulation, we were all in an angry mood, and I was again the one who was stupid enough to utter the loudest protest. I said I wouldn't do it; I wouldn't walk on that side!

"What?" said the provost marshal. "You won't do it! The general has the right to choose any place he wishes for your walk."

I answered that I knew that, but I had the right to make use of it or not, just as I pleased. I would continue to walk back and forth in front of the sentry, or I would stay in my casemate altogether.

"That is insubordination!" he said.

I answered, "I look at it in another light. We are now being assigned a less desirable area for walking, and I consider that a punishment which is completely unjustified."

I suppose it was unwise of me to talk like that. I am now as much over fifty years of age as I was over twenty at that time, but even to this day I have no regrets that I spoke up as I did. Otherwise I would never have found out what a splendid old gentleman our general was.

It was about a week later, when Copernicus and I were walking up and down in front of the sentry — Copernicus too refused to obey, because he was as stubborn as I — that we were ordered to appear before the general at the parade ground. — There he stood with his white plumed helmet among all the other black and black-and-white plumed helmets, and as I approached, he said to me, "Sir, why do you refuse to obey my command?"

All the majors and captains and lieutenants were standing there looking at me with inquisitive expressions on their faces, and in such a situation one becomes very embarrassed. I therefore said quite defiantly that I refused to walk in the area behind the carriage house.

Then the old gentleman bristled and asked if I didn't know that he was the commandant, and that it was my duty to obey his orders.

I said that I did know that, but I considered this a punishment, and I was not aware of having done anything to deserve it.

His anger seemed to subside, as he said that it had not been intended as a punishment, but that he had given the order merely because some of my comrades had requested this location for their walk.

I explained that only one person could have made that request, and he hadn't done it for the purpose of doing us a favor.

The old gentleman looked at me, called Lewandowsky aside and spoke to him, and then he returned and said, "I shall inquire into the matter, but in the meantime I suggest that you follow my orders; and tell that to the other fellow too," — he was referring to Copernicus — "and now you may go."

Thus everything remained as it had been, except that I now knew that the old gentleman had not given the order with any evil intention. He had simply wanted to do Schramm a favor, and who knows with what stories Schramm had filled his ears?

I reported everything to Copernicus. Upon hearing this he became furious and said he would not walk in that area; he simply would not do it. — While we were talking the Archbishop passed by and gave us a little sermon, in which he explained very clearly that if the general wished, he could order us to walk in the gutter pipe of the carriage house or on the gabled roof, and if in so doing half of us should break our necks, no one in Berlin would worry about it in the least.

Copernicus replied that as far as he was concerned the Archbishop could walk with the rats in the gutter pipe, if he wanted to, but he himself was not going to walk on the top of the carriage house and not in back of it either.

"Copernicus," I said, "I don't think the Archbishop's sermon is so stupid at all. What he said was meant only by way of comparison. Just think back to Magdeburg and remember that a general has the right to do anything he wishes. General Count Hacke may not have had us walking on rooftops, because he probably thought that would have been granting us too much freedom, but he did have us walking on manure piles, and because of that half of our friends became sick for life, and who worried about that in Berlin? We were just fortunate that Count Hacke died when he did. — I believe we should take our exercise walk behind the carriage house. The old man was not trying to punish us with this new order."

But Copernicus refused.

I took him by the arm: "Copernicus," I said, "just think of Aurelia!"

"I do; that's just it!" he burst out.

"I'll give you my guarantee, signed and sealed," I said, "the sooner the general sees us walking between the piles of cannon balls the sooner you will see Aurelia."

That did it. That afternoon I went walking arm in arm with Copernicus between the piles of cannon balls. It was unpleasant for both of us, and the one who was the cause of our vexation saw no friendly faces as he passed us.

I have told this story merely to prove that very often in a situation like this one has to accept some punishment, even if it is undeserved. This holds true when one has a good commandant; I won't even talk about the bad ones.

"I would not have accepted any such punishment," many a one might say; "I would not have done it!"

In that case we would have gone from the frying pan into the fire.

"But you were within your rights."

Oh, good Lord, don't talk to me about our rights! We had long ago become acquainted with what were supposed to be "our rights." We had no desire to become any better acquainted. — And what were we supposed to do? — Complain to the Supreme Court in Berlin? — We would have received the comforting reply that everything was to remain as it had been ordered. Our good old commandant might possibly have received a reprimand for granting us more privileges than the Supreme Court wished to allow. — And the old gentleman certainly didn't deserve that! We didn't want anything like that to happen to him because of us!

For two days Copernicus and I walked behind the carriage house during our exercise period. The old gentleman could see us from his corner window. — Then he summoned Lewandowsky, and when the sergeant returned, he told us very secretly that the old gentleman had asked him if the two prisoners walking there were the little jaundiced student from Halle and the stubborn Mecklenburger. When Lewandowsky had answered that they were, the general had closed the window and mumbled something to himself.

The next morning the provost marshal came with his plumed helmet and his sword and read an order from headquarters: "The political prisoners so-and-so and so-and-so were again to make use of the former walking area as far as the little linden tree in the vicinity of the water tower."

Thus we again had what we wanted, and we found out what a splendid man the general was. — I wonder what punishment Count Hacke would have given us?

Our general, however, had served as a colonel under Emperor Napoleon and he had taken part in campaigns in Spain and Russia. He had been forced to fight against Germany, although he had done so by decision of the princes and not on his own volition.[1] He had seen misery and suffering on many fields of battle, but he was a compassionate man in whose loyal heart there was no room for the meanness and harassment which other commandants practiced against us. — The fellows who became commandants in those wonderful years of peace didn't know how to command a regiment. They were peacetime heroes who found their happiness in carrying out to the letter the orders of their superior officers. They were the ones who tormented us. However, men like the general or Colonel B. in Glogau, who had experienced great trials and tribulations in their lives and who knew the ways of the world, never harassed us in the least. — Even today my heart rejoices whenever I see such an old gentleman with a white mustache through which the winds of 1813 once blew — whether he is a general or a corporal.

For Schramm this last order from headquarters was a serious blow. Now he once again had to walk around like a pariah until he was finally fortunate enough to be transferred. He departed, and I never saw him again.[2]

Winter had now arrived and with it a more peaceful time for us. There was some switching around of cell mates: the Captain moved in with his little friend from Halle, and the Frenchman, who arrived from Berlin, moved in with me.

CHAPTER 20

Z——, or the Frenchman, as we called him, was a tall and impressive-looking fellow, as I have mentioned before, but from the bad treatment in Magdeburg he had become mentally disturbed. — Instead of setting him free they had sent him to the charité in Berlin, and from there he came to us at Graudenz — but he was not cured. — He imagined that he could foretell the future. He would sit for hours telling fortunes from playing cards, and he would turn to certain pages in Virgil or in the Bible and read all kinds of fanciful stuff and nonsense into whatever passages he happened to find.

Well, to divert him to other thoughts I made the suggestion that we do our own cooking, and so we did. — We bought potatoes and then we sat down and peeled them in one of our well-rinsed wash basins. However, I couldn't get the Frenchman to cut the eyes out cleanly. On our staircase we had a large variety of soup greens packed in sand. Around the stove we had a collection of small and large pots ready for use, because we did most of our cooking in the stove. Only special dishes, for which great skill and care were necessary, were prepared, as they should be, on the open hearth fire. At great expense we acquired a tin skillet and all the other necessary equipment. Meat, to be sure, was always scarce, because that was not easy to get. Thus we started on a large scale, and we agreed to take turns cooking. It fell to the Frenchman's lot to take his turn first. — Until this time I had always prepared the coffee, but now the Frenchman had to do it. He set to work, poured coffee into the pot and lit a fire underneath, but he forgot to add the water and thus melted away the entire bottom of manufacturer Löff's most beautiful product.[1] — That was the beginning of our cooking.

"Frenchman," I asked, "have you ever done any cooking, or have you ever given it any thought, or have you ever watched anyone else do any cooking?"

"What do you mean?" he asked.

"Well," I replied, "I'm just asking if you have ever done any cooking, or if you have ever glanced into a cookbook, or if you have ever looked over the shoulder of a real cook, who is trained in her specialty?"

He answered that he had never done any cooking, nor had he ever concerned himself with any cookbooks, but that he had often looked over the shoulders of many trained cooks — and then he mentioned a whole list of nothing but French names.

"That's all very well," I said, "but all your Madelons and Louises and Charlottes are not going to help us now. Here it is a matter of 'every man for himself.' Do you think you can prepare a stew with vegetables and potatoes?"

"No," he said.

"Well, in that case we'll do it like this," I answered. "I'll do the cooking, and you can clean up all the pots and pans, but if you break one single pot, I'll deduct it from your pay. We'll both peel the potatoes and clean the soup greens, because that's pleasant work and we can talk together while we are doing it."

After this agreement we set to work. — I had a nice piece of linen covered with many pictures of faces and trees and flowers which I had used for my first attempts at painting in oil. I put this on as an apron and tied it at the back with a piece of cord, and then I was ready.

"Frenchman, first clean this pot for me, and get it very clean! — Fine! — Now get the peas! — Jackass, not these! I want those up there on the stove, the ones that have been soaked! — Fine! — Now fetch some dry kindling wood!"

My good Frenchman followed all my orders. "What kind of peas are you cooking, the small ones or the big ones?" he asked.

"Frenchman," I said, "I want to tell you once and for all: I don't like people who stick their noses into everything while I am cooking. You do what you are supposed to do, and I'll do what I am supposed to do, and when dinner is ready, you can come to the table and eat."

My peas were excellent; I had cooked them with a nice piece of bacon, but nevertheless the Frenchman chewed on them with something less than enthusiasm. — "What's the matter?" I asked.

He said he was getting too many pea pods in his teeth.

That made me angry; so I said, "You must have a damned narrow throat, if the pods can't even pass through. — Do you think we are living in such abundance that we can afford to throw the pods into the garbage? We don't even have a pig that we could feed the garbage to. — And look here! One taler and eight pennies. We're supposed to live on that for two weeks; we can't spend everything the first day. If the pods are too rough for you, then I wish you would get me a strainer."

Well, that helped. After that he said nothing, but then I always cooked the best food. I was fortunate that it was just the time for spring lamb, and also that we lived close to the gate where I had the best opportunity to smuggle in half a baby lamb. At the fortress in those days a tax was levied on slaughtered meat and also on every sack of grain ground into flour. So I made the most of my opportunities, and as far as possible made my purchases in large quantities. — At that time half a lamb cost eight pennies if it was smuggled in. Whenever I had half a lamb hanging over the staircase and a bushel of potatoes down below, I was always very happy. I would then come into the casemate and say, "Frenchman, we're not going to starve for quite a while yet!"

We could have continued to live very economically and also with very good nourishment, if the Frenchman hadn't been such a gourmet. However, one day he was walking down the lane where he met a pretty girl. He asked her what she had in the basket.

"Carp," she said, "beautiful fresh lake carp!"

Now his mouth began to water at the thought of such a dainty morsel, and he took it upon himself to encroach upon my province — for I was in charge of the cash box and all purchases — and bought the carp for a considerable sum of money.

I was just then standing with Lieutenant Cappeler of the fire brigade. He used to visit us quite often because I had painted his portrait. Furthermore, our old general no longer had any objections to such fraternization. I was telling the lieutenant about our excellent cooking arrangement, when the Frenchman came up and asked me for money from our cash box to pay for the carp he had purchased. Well, I gave him the money and acted as though carp were a very common dish for us — for who wants to be put in an embarrassing light in the presence of a lieutenant?

"Carp?" asked the lieutenant.

"Yes," I replied, "carp! Do you like carp?"

Then he began to sing the praises of carp. He told me that he had once eaten so much carp that he had become sick, but that he hadn't seen any in the last four years.

I invited him to dinner, because I couldn't very well do otherwise, but I thought myself, "I'll see to it that you won't get sick from eating too much this time."

He accepted the invitation, and I went up to cook our carp — naturally, in beer.

When I came upstairs I asked, "Frenchman, where are the carp?"

"Here, in your wash basin!" he answered.

I went closer and looked at the creatures and my arms fell to my side in despair. "You call these carp?" I exclaimed.

"Yes," he said, "fresh lake carp!"

"Well, I call them red bream," I said, and looked at them in silent rage. "It's bad enough to spend that good money for them, but with these red bream we are also making fools of ourselves before a royal Prussian lieutenant of the fire brigade. Go back to that girl right away and have her give you your money back, and then tell the lieutenant he should eat some other place. There are no carp; they have turned into red bream. Then tell him it is all because of your stupidity, so that I'll not get the blame."

Well, he didn't want to do that, and I could understand that. That was asking too much of him, and so I thought it over and said, "We'll do what we can. If red bream is well cooked, it is not all that bad. — Frenchman, my dear Frenchman, pay attention now to what I'm going to tell you. First cut off all the fins and tails, because they would give us away immediately. Then split open the fish and put all the innards on this plate. Watch out especially for the bile. Then cut them up into very little pieces, so that it looks like a very special dish, of which not too much is served at one time. I'll run over to the store and buy various kinds of spices; we'll put one over on the lieutenant."

I left, but as I was on the staircase, a frightening thought came to me. I went back and said to the Frenchman, as I gave him a friendly pat on the back, "Frenchman, watch out especially for the bile!" — He promised that he would, and then I went to the store and made my purchases.

"A bottle of beer!" I ordered.

"Real Bavarian beer?" the merchant asked.

"No," I said, "sweet beer."

"I have a very excellent Bavarian beer," he said.

Well, this was a suitable occasion to buy something especially good, and so I said, "Let me have three bottles of Bavarian beer, and also a half-penny's worth of clove, and a half-penny's worth of English spice, and a half-penny's worth of brown honey cake, and a few bay leaves."

I got everything; he had his errand boy carry the four bottles of beer for me, and I followed with my two hands filled with bay leaves.

"What do you have there?" asked the Captain.

"Bay leaves," I answered, "We're having carp today."

"Carp?" asked Don Juan; "I've forgotten how they taste."

"Fellows," I said, "I'd like to invite all of you, but we don't have enough food, because we are inviting Lieutenant Cappeler of the fire brigade to dinner."

Then the Archbishop came up too, and when he heard us talking about carp and saw the bay leaves, he said that he could tell that I knew my business. Carp must be prepared with bay leaves. Then he looked at all of us and said very emphatically, "I can tell you that bay leaves and onions will never spoil any dish. Only with baked foods and pudding one has to go easy with these ingredients."

As I left, I felt very happy that the Archbishop and I agreed on that, because he was well informed in matters involving home economics. When I came upstairs, I saw that the Frenchman had carried out his assignment, and as far as I could see, he had done everything well. He had also kindled a fire. I therefore took off my coat, tied on my motley-colored apron and went to the hearth, because this dish was one that had to be prepared over an open fire — the stove didn't come into question. I rolled up my sleeves and I was ready to go to work.

The roe was put at the bottom of the pot, because otherwise it wouldn't be properly cooked. Then came a layer of salt and onions, and then I kept alternating red bream and salt and onions and red bream and salt and onions, and so on until everything was in the pot. When the fish was half done, I called to the Frenchman and said, "Now you stand here next to me and assist me, because one man can't do this alone."

Then he held a bowl and I poured off the water in which the fish had been cooking. When I had done that, I said, "Now get the beer!" — He did that and I poured the beer over the onions and the fish and let it continue to cook.

After a short deliberation I threw the spices and honey cake into the pot, and I stood there with a handful of bay leaves. There weren't many, but the Archbishop had said that "onions and bay leaves will never spoil any dish." I had put in a large amount of onions, and so a large amount of bay leaves would have to be added too. I therefore threw in the entire handful. — "There," I said, "now get the butter, Frenchman!"

"The fresh butter or the old butter?" he asked.

"Don't you think our old butter is good enough for our old red bream?" I said.

Well, he brought it, and the butter was very good, because it had been made at home and sent to me by my father — but it was a half year old. In order to do a good job I put into the pot a slab of butter, which was inexcusably large, and then I just stood there and waited. I had done what I could, and I had added whatever ingredients were necessary for a dish like this. "Frenchman," I said, "if the fish isn't too good, at least we will have the sauce."

There we stood; I was very happy because of the fragrant aroma which came from the fish cooking on the hearth.

The Frenchman said, "Now they are done."

"No," I said, "they are not done yet; red bream has to cook a long time."

This foresight, as it turned out, probably saved my life. Just then the lieutenant arrived. He had to come in through our kitchen, and so we welcomed him there. The Frenchman did the honors, and because he himself had been a lieutenant in the militia, he kept calling our guest "Herr Comrade." I also wanted to play my part as host, and so I kept bowing to the lieutenant as I stood by the hearth. I told him how happy I was, and how good it was of him to have kept his promise. At that moment I came too close to the fire with my confounded linen apron, and as quick as a flash my whole midriff was ablaze. As soon as the lieutenant saw the danger — and as a fire lieutenant he would have to recognize danger when he saw it — he drew his sword and came at me with the sharp weapon. At the same time the Frenchman took the bowl with the hot water in which the fish had been cooked and poured it with a splash over my head. — Oh, unfortunate me! — However, the lieutenant was able to cut the apron cord with his sword, and the apron with my first attempts at oil painting fell to the ground. I jumped around and stamped on it and my arms were flaying in every direction. If I had not been so deliberate in throwing the bay leaves into the pot, and if red bream were not such a tough fish, the water would still have been boiling hot, and the Frenchman would have scalded me like a capon.

For this reason I say that it is always good to be deliberate in one's actions, even if it is only in cooking red bream. — This time I got away with a few blisters on my knees, a singed pair of old pants, a slightly scorched mustache, and a terrible headache. I was nevertheless very fortunate, merely because I had been so deliberate.

Because of the fire damage my fish was forgotten for the moment. However, when the Frenchman invited the lieutenant to come in, I said to myself, "Well, if they are not done now, they never will be."

I therefore took the pot from the fire and started to fish out the pieces. The first thing I picked out was a head — very tender! really very tender! — I wanted to find out how it tasted and so I peeled off a piece from the head — very tender! but bitter as gall! — "I can't rely on that Frenchman," I said. "He forgot to remove the bile, and not the bitter taste has even gotten into the fish heads! Just for that he will have to eat both fish heads himself!"

I searched around in the pot with a spoon — nothing but crumbs! Everything had been cooked to bits! — "That's what I get," I said, "I told him to cut the fish into small pieces, and he went ahead and cut them into the tiniest bits!"

Finally I fished out a couple of tails, which were still in one piece, because the good Lord has provided the red bream with very tough tail bones.

"They are for the lieutenant," I said, "because the bile can't get into the tails."

When the dish was placed on the table, it had a very appetizing smell. It looked appetizing too, because I had made good use of my large supply of bay leaves to cover the fish, so that the tiny bits could not be seen. — I didn't want the lieutenant to find out about my secret, and I therefore served the fish myself, and I acted as though I were very much concerned that he get a choice piece.

"The best part of a fat carp is the tail, and therefore I want you to have that!" I said as I served him both tails.

He looked at me, as though he had never heard of that before. I had never heard of that before either, but I didn't tell him that. — As punishment the Frenchman was given a fish head to eat.

Before I started to eat I observed both the Frenchman and the lieutenant to see how they would react. — The Frenchman was busy eating and enjoying the fish head, but the lieutenant was making funny faces and chewing away at the tail for all he was worth. "Chew away!" I thought. "Those are the bones, and I can't help it; I didn't make the red bream."

Then I began to eat too — good Lord! — as bitter as gall — not only the fish, but also the sauce! — "Be quiet!" I thought. "Don't say a word!"

I kept on eating in order not to give myself away, and I urged the lieutenant to eat some more. "Herr Lieutenant, wouldn't you like a few onions and a few bay leaves?" I said, and I piled up his plate with onions and enough bay leaves for one to make a wreath and crown him with a hero's garland of victory.

"No, thank you! No, thank you!" he stammered. "I don't care much for bay leaves; they taste too bitter, or piquant, I should say."

Now I was shaken, as a light began to dawn: the bitter taste came from the confounded bay leaves. For that no one was to blame but the stupid Archbishop with his stupid advice, and also the merchant who in his generosity had given me so many bay leaves. — It was not my fault, nor was it the Frenchman's fault. I had done him a grave injustice in blaming him for not removing the bile, and so I served him a couple of spoonfuls of tiny fish fragments and said, "Frenchman, later I must beg your pardon."

He continued to eat with relish, but the main person, the lieutenant, was poking around in his mouth with fingers and tongue and teeth trying to remove the fish bones. I thought to myself, "He'd be a good man to have for raking the barley field."

Suddenly I had a bright idea; there is always a solution for every problem. If I now served the bitter Bavarian beer, it was possible that the fish by comparison might taste as sweet as honey.

"Well," I said, "I think we'll drink a glass of good Bavarian beer with our fish!"

I poured out a pint glass of beer for each of us.

"It's strange," said the lieutenant, "but my beer looks so much lighter than yours."

"Yes, indeed," I said, "it is strange, because it all came from the same merchant."

The lieutenant raised his glass, but put it down again immediately and said, "They were certainly stingy with the hops when they brewed this beer."

"Was everything going wrong today?" I thought. My beer was very bitter, and so I took the lieutenant's glass: "Allow me!" — Good Lord! It was the weak beer in which the fish should have been cooked. The Frenchman had poured a bottle of Bavarian beer over the fish!

Now the mystery was solved! — Neither the red bream nor the onions nor the bay leaves were to blame; only the Frenchman and the Bavarian beer were responsible for everything! — Fortunately, the Frenchman had not as yet drunk from his glass. I therefore placed his glass in front of the lieutenant and gave the Frenchman the weak beer. — There now, drink! — I kept urging them to eat the fish, but neither seemed to be interested. When the casemate to my great relief was finally unlocked, the lieutenant thanked us politely for the excellent meal and left.

CHAPTER 21

NOW I was alone with the Frenchman; I walked around in the cell too embarrassed to speak a word.

"Well," he said after a while, as he emptied his glass of weak beer, "I would have to say that was a very inferior kind of beer you served today."

"For you it was good enough!" I answered.

Then he asked, "What did you mean this afternoon, when you said you wanted to ask my pardon?"

"Ask your pardon? That too?" I said. "First you try to pass off red bream for carp! Then you cut them up into tiny little bits! And to cap the climax you pour Bavarian beer over the fish! Some cook you are!"

"You're not much of a cook yourself," he replied. "You're always trying to take on things which are beyond your capabilities."

And so to the bitterness of the bay leaves and the Bavarian beer was added also a bitter quarrel. What was more, toward evening he was unreasonable enough to ask for supper.

"It seems to me that you had plenty to eat this noon," I said. "You can skip eating this evening. I slaved long enough at the fireplace this noon; you can let me have a little rest now."

But he wouldn't listen to reason! On the shelf we still had three eggs and also a dish with some wheat flour, and so he asked me to prepare a pancake for him.

I told him that I had no pan.

He said I should use the tin skillet.

I said we had no alcohol to make a fire.

He said I could just as well make a coal fire.

Then I told him we had no milk.

He answered that pancakes could be made without milk.

"Well," I said, "if you know everything so well, then do it yourself."

And so he did. He mixed the eggs and the flour together, placed hot coals under our expensive new skillet and kept on stirring, so that the pancake wouldn't burn. I walked by casually, but I didn't say a word, although I noticed that he had stirred so well that everything in the skillet had been reduced to crumbs. I thought to myself, "I want to see what comes of this." I was spiteful enough to be happy about the mess he had made of the pancake.

Now the little brown crumbs according to his calculation were ready to eat, and so he started scraping them together, but in doing so he pressed the spoon down with such force that the bottom of our expensive new skillet cracked in two and skillet and pancake fell into the fire.

"Now you've done it!" I said.

"Yes," he replied.

"That's what you get!" I continued.

"Yes," he mumbled, as his gaze lingered first on the molten skillet and then on his crumbs.

"That does it!" I said. "We can't go on like this any longer."

With that I went and fetched our three good pots, placed one half of the tin skillet beside them and said, "Now take a look at what we have left! When we started to do our cooking a couple of months ago, each of us contributed seven new pots, each of them worth at least a penny. And what do we have left? — Three! — You ruined all the others, and now you've ruined the tin skillet too. And before that you ruined my coffee pot. Besides, three flat plates are missing, so that this noon I had to eat my fish from a deep dish."

He answered with a sneer that one is supposed to eat mash from a deep dish and that we were both responsible for all of our kitchen equipment that had been broken through usage.

"All right," I said, "if that's the way you want to have it."

I went and picked up my pair of trousers that had been singed by fire that noon and placed them beside the tin skillet. "They belong to our inventory too," I said.

He replied that trousers did not belong to the kitchen inventory, and then he began to chew on his crumbs.

I didn't care for his attitude at all. — "Here," I said, "is all our cash and here is my daily account. And now look here! — We still have a bushel of potatoes; we can divide them and the soup greens between us. We can draw lots for the three pots and also for the tin skillet. I'll pay you for your share of the half calf that I bought yesterday. We'll also divide the plates between us. That will then be the end of our partnership."

Then he took hold of my poor trousers, held them up and asked, "Shall we draw lots for these too, because you included them specifically in the kitchen inventory?"

That was nothing but sly innuendo. I was certainly annoyed, but it strengthened me in my determination never again to get involved in any such communal project. From now on all the cooking I did would be for myself, because I had acquired the three pots.

The Frenchman had to pay good money for his meals in the lieutenant's kitchen, but the food he was given there was in no way comparable to mine. From that time on just to spite him I prepared the most tasty and delicious dishes. While he sat down to his dinner of large tough old peas with Polish sauce, I had a lovely veal fricassee or a delicious piece of mutton steeped in kümmel, and later when he walked around in the casemate with his belly full of these musket balls, I sat in all comfort and was happy that I had no musket balls rattling around in my belly.

Cooking was a useful occupation and also a great education, because through it I became interested in the subject of chemistry, and so when the old general gave me permission to instruct a couple of bright little schoolboys in science, I had enough together with my painting to keep me busy the whole day. In this way the time passed very nicely.

Word of my painting must have gotten around. Before Christmas my little Ida came to see me and she brought greetings from her mother. She told me that Aurelia's eldest sister was going to be married, and because she wanted something special for the occasion a transparency was to be set up in the casemate. Now she wanted to know whether I would paint it for her.—I said I would be delighted to do so.—Then she told me that I should ask the general for permission to visit her mother.—I did that and the general granted me this permission.

There was great excitement when this became known, because it was the first time that any one of us had been allowed to enter a private home. What was more, this private home was precisely the one around which so much attention had been centered. The Captain stood dumbfounded and looked at me as though he were about to say something, but he said nothing. Don Juan came and congratulated me and offered me many a good hint as to how to use this opportunity to my own advantage. The Frenchman assisted me in getting dressed, lent me his stand-up collar and even helped me put it on and he made a very fancy knot in my neckerchief. The Archbishop lent me a pair of his gloves. His hands were as large as a couple of wash basins. People always said that from two pair of ordinary leather gloves he would make one pair by sewing two gloves together. These gloves were wool-lined, but I reasoned that it was now winter and furthermore at that time no one considered it absolutely necessary to put on airs by wearing sheepskin gloves.—Well, I guess I looked impressive enough in my best coat and Don Juan's Polish fur cap and all the other things borrowed from this friend or that friend.

When I entered Copernicus's cell down below, that creature almost burst with anger and envy. "Well," he said very caustically, "I wouldn't have thought that you could have dug up such fancy clothes from all these hit-and-miss contributions."

"That's where you were mistaken," I replied. "I think I'll now go and pay her a little visit in this outfit."

Then he became taken aback enough to suppress his anger and say, "Charles, do me a favor and tell her . . ."

"You mean the mother?" I asked.

"No, her."

"The bride?" I asked.

"No, Aurelia," he said growing ill-tempered.

"Did you tell her anything yourself?" I asked.

"No!" he answered.

"Well, then I won't tell her anything either," I said. "Otherwise, I might be as welcome as a mother-in-law on a honeymoon. It may very well be that the poor girl has a broken heart because of the good old Captain, or it may be that the mother has come to the conclusion that I am the most suitable one for her daughter, because I know only this much: she has invited me and not you."

With that I left. I thought to myself, "There, take that! You wanted to make fun of my outfit! Well, did I borrow anything of your juvenile wardrobe?"

As I came out in the courtyard, the others looked at me with great pleasure. I was their pride and joy because I was wearing something from each one of them. I was also very pleased with my own appearance and as I walked down the lane I rehearsed the speech I was going to make to the mother: "If I have the courage to

. . ."—Well, after all this didn't take that much courage.—"If I take the liberty of . . ."—But I wasn't at liberty.—"If I obey your orders . . ."—That was too much; she had no right to give me any orders.—"If I accede to your request . . ."

Just then someone came up behind me and fumbled at my coat pocket. As I turned around I saw that it was the Archbishop who had already pulled my brightly colored kerchief from my pocket to display it properly.—"There," he said, "that looks better." Then he leaned over toward me and whispered into my ear so that Lewandowsky who was walking nearby would not hear it: "Who in eternal love would be united, should first be certain that his love will not go unrequited . . . Well, Charles, you know what I mean." With that he gave me his blessing with a pat on the back, "God be with you, old fellow!" Now I was on my own.

Lewandowsky remained outside as I went into the quartermaster's casemate.—They say that "the more stupid a person is, the greater is his luck." This must be so, because I had the good fortune to find Aurelia all alone.—As I entered the room she rose from her chair where she had been working on her embroidery and like a lovely little innocent girl held out her hand. "Good morning! Good morning! How nice of you to come!"

It was a good beginning, but I was wearing those confounded wool-lined gloves of the Archbishop and while wearing them I couldn't take her hand. By the time I had finally taken off the gloves and placed them in Don Juan's fur cap she had withdrawn her hand.—Now I had rehearsed a speech for her mother, but I was not prepared to address a young girl. In bygone days, to be sure, I had on many an occasion paid my respects to young ladies, but now I was completely out of practice in speaking with members of the opposite sex. In my six years of fortress imprisonment the only opportunity I had had to practice such amenities had been with Korline, the one with the bleary eyes in Silberberg, and here with old Frau Bütow,[1] and they were in no way to be compared with Aurelia.—I managed to mumble something or other and then finally I came out with the most asinine remark that anyone could possibly make: "May I speak to your most gracious mother?"

Good Lord, I had the game already won, I held all the highest trumps and still I went down, doubled and redoubled!

"I shall call mother," she said and went out. I stood there like a jackass and was surprised that I didn't crash against the ceiling with my long ears.

"Mother" was probably still occupied with her household chores; so I had time enough to go over my prepared speech a couple of times. When she finally appeared, I began: "If I accede to your request . . ."

"Oh, you are so kind!" said "mother." "See, here is the niche. Now if you would be kind enough to paint a transparency which we could set up in here . . ."

"Yes indeed! Very gladly!" I replied.

While talking to "mother" I had to turn my back to Aurelia, who had again taken her place at the window and resumed working on her embroidery.

"Yes, very gladly!" I said. "I have already given it some thought."

"What do you have in mind?" she asked.

"In the center I thought of having a very beautiful altar covered with ivy to express the permanence of love, and on the altar a flaming heart to express the passion of love, and above the flame two hands enclasped to indicate the sealing of the covenant."

"Mother" seemed to like that fairly well, but she thought the whole picture might look too bare. I said she should let me take care of everything; we would have to have a couple of angels hovering over the scene. They would hold myrtle and palm branches in their hands and their legs would be entwined with a garland of roses.—She was in agreement with everything else, but she didn't care for the angels. It seemed as though she didn't believe I could paint angels.—She asked whether we couldn't dispense with them.—I told her I couldn't think of leaving them out. The painting would otherwise look too lifeless; there had to be some movement or action in it.

Well, she finally agreed, and then as I turned around to look at Aurelia again, I noticed that the sneaky little thing was peering out the window. She had a big smile on her face. First she held up one finger, then she held up a bent finger and placed it beside another finger and with both hands she was making all kinds of crazy gesticulations.—"What in the world is the meaning of this?" I thought as I went closer to the window.

"Is that the way you think it should be?" asked "mother."

"Yes," I answered, "that's what I had in mind."

I looked out the window and there was Copernicus standing at the little linden tree and making the same crazy gesticulations as Aurelia.—"Aha," I said to myself, "you are not only looking at each other; you are sending telegraphic messages too."

I went still closer to the window and looked through the panes. Then that little half-pint Copernicus sent me a telegraphic message which I understood very well. He spread his fingers and placed both hands beneath his hook-nose and grinned at me: "Haha, Charles, it didn't help you any, did it?"

I returned to the niche, measured its size and thought I would then have the opportunity to engage in a genteel conversation with "mother," but she merely asked me how long it would take me to finish the job.

"Oh, about three days," I said, and then when there ensued a pause in the conversation, I took my fur cap and my wool-lined gloves and said good-by.

As I went out the door I had the feeling as though I had acted like a shoemaker, who had come to fit "mother" for a pair of new shoes.

Oh, how angry I was with myself! I was no longer able to engage in any conversation with a lady. During my imprisonment at various fortresses I had forgotten all those lovely phrases. If I had been treated like a shoemaker, it was only because I had acted like a shoemaker. However, when I saw Copernicus standing outside, defiance flared up within me: "Lie if you have to, but don't let him know what happened!"

"Are you back again so soon?" he asked with a mocking grin on his face.

"Yes," I answered, "if you had been invited, you would probably have inflicted yourself upon the people for an entire forenoon. Thank God, I have enough good manners not to do that." I walked past him very quickly and went up to the Frenchman and Don Juan.

"Well, how did it go?" asked Don Juan as the Frenchman came up to loosen my stand-up collar a little.

"Very well," I said, "very well!—When I came in there was a nice breakfast already set on the table. Aurelia took me by the hand and invited me to sit down on the sofa, and then she poured me a glass of Madeira wine."

"Madeira wine?" repeated the Archbishop, licking his mouth.

"Real Madeira wine?"

"Of course," I answered; "would you expect her to serve me a glass of bitters? And there we sat on the cozy sofa and in our conversation we soon came to the topic of love."

"You're adding all that," said the Frenchman; "you didn't have that much time."

"Well," I said, "if you know everything so much better, just ask Don Juan. He'll tell you whether anyone who knows his business needs so much time."

Don Juan replied that he had expressed his everlasting love to many a girl within the first five minutes, and that had always been without any Madeira wine.

"And so we sat together," I continued; "I held her hand and squeezed it now and then, and then in turn she squeezed my hand . . ."

"You're lying!" a loud voice behind me cried out, and as I looked around I saw the Captain glaring at me with anger in his eyes. "You're lying, Charles, and you ought to be ashamed of yourself for compromising a fine young girl with such lies."

That had certainly not been my intention, but I didn't want to admit how badly I had fared with my genteel conversation and that I had left feeling like nothing better than a shoemaker.

"What do you mean?" I asked perplexed.

"Come along," he replied, "I'll prove it to you."

I shuffled along after him, because when one is caught red-handed, he submits to everything.

"I'll tell you what a big liar you are," he said. "Aurelia merely said 'good morning' to you, and then she called for her mother without exchanging one further word with you."

Oh, how taken aback I was! How did he know all that? — I told him I would reveal everything just as it had happened, but he would have to tell me how he came to know.

At first he tried to wriggle out of it, but finally he said, "Charles, you know that I used to be a rival of Copernicus for the hand of Aurelia, but now I have become his confidant and even the protector of his love."

I didn't exactly know that, but I pretended that I did.

"You know," he continued, "there is a poor deaf and dumb girl who is living here at the fortress. She was formerly in an institution where she learned this deaf and dumb sign language. Every Saturday this poor girl is given her dinner at the quartermaster's house, and from her Aurelia has acquired this particular skill—just incidentally, and for no special reason. I used to room with a student at Halle who was being trained to be a teacher in an institution for the deaf and dumb. He taught me this sign language and I in turn taught it to Copernicus."

"Just incidentally," I remarked, "and for no special reason!"

Now the Captain became a little embarrassed: "No," he said, "this time it was for a very definite reason, for as I have said, I consider myself the protector of this love."

"Aha!" I said. "Now I can understand the meaning of that telegraphic communication which they were carrying on behind my back. It's really nothing but that same old sign language which we used in every cell of the city jail.[2] Is that why you have again been standing at the little linden tree all the time—to give Copernicus private lessons?" I asked.

Now the Captain blushed from embarrassment and his glance became unsteady.—"No, that's not the reason," he answered.

"That's very nice," I said; "you expect me to tell the truth, but you have secrets which you keep from me!"

"No, Charles," said the loyal old fellow, "I'll tell you, because I know that you will reveal nothing; I am in love."

"Good Lord!" I said. "Not again?"

"Since that time when I renounced my love for Aurelia have you ever seen me standing at the little linden tree looking over toward her?"

"No," I answered, "I can testify that you always turned your back toward her and kept looking in the other direction toward Major Martini's[3] windows. Lewandowsky no longer has to straighten the pole, because you and Copernicus on either side have been taking turns in bending it crooked and then straightening it out again."

"Yes, Charles, she is the one for me," he said thoughtfully passing his hand over his eyes. When his hand came down to his splendid nine-month-old mustache he began to twirl it, and when the ends stood straight up he added, "Yes, Charles, Auguste von Martini is the one for me, now and forever."

I couldn't say much to that, because in my opinion he was on the right track; between the quartermaster's daughter and Queen

Victoria he was taking the middle course and choosing a young lady of the nobility. The middle course was then very popular, because the two most famous people of the time, Guizot[4] and Louis Philippe,[5] had made the same choice.

"Captain," I said, "this time I don't think you are making any mistake, but how did all this come about?"

"I think it is very clearly God's will," he replied. "At that time when Copernicus and you both refused to walk behind the carriage house, it happened that Schramm's fiancée was visiting him, the Archbishop had a cold and therefore didn't go out, and Don Juan was trying to catch a friendly smile from the tavern maid at the further end of the carriage house. In short, I was all alone because Lewandowsky was busy watching Don Juan. Then I walked past the gateway of Major von Martini's house; the gate was open and I caught a glimpse of a lovely young lady who was hanging out some things to dry.—You probably think she was hanging out such articles as bed linen, hand towels, or tablecloths, but the fact is they were the most dainty and elegant articles of wearing apparel from which we derive so much joy and pleasure because of their delicacy and tenderness, namely undersleeves, shirtwaist ruffles, and nightcaps. From behind all this linen she peered forth like a fully blown rose between white lilies."

"Yes," I said in order to make him feel happy, "she is a little plump; she's got it over Aurelia in that respect."

"Yes, don't you agree?" he answered, putting the lovely Aurelia completely out of his thoughts. "She is a vision of beauty! As I stood there absorbed in the completeness of her beauty, a gust of wind came up and one of the nightcaps came fluttering through the open gateway right up to me. I caught it before it fell to the ground and said, 'Happy the man, my young lady, who at least has the privilege of becoming acquainted with the nightcap in which your dreams are enveloped.'"

"Well, I'll be damned!" I thought to myself. "The Captain hasn't forgotten how to converse with ladies; why have you?" I was quite angry with myself.—"Well," I said very spitefully, "and then she laughed and that was that?"

"Charles," he said seriously, "shy love never laughs. We stood in the gateway in silence and it was so charming to see her embarrassment as she plucked at the ribbons of her nightcap. Suddenly from the window a man's brusque voice called out into the courtyard, 'Auguste, my sash!' She was startled and called out nervously, 'Good Lord, father has to go to the dress parade!' She pulled more vigorously at the ribbons, ran through the gateway and left this souvenir in my hand."—With that he pulled out a nightcap from beneath his vest.

"Captain," I said, "I won't say any more than that you're on the right track! A real courtship begins with all kinds of loose ribbons and later it ends with a bond tied into a tight knot."

I became mellow and began to reminisce, "I've had the same experience, although not exactly with the ribbon of a nightcap! I too once carried under my vest a beautiful blond girl's beautiful blue hair ribbon,[6] and I might very well have had a wife and children by this time except for this damned imprisonment.—Oh, Captain, what romantic things I have done!—Things you have never dreamed of doing!"

He wouldn't agree to that because he didn't want to be outdone.

"Well then," I added, "did you ever sit in a little plum tree with all those confounded branches such as a plum tree has, just to get a look at her bedroom window?"

"No," he answered.

"Well," I said, "I have, and standing below was my friend Wählert[7] —by this time he's probably a pastor with wife and children—playing a guitar and singing: 'Hear the raindrops falling on the ground, hear the howling of neighbor's little hound!'—He sang well, but there were no dogs around, and the only ones doing any howling were he and his guitar. It was unfortunate for me that the raindrops were not falling and that the moon was shining so brightly, because she—the young lady in question—saw me sitting there in the branches and called to her sister. Then they both looked at me in my embarrassment and the sister, who was very nearsighted, even looked at me through her lorgnette. Wählert ran away and left me sitting there as though I had been placed there as a scarecrow. When I finally did jump down I ripped the back of the only pair of trousers I owned. I won't say anything of the cuts and bruises I got because they all healed in due time. My tailor in Parchim couldn't match the material of these trousers anywhere in town—they were of the most unlikely color and had been made in Stavenhagen. All that autumn—and it was a windy autumn—I had to hide my rear with my coat tails, so that people couldn't see how poorly the back of my trousers matched the front. However, the little fifth-class pupils noticed the difference and called me 'goldfinch'!

"But the worst was yet to come. The next morning the privy councillor dispatched his lackey to my room with the message that if I did not refrain from disturbing him at night while he was trying to sleep, he would have me reported to the headmaster of the school. — Captain, I can tell you that I've been through all this myself!"

The Captain had not expected this of me, but he was evidently happy to hear it, because he now confided to me that he had spoken to Auguste several times after that when her father had gone to dress parade. She had once been trying to hang up a clothes line, but she was so short that she could not reach the pole. He had rushed up and helped her, and so they had talked together in the courtyard. She had shown him their private stables and their seven beautiful cows, for her father, the major, in addition to his regular salary received as additional income all the hay that grew at the fortress. She herself managed her father's dairy and was in charge of all milk sales. However, at the moment things were not going too well, because there were too many cows at the fortress.—Thereupon the Captain hit upon a very romantic idea: we should all buy our milk from Auguste.

"The rest of us will be glad to do so, Captain," I said, "but the Archbishop will certainly not do it, because he is already too greatly committed to the baker's wife."

"That's true!" he said, walking around in deep thought. "The sale wouldn't amount to much."

Suddenly he turned toward me and asked, "Charles, what's your opinion of Surgeon-Major Reich in Magdeburg?"

"He's a splendid fellow!" I answered.

"I mean, what do you think of his medical qualifications?"

"Oh, I consider him an outstanding physician."

"Do you know what he once said? All of us in Magdeburg should go on a complete milk diet."

"What is that?" I asked.

"One consumes nothing but milk; the first three days he is allowed to have some dry rolls, but after that he has nothing but milk for four weeks."

"God help us!" I said. "It's enough to turn a man into a young milk-fed calf."

"Yes, he becomes rejuvenated," he said, "completely rejuvenated!"

"Rejuvenated?" I asked. "In that case you can dismiss the whole idea from your mind. That's nothing for us. Now if through this treatment we could *add* twenty-five years to our lives within four weeks, I'd be all in favor of it, because in that case our sentence would be up and we would be set free."

The Captain took that amiss and left in a huff, because he thought I was making fun of him.

CHAPTER 22

I went into my cell and began to work on the painting. I painted for all I was worth and moved around from one corner to another to get the best light because the days were getting quite short. I had blisters on both hands from cutting the stiff cardboard with a dull table knife. Finally it was finished except for the two angels. "Frenchman, do you think I should paint the angels with or without trumpets?" I asked.

"It all depends on the cheeks," he answered; "if you want to paint the angels with chubby cheeks, then you should have trumpets, otherwise not."

He had a point there, and while I was still trying to decide whether it would be easier for me to paint them with or without chubby cheeks, the Captain came in.

"Charles, have you made up your mind yet?"

"No," I answered, "I'm still thinking about it."

"Well," he asked, "do you want to start on a complete milk diet or not?"

"Oh, I haven't given that any thought," I said. "I was just trying to decide whether a couple of angels would look more beautiful with or without trumpets."

The Captain still thought I was trying to make a fool of him and so he left the cell in anger and slammed the door after him.

The next day I was again busy painting my angels. The Frenchman was looking over my shoulder.

"You know what?" he said. "Your angels are nice and plump. but the trumpets are too short!"—We had decided to add the trumpets.

"That's what you think," I said in anger; "but where am I supposed to find the space for longer trumpets?"

At that moment the Captain came in again, and when he saw my painting he asked why I had painted the two little cherubs with such post horns.

"Yes, that's the correct word," said the Frenchman, "but on a horn you should have tassels."

"Don't get me all heated up!" I said. "My head is already warm enough from all this thinking."

"That's not the reason I came," said the Captain. "I just wanted to ask how much I should order for you."

"Order what?" I asked.

"Milk," he said.

"Oh, nonsense!" I said. "Don't bother me with such questions while I'm trying to create something. Ask the Archbishop; he knows more than I about such matters!"

"It's impossible to talk to you," he said and went away.

Now they had put a bug in my ear with this suggestion of tassels, and even though I knew very well that angels are usually portrayed without tassels, I liked the idea, because in this way I would have the best opportunity of showing off a little with very bright colors.

"Frenchman," I said, "do you think I should use my Mecklenburg colors: blue, red, and yellow?"

"God forbid," he answered, "you should use black, red, and gold, because that's the reason we are doing time. Furthermore, you should provide the two little cherubs with a sash around their middle, because otherwise it looks a little embarrassing."

He was right about the sashes, but he was wrong in suggesting that they be painted in the Prussian colors: black and white. That would not have been appropriate, because I wasn't painting a portrait of a couple of Prussian lieutenants. So I used my Mecklenburg colors and because I still had some space at the rear I let the ends of the sashes hang down somewhat.—Then I placed candles behind the transparency, and because I had painted the little cherubs with blue and white wings, they were really as colorful as a couple of peacocks.

The Frenchman said they looked beautiful, and as the two of us stood there admiring the painting, the Captain, that killjoy, came up with Copernicus and said, "Charles, I asked him."

"Whom?" I asked.

"The Archbishop," he answered.

"Well, what did he say about the black, red, and gold tassels and the sashes?"

"He thought about eight to ten quarts," he said without looking at my painting.

"All right," I said, "as far as I'm concerned, you can make it sixteen!" I was really angry because with all his love for the fair sex he had no appreciation of art at all.

Then that sneaky wretch Copernicus came up and looked at the painting.

"How do you like it?" I asked.

"Well," he said, "it's all right, but there's a little too much color in it; I think it lacks harmony of color and in proportion to the rest of the painting it seems to me that the angels are too small."

That was a little too much for me—a fellow who just barely had the minimum height required for military service talking about something being "too small!" And this fellow who had a yellow and green complexion talked about "harmony of color!"

"Copernicus," I said, "you know I'm usually as gentle as a lamb, but if someone willfully steps on a lamb's toes, that's the end of the lamb's gentleness! This is nothing but your green and yellow envy speaking. You can't paint a transparency like this; you're not the one who will deliver it tomorrow, but I'll be the one!"

Then I took the Frenchman by the arm, walked back and forth with him and said, "Frenchman, why should we let ourselves be annoyed by such a person?"

"Charles," said the Captain, "Charles, please calm down; it wasn't meant that way!"

Then he too walked back and forth with me while Copernicus stood there looking at the painting. He wanted to say something, but couldn't do it.

"Charles," said the Captain, "will you stand by what you said?"

"Yes," I said as I tore myself free from him, "if I have to see it through, I will!"

Then the Captain went over to Copernicus, took him by the arm and the two left. However, while still in the doorway the Captain turned around and said, "Charles, I'll let you know tomorrow afternoon."

"Fine!" I said. "Just fine!" but I was hissing like a snake.

"This is a fine mess," said the Frenchman, when they had left. "As a Jena student you will probably want to duel with foils, but as a Halle student he'll choose rapiers, and where will you get the weapons?"

"It's all the same to me," I said.

"Pistols would be best; we can probably get them from the lieutenant of the fire brigade," the Frenchman said.

"It's all the same to me," I answered.

"You can't duel out in the courtyard," continued the Frenchman,
"and you can't do it in the casemates either, because it would make
too much noise. The best possibility is the kitchen, but in that case
we would have to place the beds up against the door so that the noise
couldn't be heard."

"It's all the same to me," I said—"but in the dark kitchen and at
three paces?"

"That's the usual regulation in the army," he said, and he should
have known because he was a lieutenant in the army reserve.

"Very well!" I said. "In that case I guess it will have to be in the
dark kitchen."

I lay down, but I can't say that I slept very much—pistols, at three
paces, and in the dark?—That's not exactly child's play!—I looked
upon the whole incident as an affair of honor.—He had wanted to
insult me; otherwise how could he speak about "harmony of
color"?—Had he ever painted anything in his whole life?—Did he
know what effort this painting had cost me?—I lay there the whole
night and racked my brains as to what I should do, but when I got up
I knew exactly as much as when I had gone to bed.—But my
transparency was finished and I would have to deliver it; the general
had given me his permission. Frau Bütow had to carry it, and
Lewandowsky and I walked behind her. Whenever we met anyone
we had to stop and exhibit the painting just like an organ grinder at a
carnival who displays a canvas depicting some horror story for which
the organ blares out the appropriate music.

As I left, Don Juan and the Archbishop wanted to dress me up
again—or make me "civilized," as they expressed it—but I was in no
mood for that and went on my way. However, as I walked down the
lane with Lewandowsky and Frau Bütow, a strong gust of wind
came up, took hold of Frau Bütow and my transparency, and if Don
Juan had not come to the rescue, my transparency together with
Frau Bütow would have been wafted into the air like a
kite.—However, Don Juan saved the situation for both, and as he
helped us get the confounded thing into the doorway, he whispered
to me, "Charles, I'm going in with you!"

"It's all right with me," I said to him, and to Lewandowsky I said,

"You saw how much difficulty we had with this thing. If this gentleman doesn't come in with me, I'll never be able to manage it."

Lewandowsky took one quick look out the door, saw that the coast was clear, and then winked at Don Juan: "All right, go in with him!"

With great effort we managed to bring the "thing" into the room and Aurelia came up to meet us.

"Is it finished?" she asked.

"Yes, it is," I answered.

And now Aurelia began to express her thanks to Don Juan for having been so helpful, and Don Juan replied with all kinds of well-phrased words. "Mother" took me in hand and praised me to the skies for my friendliness. If Don Juan and I could have measured our good fortune in terms of pounds, I would have been far better off than he, because not only was "mother" stouter than Aurelia, but her thanks were also more profuse.

Nevertheless, I was not a little annoyed because I had had all the work and now Don Juan was stealing the honey right out of my mouth. .

Mother called, "Aurelia, draw the shades; I'll get some candles and we'll see immediately how it looks."

She hurried out and there I stood in the darkness holding the transparency in my arms and before me I heard some stirring and commotion. "This is a fine state of affairs," I thought; "I'm standing here with my hands full of blisters and he's probably squeezing Aurelia's soft little hand."

At that moment "mother" made a grandiose entrance with two candles in her hands and Don Juan stood there with a knitting frame in his hands. In his left hand he held "mother's" soft warm flannel petticoat and with his right hand he was squeezing very gently the toe of "father's" stocking, because Aurelia, that tricky little thing, was just in the process of knitting a pair of warm stockings for her dear father for Christmas, and instead of offering Don Juan her hand she had given him her knitting to hold.

"Mother" laughed heartily, because there I was standing with my transparency and looking for all the world like a lion in a coat-of-arms and Don Juan with his knitting frame looking like a mythological griffin. To her mother's hearty laugh Aurelia added her own gentle laughter which was just as sweet as honey.

This time the joke seemed to be on Don Juan, but before long I

was the one to be put in an embarrassing position.—The confounded transparency was set up and candles placed behind it.—I
thought to myself, "Now folks, just take a look and see what a man
can accomplish with deliberation and artistry!"

I didn't even bother to glance at the transparency because I knew
what it looked like. I turned my back to my painting and from the
standpoint of the artist I began to evaluate my work. Suddenly a roar
of laughter broke out behind me: "mother's" laugh was obtrusively
loud, Don Juan's was insolent, but that little wretch Aurelia's was
lovely, so lovely, ever so lovely! However, to me it was disagreeable
and annoying.—I looked to see whether there was anything amiss
with my clothing.—Everything was in order!—I tried to look at my
back to see if they had attached something to my coat as a joke. As I
turned around I caught sight of my painting, and my two little
trumpeting angels were looking at me with the most despondent expression possible—each of them had a big black mustache!

That scoundrel Copernicus had done that!

"Don Juan," I said, "you know what's going on. Isn't this
mustache an added insult from Copernicus?"

He said that it indeed was.

I rushed over to the transparency, pulled it down and was about to
trample on it with both feet, but "mother" came up and said, "Sir,
didn't I tell you to leave out the angels?"

However, I turned to Aurelia and said, "Are you in love with
him?—Are you trying to make a fool of me?—Young lady, it doesn't
pay to laugh too soon! Good-by!"

With that I went out the door and Don Juan and Lewandowsky
carrying the transparency followed me.

I returned to my cell and Don Juan and Lewandowsky placed the
transparency very carefully against the wall. Immediately I went to
the pot containing the pine soot and dipped my brush in. The
Frenchman came up and asked, "What are you doing?"

I told him I was going to paint over both angels with pine soot. I
was also going to paint over both trumpets and tassels, but the
Frenchman would have none of that.

"Stop!" he said. "Leave them as they are; they are so beautiful."

"Nonsense," I replied, "I'm going to paint over the whole mess."

"You can't do that," he said. "Tomorrow is the wedding; you
made a promise. Can you paint a new one by tomorrow?"

What he said was true. As I stood there seething in silent rage Frau Bütow came in and set down a pail at the door and said that she didn't have a pot big enough and that she would have to have the pail back again very soon.—Then she handed me a note—it was from the Captain.

"Frenchman," I said, "what's the meaning of all this? Since when has Frau Bütow been employed as a messenger? Here, you take this note; you understand these things better than I."

The Frenchman took the note and burst out laughing as he began to read.

"Well," I said angrily, "it can't be that funny.—What does it say?"

He began to read: "Dear Charles, eight quarts a day at a silver penny per quart makes exactly eight talers a month.—Since it is only proper that we pay the major in advance I should like to ask you to remit the money to me today.—Your etc.—P.S. I think we'll start with eight; we can always increase it to ten or twelve later."

"Good heavens, what is this?" I called and went over to the pail.—It was nothing but milk! Milk almost up to the rim!—"I'll be damned! Am I supposed to pay for all this?"

"Yes," the Frenchman replied, "and you're supposed to drink it too!—In my opinion it would be best if you started right now; otherwise you'll not be able to drink up your assigned quota for today."

"The Captain's crazy and so are you," I said.

"But you said you would," said the Frenchman. "He asked you explicitly if you would stand by what you said and you said 'Yes.'"

"Yes, but I was talking about Copernicus."

"And he was talking about the milk. I think you had better start right now."

How was this possible? I was supposed to drink eight quarts of milk every day for a month and pay eight talers in advance, and all that just because the Captain had fallen in love with Major Martini's daughter! Nothing doing! I'd rather choose pistols at three paces in the dark kitchen!

I took out my paltry money purse from the trunk and counted my fortune.—All together—including the small change—it amounted to just about three talers.—"Frenchman," I asked, "do you have any money?"

"Yes," he answered, "but I need it myself."

Hm, he needs it himself.—No luck there.—"Frenchman," I continued, "milk is supposed to be good for the health."

"I don't question that," he answered.

"Do you want to share this milk with me?" I asked.

"No, thank you!" he said grinning at me. "Since the time I stopped eating your confounded cooking I've been enjoying very good health."

Hm! he's enjoying very good health.—No luck there either.

"Look here," he said with his sarcastic smile, "things are different in your case. Recently you have been eating a considerable amount of veal. That means that many young calves were slaughtered without living long enough to drink much milk. How about pouring the milk down your own throat now so that things will be evened up again?"

"Why do I let myself be annoyed by you in this way? There's only one way to settle this," I said and went downstairs to the Captain.

The Captain was sitting at a table with a large bowl of milk and he was drinking with obvious relish as I came in. Triumphantly he called out, "Charles, I've started already!"

"I see that," I said, and then I explained that for me it was too much milk and also too much money, but he wouldn't accept that as an excuse. He said he thought he was dealing with a man of his word.—Copernicus was sitting there and grinning at us, and so I couldn't explain to the Captain that the whole thing had been a misunderstanding.

"Copernicus, you wretch," I thought to myself, "you ought to go on this milk diet yourself, so that the milk of human kindness might rid you of your hateful venom."—Finally I said, "Well, I guess I'll have to go through with it, but the major will have to give me the milk on credit!"—I started to leave.

"But he won't do it," the Captain called after me.

"Then he can keep his milk!" I called back. I went up to my cell and although I was very angry I managed with the greatest of effort to drink a considerable amount of milk—but, but! struggle as I might, I couldn't drink it all.

Early the next morning I again set myself to the task, but it was simply impossible to drink all the milk. I kept losing ground; each day, when I thought I was just about to finish drinking the stipulated

quota, Frau Bütow would come in with a fresh supply. All my bowls
and pots and dishes were filled with milk.—Down below it was no
different either.

Once when I came walking through the Captain's casemate, Frau
Bütow was standing there looking very disconsolate. She said she
didn't know what this was all coming to, because conditions were
even worse here than upstairs.—The Frenchman and Copernicus
who could have been of help to us would not let themselves get involved, and they even seemed to derive pleasure from our discom-
fiture. Copernicus once told the Captain that if we purchased a pot
of honey, we could really say that we were living in the Promised
Land.

The Captain was angry at me because I didn't pay, but misfortune
brings people together, and we both did in fact share the same misfortune. The third day when Frau Bütow again brought our daily
allotment and the Captain again began to bewail his predicament, I
said, "Captain, I have a good idea. We have to be practical about
this. Let's make butter and cheese.'

"How will we do that?" he asked.

"I'll tell you," I answered; "from the cream we'll make butter and
from the rest we'll make cheese. We don't have a vat, but we can
make the butter in a bottle. We'll shake the cream until it turns to
butter and it will be even simpler to make the cheese, at least it
demands less effort."

I explained everything to him in a scientific manner and why it
had to be done in such and such a way, just as I had been taught by
my aunt Schäning[1] and old father Thaer's book on scientific husbandry.[2] "That will take care of everything except for the cheese bags.
Where shall we find two cheese bags?"

I went to my trunk and looked at my supply of linen.—It would be
a shame to cut that up and besides it would have to be sewn together
again.

"Just a moment!" said the Captain. He went below and returned
with a pair of white trousers made of English leather.—They are
clean and in good condition," he said, "but I can't wear them any
longer because they are too short and also too tight around the
waist."

"Splendid!" I said. "Now we won't have to sew anything

together. We'll simply cut the two legs off, tie each one together at the bottom and pour the milk in at the top."

CHAPTER 23

W E did just that; I skimmed off all the milk, poured the cream into a couple of two-quart bottles and the curds into the two trouser legs, which I then hung up carefully against the wall, and under each one I placed a wash basin to catch the whey as it ran off.

"There," I said, "now we can start making the butter."

I gave him one bottle and I took the other, and then we walked back and forth, each one with a bottle in his hands and shaking it for all he was worth, so that it was just a joy to behold. In the meantime the whey continued to run off from the cheese bags.

"But what are we going to do with all the butter, if we are not allowed to eat any in the next four weeks?" asked the Captain.

"I have it all figured out," I said. "We'll sell it; if the Archbishop can get it from us a shilling[1] cheaper than elsewhere, he'll buy it and thank us in the bargain, and as for the cheese, we will still have plenty of time before it becomes firm."

And so we were talking and making butter and making butter and talking when there was a knock on the door. "Come in!" I called, and who should come in but my little Ida with a big basket? She said, "Greetings from mother, who would like to have seen you at the wedding, but since that was impossible, she is taking the liberty of sending you this. She also said that the transparency was just beautiful."

"I put my bottle aside and unpacked the basket — cake and more cake and four bottles, but these bottles contained something other than what was in our bottles.

I asked Ida to express our most sincere thanks to her mother. After she had left, the Captain put his bottle aside too and we looked at our present.

"It's unfortunate that we are just now in the process of making butter," I said, "because that doesn't allow for any interruption." — Then I picked up my bottle again.

"Yes, right in the middle of our diet," said the Captain, as he too reached for his bottle. "Charles, you're not going to make the mis-

214

take of discontinuing the diet, are you?"

"God forbid," I said.

And so we continued to walk back and forth making our butter. However, whenever we came to the table where our magnificent present was displayed, we spent a long time there, although we did not stop shaking the bottles.

Finally I said, "Captain, during the first few days of our diets we are allowed to eat some rolls; we are in fact still in the first days, and here are some biscuits which are sometimes expressly prescribed for people who are on the verge of death. They can't do us any harm."

"I don't think they can either," said the Captain. — And so we put down the bottles and ate the biscuits.

When we had eaten them I sniffed at another piece of cake and said, "This smells just like almond cake. It seems to me that this harmonizes very well with milk, because milk is produced from almonds too."

"That's correct," he said, and so we also ate the almond cake.

"I wonder what's in the bottles!" I asked.

"Yes," said the Captain, "I wonder what sort of a drink it is!"

I removed the cork, poured out a few drops and said, "Here, try it!"

"It's cardinal,"[2] he said, "excellent cardinal!"

"Well, I'll be damned!" I said. "Here we are in the middle of this stupid old diet, but cardinal becomes sour if one lets it stand four weeks."

"That's a fact," the Captain said in agreement.

"Captain," I continued, "do you have a smidgen of butter in your bottle yet?"

"No," he replied.

"I don't either," I said. "It's an old story: if it doesn't turn into butter, there's simply nothing one can do about it."

Then I went over to the cheese bags and said, "The whey has all run off; now we have to put the curds under a hard press."

"We'll probably have to get some stones," he said.

"No, we can take care of this ourselves," I answered.

I placed one trouser leg on the Frenchman's stool and the other on mine; on top of each I placed the lid of a wooden crate and said,

"Now you sit on this one and I'll sit on that one."

And so we sat there facing each other and making butter and cheese, and between us stood the four bottles of cardinal.

"You know, I'll have to try it too," I said, "just once." — And I did. — 'Look here," I said, "this is very good stuff. Aurelia did a good job in making this."

"Aurelia?" he asked.

"Yes, Aurelia!" I answered. "Her mother didn't make it; if she had, it would be sweeter. The older women get to be, the more sweet-toothed they become."

"And so do you really think that Aurelia made it?" he asked. "In that case I'll have to try it again."

He poured out a few drops for himself and for me and we tasted it again, this time, however, more carefully, insasmuch as we wanted to evaluate Aurelia's skill in making cardinal. — It met with our approval and so I said, "Captain, she is after all a lovely little girl and I think we should drink a toast to her health."

"That she is," he said, "and so that you may see that I bear her no grudge . . .," and with that he emptied his glass. — And I — well, I concurred with his opinion and emptied my glass too.

However, after a while his conscience began to bother him — not because of the cardinal and the milk diet, but because of Auguste, his new love, and he said, "Charles, while we're drinking toasts — there is another very lovely creature here at the fortress — you know the one I mean" — and with that he refilled both glasses.

"Stop!" I said. "Her health we shall have to drink from a cream bottle, because every bird has different feathers."

"Charles," he cried out, "are you trying to hurt me?"

I had no intention of doing that; so we touched glasses and drank to Auguste's health. He placed his hand over his heart and with his thoughts solely on the major's daughter he again emptied his glass. Beneath him very gently and quietly little drops trickled out of the cheese bags and fell to the floor. It was a very solemn moment and we sat there in silence.

Without saying a word I refilled the Captain's glass and I was just about to say in mournful tones, "What do you know, the bottle is empty," when I heard a loud commotion down below. The Frenchman and Copernicus had just returned from their exercise period and had noticed that the whey had seeped through the floor

and the drops were gently trickling down into their cell. — The
Captain came out of his silent reverie long enough to ask, "Shall we
give them some?"

"Why should we?" I answered. "They didn't help us with the
milk, and so we don't need them now to help us with the cardinal."
Just to show them that I wanted to have my revenge I opened the
second bottle and filled two glasses for the Captain and myself.

The Frenchman came up making a great deal of noise and asked
what in the devil's name we were doing.

"Making cheese," I said coldly.

"Cheese?" he repeated very perplexed. Then he came closer, and
when he saw the cake and the bottles, his curiosity was aroused.
"What is all this?" he asked as his eyes lit up.

"Get a good look," I said to myself, "because there is no place set
for you at this table."

"Good heavens, what's this?" he asked as he held up one bottle
to the light.

"Cardinal," I answered.

"Where the devil did you get that?" — Then I stood up and
decided to put it to him in plain language, so that he would certainly understand what I meant. I said:

> "He who can do something, gets the nod;
> No one is ever in need of a clod."

But he didn't understand, and so when he continued to look at
the Captain and myself with questioning eyes, the Captain said,
"It's because of the transparency; we have derived this profit from
Charles's art."

"Charles, old fellow, didn't I help you with it?" he asked.

That was true; he had suggested the trumpets and the tassels. —
"All right," I said, "go get yourself a glass and we'll drink a toast to
art."

And after I had drunk still another glass of cardinal I became so
mellow that I stood up from my moistened seat and said, "Come
over here, Frenchman, you can do something too; sit right here on
this chair, but when you sit down, do so very gently!"

Then unnoticed I left the cell and went down below to Copernicus. I talked to him in a friendly way, extended my hand and said,

"Come now, Copernicus, let's be friends again. I want you to come upstairs with me, because we're making cheese and at the same time drinking some of Aurelia's cardinal."

The stubborn little fellow was so moved that the tears rolled down his hook nose and he followed me like a lamb. — Later on, to be sure, he maintained that it had not been tears but drops of whey that had fallen on his nose — but I know him better than that — he also had his sentimental moments.

When I came up with the little fellow, we were received with loud cheers. The two cheese-bag-sitters during my absence had made good use of the time to drink cardinal, the Captain in the van making steady progress and the Frenchman in the rear hurrying with all speed to catch up.

With Copernicus present we had to drink another toast to Aurelia and then one also to her mother, and there was great merriment, but it did not get out of hand. And why was that? — Because we knew how to combine useful work with our fun, for before long we two, Copernicus and I, were have our pleasure walking back and forth in the casemate and making butter, while the other two were sitting securely and firmly on their trouser legs. However, the Captain's head was already somewhat befuddled, because he had had a considerable head start, and so when we had almost finished the third bottle, he slapped himself on the chest and said, "Copernicus, you got her from me; I ceded her to you."

Copernicus wanted to know what kind of stupid talk that was, and I was terribly frightened because I thought that we were again to be shown an example of the Captain's magnanimity. A situation which on that earlier occasion had been resolved moderately well over a cup of coffee could now over a bottle of cardinal bring dire results. I tried to act as a mediator and the Captain seemed to be accepting everything in good spirit, "because," he said, "I have found a consolation, a replacement — and what a replacement! — a wonderful replacement!"

Then in all confidence he also told the others about Auguste and how it had all come about, and whenever he got stuck I helped him out. — I then started to open the fourth bottle while Copernicus continued to walk back and forth shaking his bottle of cream. Suddenly the Captain caught hold of the dressing gown of the un-suspecting Copernicus as he was passing by, pulled him down into his lap, kissed him and said, "Copernicus, we shall be friends forever."

"Yes," said Copernicus and calmly continued to churn the cream.

The Frenchman and I observed this tableau of eternal friendship, I chilled to the heart, and he chilled to the knees, because he was being spattered with whey.

Out of gratitude Copernicus wanted to drink a toast to the Captain's new love: "To Auguste Martini!" he cried as he jumped up from the Captain's lap, and then we heard something that sounded like "puff" from under the Captain and he sank down about four inches. The trouser leg had not been strong enough to withstand such a friendship and such a toast; it had split and the cheese had all poured out.

Good heavens above! There was the beautiful white cheese all over the sandy floor, and whatever was not on the floor was sticking in strips to the new bright green patch which the Captain had sewn on the backside of his dressing gown. The whole cell looked like a beautiful green field of rye when it is still covered with a thin layer of snow in the early spring.

"There, that's what we get!" I said; the Captain also said, "Yes, that's what we get!" but Copernicus merely said, "Oh!"

The Frenchman was just about to get up to view the damage, but I made him sit tight and said, "Frenchman, I beg you for heaven's sake, don't move or you will bring about another disaster!" but he paid me no heed.

When he saw the damage, he broke out into a foolish laugh, took his glass in hand and called out, "Charles, long live your dairy business!" — When he saw the Captain's backside, he again broke out into unrestrained laughter and in the most foolish manner threw himself back on his chair: "Puff!" said the trouser leg, and there lay the whole mess.

"There," I said, "that takes care of that business. The only thing I need now would be to have a couple of you come up with the brilliant idea of taking the cream bottles and with them drinking a toast to Auguste's health. — How about it, Frenchman? — How about it, Copernicus?" — I held out a bottle for each of them; they didn't want to, but the Captain did. — "Auguste," he said, "for Auguste nothing is too good!" and — bang — he slammed one cream bottle against the other, so that all our butter and all the income from the sale of the butter ran out over the table and chairs.

"Oh, there is still a bottle of cardinal here," I said, "don't you want to break that to pieces too?" — And he would have done it, he would actually have done it, if Copernicus had not had enough compassion and good sense to prevent him from doing so, "because that would be a shame."

I stood there like a man who had lost his best friend and reflected upon the complete failure of my first business enterprise. The Frenchman and Copernicus were preoccupied with the very urgent business of emptying the last bottle of cardinal and making many poor jokes about dairy farming, with which they may possibly have wanted to cheer me up. After making his sacrificial offering of butter at the altar of his beloved Auguste and after all his other heroics the intrepid Captain was walking back and forth in a military goose step and addressing his trouser legs. He said they had served him faithfully for many years, they had always stood him in good stead, and they would have performed this most recent service too if human folly had not expected the impossible of them.

Because there was no place to sit down we drank the last glass of cardinal while standing. Frau Bûtow came in, threw up her arms and said, "Good Lord, down below it is just as bad! The whole cell is dripping! — Well, cleanliness is half the battle," and with that she swept off the table with a broom.

That was the end of the transparency episode and also of the Captain's white military trousers; or — to be more precise — it was not quite the end, because that night I became sick, so sick that even the Frenchman took pity on me and stood at my bedside all night with the only medicine we had, a pot of camomile tea. When Frau Bûtow came in the next morning and saw my miserable condition, she again threw up her arms and cried, "Good Lord, down below it is just as bad! The Captain is so sick that he doesn't know what to do either."

And so he was sick too! In that case I knew what the trouble was, and so as soon as the others had left to take their walk, I crawled down to the Captain, and there the two of us sat looking at each other like two lost souls. I said, "That's what happens!" — And he said, "Yes, that's what happens with cardinal!" — "No," I corrected, "with milk!"

And we argued about that, but only half-heartedly, and finally I said, "Captain, let's not argue about it any more; so much is certain: cardinal and milk do not mix well in the human body, and the way we feel we won't be able to eat anything for the next three days. Look here! Behind your bed there are already another eight quarts. I've already given Frau Bûtow my eight quarts, because I no longer want to have anything to do with a dairy business. How would it be, Captain, if you put on your best clothes, that is, after you have recovered somewhat, and went to the major and called off this milk transaction?"

He said he couldn't do that. What would the major and his daughter think of him?

"Captain," I said, "you're too timid; you don't know how to take advantage of a good opportunity. The general will certainly permit you to cancel the deal, you will come into a very pleasant relationship with the fat major, and if you give a detailed description of our present state of health, then it would be most strange if Auguste were not moved to pity. — A woman is already very much in love when there is pity in her heart."

Sure enough! — Three days later the Captain called on the major, and during that time Frau Bütow was fattening up her five little children with sixteen quarts of sweet milk daily.

CHAPTER 24

THE Captain had gone in to see the major and I was waiting to see what kind of an expression he would have on his face when he came out again. — But who was it that came walking along? — Aurelia. — Because I am a well-bred man I wanted to thank her for the gift of cake and cardinal, and so I sauntered over to talk to her. She was in no particular hurry; so we stood there chatting for some time at the corner of the smoke-house. Well, I thought nothing of this, but after she had gone, Copernicus came up to me and said that he considered it very ill-bred on my part to speak to a lady on the street. — I replied that she had spoken to me first. — He said that made no difference; I should not have entered into any conversation with her.

Just then the Captain came by looking as mad as a hornet. He said that he had had a most unpleasant experience as a result of my underhanded advice. The old major had been sharp and caustic to him, and of Auguste he had seen just the tip of her bed jacket, and no more, as she had skipped out the door.

Since neither had been able to pay court to his beloved, both Copernicus and the Captain took it out on me. Finally I became angry and asked whether they thought they could use me as a lightning rod every time a dark cloud appeared in the skies of their romance.

There was much grumbling and complaining, because with so much romance Copernicus and the Captain were afflicted with all the trials and tribulations which accompany love affairs. If it hadn't been for the fact that spring with all its beauty arrived just at that time, I would probably have become completely "musical," [1] as old Frau Jakob in Stavenhagen said when they locked up her husband for stealing sheepskins.

However, springtime freshens the spirit, and so I again spent as much time as was permitted walking back and forth beneath the green linden trees. One day just as I was about to pass the narrow side-path between blacksmith Grunwaldt's house and the baker's house, what did I see? — My good friend Copernicus and Aurelia, and they were holding hands and talking with great animation, and then — well, I'll be damned! — that little shrimp Copernicus got up on tiptoe and gave her — smack — a kiss right on the mouth. — Well, that was a fine howdy-do! He wanted to forbid me to speak to people on the street, and here he was at the kissing stage! Just wait till I see you again!

And in due time I did see him. — "Copernicus," I said, "I consider it a mark of ill-breeding to speak to a lady on the street."

He gave me a questioning look and finally asked, "What do you mean?"

"But it reveals even more ill-breeding when a man kisses a lady on the street."

"Charles," he whispered softly but very forcibly, "I beg you, don't tell anyone, but we have become engaged."

"This is amusing," I said looking just as perplexed as Herr Smidt of Klocksin when Herr von Frisch told him he was a jackass.

"Yes," he continued, "and everything is in order because mother knows about it."

"This is getting more and more amusing," I said repeating the words of Herr Smidt of Klocksin when Herr von Frisch gave him a box on the ears and then threw him out the door.

"Charles," he said, "I'm making you the confidant of our love; you can help us."

"Another new assignment for you!" I thought to myself, and then I asked, "I guess I'm supposed to be a surrogate for your father?"

He said it wasn't that, because his father was going to be informed about this in a few days anyway. However, the next day was Sunday and the Captain, the Archbishop, and I were supposed to have our turn to go to church in town. Now Copernicus wanted to know whether I could arrange to have the Captain give up his turn to him and to have the Archbishop stay home. He would then make use of the opportunity to talk to Aurelia on the way to church and to discuss with her all necessary matters. I, however, would have to divert the attention of the sergeant.

"Confidant of our love!" I said to myself as I came back to the casemate. "That's something you have never been before." — I thought it over for a while and finally I said, "I won't be able to accomplish this without some terrible lies." — And so I took action immediately.

I went down to Copernicus and the Captain and said, "Copernicus, recently you were talking about a ham. I know where you can buy one in town, a very good one."

"That's well and good," said the sly little fellow, "but I'll have to see it for myself."

"Well, then go into town with me tomorrow," I replied. "The Captain will probably let you go in his place."

' The good old Captain suspected nothing and was satisfied with the switch; it's possible that he too was thinking about the ham.

But now for the Archbishop! — I worked on him all afternoon, but with no success! He said that he wanted to hear the preacher, dull as he was, and after that buy a couple of pounds of soft soap, because he was going to do his laundry. — I tried every possible trick, but all to no avail; the practical as well as the spiritual side of his nature asserted itself again and again. — Finally I had a brilliant idea. Just as we were passing the bakery I said, "He's not going to pull through."

"Who?" he asked.

"The baker," I replied; "he's having dizzy spells. This morning his wife was standing at the door and she was looking very sad and dejected."

"The poor woman!" said the Archbishop.

"Yes, and she has nobody around the house who can be even of a little assistance to her. Furthermore, the baker is also very stout and short of breath."

Our free time was now up. In the evening when Frau Bütow came in, I said, "Frau Bütow, it's too difficult for one person to tell a lie all by himself; you must give me a little help." — I reminded her that I had given her all that milk. — "Tomorrow when the Archbishop asks you about the baker, just tell him that he's getting worse; that's all."

Frau Bütow promised me that she would and indeed she did. — The next morning, as we were ready to go to church with the sergeant, the Archbishop was looking over the fence of the baker's house. He said he didn't care to go along with us because he wanted to console the baker's wife.

So just the two of us went down the road which led to the church in town. I said, "Copernicus, you will have to buy the ham — and I really know where there is one for sale — because if you come back without it, they will know we were lying."

In the church Aurelia sat diagonally across from us. Not counting the sergeant, I was probably the most pious of us three on that day, because as soon as the sermon was finished the telegraphic communication between Copernicus and Aurelia was again in full operation. We left the church and Copernicus bought the ham. As we went up the road and back to the fortress, there walking ahead of us with little mincing steps was Aurelia and she was constantly looking back at us.

"Now keep the sergeant away from us," said Copernicus, and with his short legs churning he hurried ahead.

Suddenly I became winded, so that I had to stop to catch my breath! — Now we were separated, but the sergeant was trying to make us stay together, and that was just what I was trying to prevent. — And so I began to view the landscape and pick flowers at the edge of the ditch, and when the sergeant hurried on ahead, I quickly jumped over the ditch and called to him from the other side, "What if I should escape now?"

He said I certainly wouldn't do that and I answered that it was just possible that I might. — As soon as I was certain that I had him worried I crossed back over the ditch and had the pleasure of noting that he stayed close to me, so that Copernicus was free to carry on his romance undisturbed. In short, I was playing the part of a protective angel and it was a joy and a pleasure for me just to look at the two. Aurelia, slender as a reed, was walking along gracefully and her cheeks were fresh and rosy with hope and from the spring breeze. And there was that little shrimp Copernicus with his short legs struggling to keep up with her, with love in his heart and under his arm the smoked ham.

"That's the way it should be," I said to myself, "because what good is love if food is lacking!" And since that time I have always thought of Copernicus and Aurelia and the ham whenever I have thought of a practicable love.

However, I can testify to the fact that even with such practical considerations they had not forgotten the pleasant aspects of love, for when we came to the area of the fortress where the road makes a turn, they were suddenly no longer to be seen. Then after we had continued a short distance they came out from behind the rifle range and were now behind us. They said they had been picking flowers and I believe it. Copernicus had picked some red primroses and Aurelia some yellow buttercups, because her lips were bright red and he had his jaundiced coloring again.

"Charles," said the little bridegroom-to-be after his beloved Aurelia had left, "now her father knows about it too and has given his consent."

"That's very nice, but wait till you see what trouble I'm in now," I said, for I had just then caught sight of the Archbishop pacing back and forth under the linden trees.

As soon as we approached him he snorted at me, "Nothing but lies! Nothing but stinking lies! The baker is sound and healthy."

"I'm glad to hear that," I said. "I'm happy for the sake of his wife. Has he recovered?"

"He wasn't sick at all."

"He wasn't? So much the better."

"Just think of this," said Don Juan who was standing beside us, "out of compassion for the baker's wife the Archbishop stole into the house. When he came into the kitchen there was the baker sitting at a table and partaking of a breakfast of smoked eel, pickled meat, and a bottle of kümmel and eating like a man who is enjoying the best of health. The Archbishop was so startled to see the baker that he began to talk about death and ghosts, whereupon the baker escorted him out the door, because according to Emilie Grunwaldt, the baker can't bear to hear the word 'death.'"

Then Don Juan took me by the arm and led me aside. "Tell me, is everything in order?" he asked.

"What do you mean?"

"Oh, I just mean between Copernicus and Aurelia. Emilie Grunwaldt says that it has been going on for a long time."

So, that's the way it was; everyone knew it! — As a "confidant of their love" I began to feel very superfluous.

So I went to Copernicus and said, "Copernicus, you know it, mother knows it, father knows it, Aurelia certainly knows it, I know it, Don Juan knows it, and Emilie Grunwaldt knows it too. Please release me from my position as confidant, because I am already on bad terms with the Archbishop. Today is Sunday and this afternoon when we are all having coffee together you would have the best opportunity to inform the others about your status as groom-to-be."

And so it happened. When Copernicus had told us all about his good fortune, my old Captain was the first to congratulate him, because he was probably thinking about his Auguste. After things had quieted down the question was raised as to how we should now proceed. We all agreed on this: Copernicus would have to inform the general of his engagement and request permission to visit his fiancée. The motion was carried, and so on the next day Copernicus requested an appointment with the general and received the answer: the general would see him the following day on his way to the parade grounds.

At eleven o'clock the next morning when it was time for the dress review I accompanied Copernicus to the little linden tree and I stationed myself behind a big poplar tree. Copernicus waited for the general and I waited to see how well Copernicus would conduct himself in this matter. Off and on I offered him a word of encouragement such as "Go to it, Copernicus!" and "Keep a stiff upper lip, Copernicus!" and "Remember the eleventh commandment — let not thyself be thrown!"

Finally the old gentleman, tall and stately in his three-cornered hat and ornamental plume, came walking along slowly, and our little groom-to-be stepped up gingerly to meet him. I saw immediately that this was going to be a difficult task for Copernicus, because the old gentleman towered a foot and a half over him and would talk downhill to Copernicus, whereas Copernicus would have to talk uphill to the general.

"Why did you want to speak to me?" asked the general in a very friendly manner.

My heart was pounding as I stood behind the poplar tree.

"Herr General," said the cocky little fellow, placing his weight on his left foot and cocking his head a little to the side, probably for the purpose of having his saucy beak appear in the proper light, "I have come here to inform you of my engagement."

"What in the devil's . . ." called the old gentleman, and it was actually as though the hair of his white wig were startled, because the ornamental plume shot up another inch and a half.

"Yes," Copernicus said very boldly, and his candor was a credit to his new status as bridgroom-to-be, "yesterday I became engaged to the daughter of Quartermaster Lucke."

"The devil you say!" shouted the old gentleman.

Copernicus, as high-spirited as a thoroughbred pony, hadn't said anything about the devil, but had merely reported that he had a fiancée.

"And you tell me that? And I'm supposed to report that to Berlin? Thunderation, what would they say in Berlin if they were to learn that all the demagogues here are getting engaged?"

However, Copernicus wouldn't let himself be thrown. Just for a change he shifted his weight to his other foot, placed his hands on his hips and said, "Herr General, you can't object to the engagement itself, because that is my personal affair. I have come here merely to ask you for permission to visit my fiancée."

"And you think I'm stupid enough to grant you this permission? — By no means! — As soon as the other political prisoners find out that they can have access to private houses in this way, they will all want to get engaged by tomorrow. — No, indeed! I'll have nothing to do with that kind of business," he said, and he left without even saluting.

"Charles . . ." said Copernicus to me as I came out from behind the big poplar tree — "Charles . . ." he said and he was all broken up.

"Never mind; no tree falls at the first stroke," I said and I tried to console him as much as I could.

When we returned to the others they too tried to cheer him up. We were all very much saddened because Copernicus was *our* groom-to-be, and what had happened to him had effectively happened to us too. We didn't count Schramm's engagement; that had happened before our time.

We racked our brains for some solution, but everything which in such situations would otherwise have been suitable or convenient was out of the question. Don Juan suggested an abduction, which he was convinced he could arrange, but we couldn't approve of that, because in that case Copernicus would have to keep fleeing with his fiancée within the encircling walls of the fortress. The Archbishop suggested a secret wedding. That could be arranged, but in that case Copernicus would again have to have one of his yellow jaundice attacks, and while Lewandowsky was under the impression that Copernicus was looking into Grunwaldt's tar barrel, the young couple could be married while standing in the gateway.

But where was a priest to be found? The Archbishop was Catholic, but his high office in the Catholic hierarchy was suspect. — It was a very difficult problem, but finally we agreed on one point: Copernicus had done everything he possibly could and now she, that is Aurelia, would have to do something about it too.

She was so informed and the prospects now looked much brighter, because Aurelia happened to be the best friend of the general's adopted daughter. The old gentleman liked Aurelia very much and used to joke with her. A few days later when he was on his way to the flood-gate and she — purely by coincidence — was looking over the breastwork of the fortification, he pretended to be angry with her by shaking his finger and saying, "You just wait; you have led one of my demagogues astray."

She said she had indeed, but she derived no benefit from it, because her fiancé was not allowed to visit her.

The old gentleman twirled his white mustache, straightened his white wig and finally said half good-naturedly and half in vexation, "Well, have your papa come and see me this afternoon."

And her father had gone to see him and the old gentleman had asked him whether he would give him a guarantee that Copernicus would not escape. Aurelia's father had replied that he couldn't do that because he wasn't Copernicus nor could he read his mind. However, he had added very sensibly that he had never heard of a man escaping because he had a fiancée.

The old gentleman saw the point and that afternoon the groom-to-be had to appear before him.

"Now the matter is coming to a head," we said as we stood in a little group at the little linden tree and waited for little Copernicus.

Finally he came and how he was strutting! He walked as fast as his little legs would allow, and when he reached the linden tree he waved his white handkerchief three times toward Aurelia's window and she returned his greetings three times. Lewandowsky said that he could see that Herr Copernicus now had his knapsack all packed and that he was prepared to march fully armed into the state of matrimony.

When we had returned to our casemate the Frenchman and I took hold of Copernicus and placed him on the table. He was our pride and joy because he had fought the good fight for all of us. Copernicus gave a speech and it began: Just as Aurelia was the most

beautiful young lady in the whole world, so too was the general the
best fellow in the whole world, and the speech ended with: just as
the general was the best fellow in the whole world, so too was
Aurelia the most beautiful young lady in the whole world. We
agreed with him out of honest conviction as far as the general was
concerned and out of courtesy as far as Aurelia was concerned.

But then we were all given a jolt just when we thought the whole
matter was settled. Copernicus reached into his coat and drew out a
document which he said we would all have to sign to insure his
complete happiness. And he read aloud what the old general had
written: we others were all to swear that none of us would become
engaged because he had enough with *one* betrothal.

Now that was really too much and we all had very long faces, but
there was nothing we could do about it. After reviewing in my mind
all the women at the fortress who were still available, and finding
no one suitable for me, I signed:

Charles douze.

After me it was the Frenchman's turn. He said that as long as he
was imprisoned he wouldn't think of getting married, and whenever
he were to be freed he would again be a Prussian lieutenant and
then he would have to produce 12,000 talers if he were to get
married. He didn't have the 12,000 talers and so he signed:

Frenchman, Royal Prussian Lieutenant,
temporarily unattached.

Then came the Archbishop. He said he would not have signed a
couple of days ago, but now that he had seen the baker at breakfast,
he was prepared to sign, because the man looked as though he
might still live a long time:

F.W., Archbishop.

Don Juan said he wasn't going to be fool enough to tie himself
down. He was still young and the whole world belonged to him. He
was therefore happy to do Copernicus this favor:

Don Juan, Poet.

Now it was the Captain's turn, but he wouldn't sign. — "But
Captain," I said, "surely you of all people want to help make these
young people happy."

No, he wouldn't do it, and when we pressed him, he said we
should judge him fairly; he had most certainly done enough for
Copernicus already. He had ceded to him a girl whom he himself

had loved, and only he, the Captain, could know what anguish that had caused him. But he could not sign away his future just to make Copernicus happy, because the happiness of another person was dependent on his own future. This other person was a delicate and sensitive young woman, and it was his responsibility to insure her happiness.

There we were again not knowing which way to turn. I was very much annoyed with the Captain; I took him aside and asked, "Is everything again straightened out between you and your Auguste?"

"No," he said, "not yet."

"Well, then you had better hurry," I added, "because the rumor that has been circulating for the last three months has been verified: the old major is being transferred and is leaving this week, and the new major is already here."

He would not and could not believe that. However, after he had spoken to Lewandowsky, and the following day after the loquacious Archbishop had asked the loquacious major in the Captain's presence how matters stood, and after the new major had informed them in all detail that the old major was to leave that very week and that Auguste had already departed to make the necessary arrangements in their new home across the river, then all the stars in the Captain's heaven, one after another, fell to the ground. As he sat in the darkness of the casemate he signed away his future for the sake of the happiness of Copernicus. "But," he said to me, "Charles, I have signed this with my heart's blood."

The next day the document was returned to the general and the commandant's order was then entered in the guard-house record. It read: Inasmuch as this unfortunate incident has taken place, Copernicus will be permitted to visit his fiancée once every three days beginning today. Lewandowsky is always to accompany him as far as the door. For the rest of the political prisoners things are to remain as they were.

And so we dressed our little bridegroom in his best finery, and as he stood before us in his new blue dress coat which he had had made for this occasion he looked as neat as a Christmas puppet. He went around and thanked us all for helping him to find such happiness and then he went to his trunk, took out the ham, tossed it on the table and said, "There, I'm treating you all to this ham."

We took him in our midst — that is, all of us except the Captain

who said he was too emotionally drained — and escorted him to the
little linden tree. From there he dashed away from us and rushed
over to his rosy-cheeked sweetheart who was standing in the
doorway. Like a bee he buzzed up to the rose and quick as a flash
he disappeared within the door and — bang — the housedoor was
slammed shut. What the bee and the rose talked about Lewandowsky never did find out, for by the time he came lumbering up to
the door with the bayonet at his side they were already in the house.

We stood there and waited because they would surely have to
appear at the window. After an initial hasty exchange of words
between lovers they came to the window arm in arm. They bowed
and nodded and that little thing Copernicus looked just as
aristocratic as a count and Aurelia curtsied as gracefully as a lily
stem. Little Ida had pushed her way in front of the two and was
clapping her hands and laughing and waving and pointing at her
new little yellow brother-in-law as though he were a honey cake
which she had just received for Christmas. Behind all of them stood
"mother" and she kept popping up and down, so that the
Frenchman said to me, "Look, I think 'mother' is churning butter
back there." — And Don Juan, who was bareheaded and had
nothing to wave, grabbed the Archbishop's "pumpkin cover" from
his head, waved it in the air and shouted, "Hurrah for both of
them!"

We others all joined in shouting "Hurrah" and waving our caps
— that is, all of us except the Archbishop who was at a loss for
words because he was too busy searching for the cap on his bald
head. — The old general also heard all these shouts of "Hurrah"
and later he told Lewandowsky that it had not been quite proper,
but nevertheless he was happy to think that we stuck together like
loyal friends.

Joking and laughing we returned to our casemate and there we
found our loyal old Captain still sitting at the table in his great
sadness. He had cut up the ham and was now feeding his love-sick
stomach with ham and bread. We all stood around him in our joy
and happiness, but at the same time we were wondering whether
ham was such a good remedy for heartache. With the most
woebegone expression he explained that he had felt the need of oc-
cupying himself in some useful activity in order to rid himself of all
melancholy thoughts. In this condition the ham had been the first

thing to come within his reach and he had merely wanted to cut it up into small pieces for us.

"And he has done precisely that!" said Don Juan. "And so let's help ourselves. But just wait one moment; I want to fetch something."

He beckoned to the Archbishop; they left and soon returned with a half anker[2] of wine. Don Juan said that he had really been saving it for the day when he would be released — for his time was almost up — but this too was a wonderful day, just as wonderful as any other.

I said that I agreed with him, for it was a memorable day for all of us. — Because of his great sorrow the Captain was given the first glass and he emptied it very quickly in the reasonable conviction that ham alone could not solve his problem.

Just as the celebration was in full swing the lieutenant of the fire brigade, together with a couple of other lieutenants whom we knew, walked past our window. They had to come in. The sergeant on guard duty out of respect for his superiors wouldn't come in, but he stood behind the door and drank one glass after another. Finally, when Lewandowsky returned with our little bridegroom in tow he joined the other sergeant and they talked together and drank together from *one* glass. — However, our little bridegroom-to-be was given a seat at the head of the table and we drank alternately to the health of Copernicus, then of Aurelia, and then of both of them. For the betrothal Don Juan composed a poem right there on the spot, but everyone said that it was more suitable for a wedding than an engagement because of the allusions in it. The Frenchman and the lieutenants kept calling one another "Herr Comrade," and one of the lieutenants in a jocular vein mentioned that the lieutenant of the fire brigade and the Captain were actually rivals for the hand of Auguste Martini. Hearing that, the two rivals became very mellow and crept into the darkest corner of the casemate where they exchanged vows of eternal friendship. The Archbishop told the other two lieutenants about his imprisonment in the magistrate's jail[3] and he showed them his bald head. He explained that he had gotten it because he had been given a bedstead which was so short that he hit against it at either end, and it was at the upper end where he had had all his hair scraped off.

And so the engagement festivities came to an end when the half anker of wine came to an end, and Copernicus remained a groom-to-be until he became a married man, and the Captain remained single and free until he became a groom-to-be. And if the two of them are still living, I wish them happiness, much happiness, because they were a couple of fine fellows and did me many a good turn.

CHAPTER 25

D ON Juan had been set free, but the rest of us quietly continued to rot on the vine. I had already been imprisoned for six years and had just twenty-four more to go. My Mecklenburg government had requested my release; three times it had demanded my release.[1] However, the Prussians wouldn't do it, even though I wasn't a Prussian, had never studied in Prussia, and therefore could not have committed my horrible crime in Prussia. — At the request of Denmark the prisoners who were from Schleswig and Holstein had been released[2] — why just they? Probably because at that time just as now Denmark had spoken up against Prussia. My Mecklenburg friends who had been my fellow students in Jena had gotten off with six months, nine months, or a year at the most,[3] and while I was still being held on remand in the magistrate's jail one of them was again studying in Berlin as though nothing had happened, and yet he had been more deeply involved than I.

That's the way it was in Germany at that time — God grant that conditions will improve! — They say that Prussia has now taken over the leadership in Germany — I hope it will be for the best! — but Prussia had the leadership at that time too, at least in North Germany, and what did it get us? The whole cart with all our goods and possessions which had been pulled out of the French morass[4] at the expenditure of every ounce of our strength and paid for with the tears and blood of the common people was again thrown into the ditch by Prussia, which continued to persecute so many people with injustice and cruelty. — But never mind! It's all water over the dam and it's best to forget about it now. The writing on the slate where the bitter thoughts of each one of us were recorded has almost faded away now — and should fade away, if the great and mighty leaders of today would only be willing to read that writing which from time immemorial was hewn in stone.

Nowadays everyone is hopeful again and all the people around me are talking politics. In each case they have everything all figured out; one person has it figured out to his advantage in one way, and another has it figured out to his advantage in a different way. They talk politics with their heads; we did it with our hearts. In their heads the figures stand out very clearly and the addition is correct, but that which was written on our tortured hearts lasts longer and flows through our souls with much more warmth than their sacred laws of interest and compound interest.

But things were to change, and the one who foretold that first of all was my Frenchman, — I have already mentioned that he was very much preoccupied with prophecies and the interpretation of dreams. One morning as we awoke he said to me, "Do you know what I dreamt?"

"No," I said.

"I dreamt that you would receive a letter from your father today."

"That's possible," I said abruptly, because if one showed any interest in his stories, there was no stopping him the rest of the day.

"You're also going to receive some money," he said.

"No," I answered, "my father sent me some money as recently as two weeks ago; I'll not be getting any again so soon."

"You're going to receive money and also some other good news," he added.

Well, I gave the matter no further thought, but at the scheduled time I went down into the courtyard for the free exercise period. As the other prisoners and I were standing before the gate, which was just then being unlocked, the merchant Swarz[5] passed by. My father had made some arrangement with him whereby I was allowed to make purchases on credit. The merchant also used to deliver most of my mail, that is, after the general had read it.

"It's good that I met you," he said. "There's a letter for you down at the post office."

"Do you see?" said the Frenchman who was standing behind me.

"But it's a letter containing money," continued the merchant, "and I have to send down the post office receipt first."

"Do you see?" repeated the Frenchman.

"This is most strange!" I said.

We spent our free time there and nothing further happened, but in the afternoon the Captain and I were playing a game of chess under the green linden trees and the Frenchman was standing beside us looking on. Well, I happened to look down the lane and saw the merchant coming along with a handkerchief in his hand and he was waving it back and forth in the air.

"What's the matter with him?" I said. "It's not so warm that he has to fan himself."

"He's bringing you the good news," said the Frenchman.

As the merchant came closer, he called out to me, "You are being transferred; you are going to be extradited to your native land!"

"This is most strange," called the Frenchman and he walked off to the side quite perplexed, as though he were frightened at his own skill.

And it was indeed strange that for once his prophecy had come true, but it would have been even more strange if all his prophecies had come true, because my good Frenchman had forecast the strangest things, and if all of them had actually transpired, the entire world would have gotten a wrench and we would probably all be walking around on our heads.

When I received this news I felt as though I would first have to turn a couple of somersaults just to straighten my brains out again. It took me considerable time before I could collect my senses and read my father's letter. But there it was in black and white. I was to be extradited to my native land, although, to be sure, only to Däms,⁶ which was located in a most unattractive area in the outermost corner of the country. My father explained very clearly that I owed my extradition to the personal intercession of Grand Duke Paul Frederick with his father-in-law, the old King of Prussia.⁷ To be sure, there was an unpleasant addendum: the King reserved the right of granting me full pardon; my own Grand Duke would not be permitted to release me.

That was very unfortunate, but nothing could be done about it. "Every bit helps," said the gnat as it spit into the Rhine, and so I thought to myself, "Once you are there, things may turn out better than you expect."

And that's what Paul Frederick had done for me! Whenever I come to Schwerin I shall visit his statue before the castle and I shall pay my respects to him in the quiet of his mausoleum, and the heartfelt words will express my gratitude that he once awakened to new joy a pain-tortured soul.

Two weeks and more passed until everything was "officially" in order. I was then summoned to the office of the clerk where I had to swear an oath that I would never again set foot on Prussian soil;

otherwise the gendarmes would seize me and do something terrible to me — I don't know exactly what.[8] — Good God! how things have changed! Now I am a Prussian — it cost me 27½ silver pennies — and yet I live in Mecklenburg.[9] — Who knows but what the Mecklenburgers might not make me swear a similar oath some day, for "What is the German Fatherland?" may be a beautiful song, and I have often sung it myself, but I have never found it, even though I have wandered and been buffeted about in it for twenty-five years.

After the solemn swearing of the oath I took leave of my splendid old general and my loyal comrades and went to the city magistrate. The man was very friendly to me and made a special notation in my pass: "Escape attempt unlikely; extradition to native land." Nevertheless, I was given a gendarme as an escort for the trip, and so once again with this millstone around my neck I traveled for 120 miles through the free German Fatherland.

The first day I had the good fortune to meet Auguste von Martini standing before her new home on the other side of the river, and I brought her greetings from my good Captain.

"Herr Reuter, what's the meaning of this?" she called to me as I sat in the carriage. — We had never before exchanged a single word.

"I'm being extradited," I called back, "and the Captain sends you his best wishes!"

"Is he also going to be set free soon?" she asked.

"Soon," I said, "soon."

The postilion blew his horn, she waved to me and I waved to her — and yet we scarcely knew each other. However, real joy like a flash of lightning can immediately strike a responsive chord in hearts which are otherwise beset with sorrow. People who are otherwise cold and indifferent to strangers feel a warm glow when they share in the joy and happiness of another, for every human being has been created by our Lord not for himself, but for all creatures.

The next day we came into a forest; it was an oak forest, and that was something I hadn't seen in six years. — "Oh," I said to the gendarme, "will you do me a favor? Let's *walk* through the woods." — And so we did.

The postilion blew his merry tune and I took a deep breath of the fresh air and the fragrant smell of woodruff. The butterflies were playing in the sun — there was a swallowtail and there a purple emperor and there a mother-of-pearl butterfly! — It was truly enough to make a person feel like a child again! And when we came out of the forest there lay at the left a white field of clover and it smelled as sweet as honey. The bees were just as busy as housewives and they were humming to themselves just like young girls whenever they start to sing a tune which will move and win hearts — and above all this there shone God's sun in the wonderful month of June! — I threw myself on the road embankment and large tears ran down into my beard. The gendarme stood there and said we would have to move on as the postilion was waiting for us.

And what did it all amount to anyway? — In a week the field of clover would be turned to stubble and the bees would be collecting nectar elsewhere; the oak forest would lie far behind me and I would be sitting in Däms. — But to think that I had seen all this beauty in nature for the first time in six years! — And then I also thought back to Criminal Councillor Dambach who said: "They must be imprisoned!" and to Herr von Tschoppe who said: "They must be imprisoned!" and to the bloody Herr von Kleist, the President of the Supreme Court, who said: "They must be imprisoned!" and to Frederick William the Just[10] who said: "They must be imprisoned!"

The following day we came to Berlin where I again had to stay for three days, this time, fortunately enough, in the city jail where otherwise only thieves are locked up. But I didn't mind; it was in any case better than to be with Criminal Councillor Dambach. In general I have made the observation that the real criminals, especially if they were of the nobility, were at that time much better treated in Prussian fortresses than we. — In Silberberg where I had at first been imprisoned I had the opportunity of becoming acquainted with this particular class of people. A Herr von B . . . had absconded with the entire tax receipts of Grüneberg. He had deserted his wife and only child and run away with his sweetheart. After he had squandered the 40,000–50,000 talers in Italy he had then been arrested as a crooked gambler in Frankfurt am Main. He was sentenced to fifty years in prison, was to be put in the pillory and flogged, and further penalized with loss of nobility and all honorary titles, but instead of that he was living in all comfort in the city. A Herr von Sch . . . had stolen the entire royal treasury and made fluid assets of it in the form of Oeil-de-perdrix[11] and Chateau,[12] but he was likewise living in town with his wife and children just like all other honorable people. Neither of these two fine gentlemen could stand the air at the fortress, but for us it was good enough. A Herr von O . . . — the scoundrel was just a plain thief — was allowed to go wherever he wished, and so as a gay and dashing blade he went visiting in town and in the neighboring villages. While we poor wretches were eating our breakfast of army bread and pork fat — and sometimes we even had to share that with a married lieutenant — Herr von O . . . was enjoying a warm breakfast in the best inn in town and washing it down with Hungarian wine. For people of that type an affluent way of life had to be preserved, but we traitors and regicides didn't count. Unfortunately we were neither thieves nor of the nobility.

It is probably not relevant at this point, but I am always enraged whenever I now think back to those times and realize that Prussia inflicted such scurrilous treatment upon us merely in order to push the wagon backwards and furthermore used us to grease the wagon wheels.[13]

But now it was all over — at least for me. I was on my way to Däms, back to my native land. Three days later I was sitting in a special mail coach with a new gendarme beside me and traveling toward the Mecklenburg border. — Good-by, Prussia! — But before we came to Warnow,[14] where I would be able to shout out this farewell, something happened which cut deep into my heart. I was to find out that the ax which had been sharpened to carry out the death penalty had struck not only us, but also our parents, relatives, and friends.

On the trip we stopped at a post house, and as is my custom I was standing there looking at the pictures on the wall. It is a good custom, for from the pictures on the wall one can usually form some judgment about the people who have put them there. Behind me I heard someone crying softly, and as I turned around I saw a woman sitting in a chair with both hands before her face and the tears running down through her fingers. — Good God! I thought that the woman had met with some mishap. — "What's the trouble?" I asked.

"Oh," she cried, "I have a son who is imprisoned too!"

Then she stood up, placed her hand upon my shoulder and looked at me through tear-filled eyes with such sadness and despair that I became emotionally upset. She reminded me of my own mother who had long since passed away.

"Who is he?" I asked. "Who is your son!"

"Wuthenow;[15] he's imprisoned in Silberberg."

She apparently didn't realize that I knew him. — But I knew him very well, and it was a great joy for me that I had good things to report about him, for he had remained well in body and soul. Before long his father and also his sister, a young girl of seventeen years, joined us and I had to keep telling them over and over again all about their son and brother until the gendarme came and said that it was time to leave. — Good God, that's the way it might have been in my home too, or possibly even worse!

As we crossed the border at Warnow — good-by, Prussia! — it had become dark. We came to Grabow[16] and stopped before the cellar where we were to spend the night. On the slope which led up to the house I heard a voice say, "Good night, we'll discuss the details tomorrow."

The last time I had heard this voice was eight years ago. In the oral examination at school[17] this voice and mine had answered in unison to the assistant director's question: "How many times was Constantinople captured?"

I recognized this voice in the dark, and if anyone doesn't believe me, he can ask Councillor Franz Flörke[18] in Grabow. — "Good evening, Franz!" I called out from the coach. "Just wait a minute!"

And as I came out into the light with the gendarme, my old friend was overjoyed and he completely forgot the fact that he was the mayor and I a criminal. — The eight years had raised a barrier between us and because he had the title of councillor, the barrier had become even higher. I am certain that before long he will also be given the title of Privy Councillor, and I shall be very happy, for then I shall have a privy councillor with whom I can exchange the familiar term of "Du."[19]

That evening the gendarme was completely flabbergasted when he heard the mayor address the vagabond with "Du" and when he saw that they drank a bottle of wine together. He must have had a very bad opinion of the Mecklenburg officials, but in spite of that he drank with us. — Do you still remember that, Franz?

V Däms[1]

CHAPTER 26

T HE next morning we continued on the Däms. — In those days whenever anyone in Mecklenburg heard the word "Däms," he reacted in much the same way as some people do when they hear the word "scurvy." However, such people had a completely false notion of what Däms was like, because almost without exception I have known nothing but decent people there. At that time Däms had the reputation of being the horror of all Mecklenburg, but unjustly so. It had its weak points to be sure, just like any other human institution, but as a fortress it had only strong points. It was protected on one side by the Elbe — great Elbe, little Elbe, old Elbe, Elbe moat — and then by the Elde — great Elde, little Elde, old Elde, and seven Elde moats. On the other side it was protected by its geographic position and by the Bokup-Eldena wilderness[2] — an ideal location for a fortress. — This wilderness was a vast godforsaken region; no people lived there. It was said that even the French had turned back when the mud came up to their thighs.

Däms was furthermore protected by a toll bridge which the magistrate had very wisely set up at the town's one and only gate and where a penny had to be paid for every horse crossing it. However, that was too expensive for the enemy and so he preferred to ride to the Red House[3] outside the city limits and there spend his money on roast eel and sour cucumbers.

No one knew to whom Däms belonged at that time. The fortress belonged to the grand duke; not only he said that, but also his lieutenant colonel,[4] whom he had stationed there as commandant. There was no disagreement about that, but who owned the city? — The lieutenant colonel maintained that he was not only commandant of the fortress, but also governor of the city, because the city likewise belonged to the grand duke. Furthermore, he maintained that whenever he set the clock at the fortress the sexton in town was supposed to set the church clock accordingly. — The sexton, however, said he set his clock by the sun and neither the lieutenant colonel nor the grand duke had jurisdiction over him.

While this quarrel was in full swing there suddenly appeared a third pretender. It was Herr Zachow,[5] the town's chief government official. He based his claim on the *superficies*.[6] He contended that legally all the manure on the streets belonged to him, and anyone could tell by looking at his boots in the evening on whose property he had been walking. Without wishing to anticipate the verdict of the Supreme Court in this matter I would have to say that the man was right: Däms belonged to him. And to his very end he was a good regent, for he ruled calmly and peacefully and made good use of the manure to fill all the pot holes in the streets of his realm.

Toward the city musicians, however, he was very strict, because he himself had a violent dislike for music, and if his reign had lasted longer, Däms might possibly have become the only fortress where music had not been able to gain a strong foothold. — Zachow shared the same fate as Louis Philippe: Louis Philippe was never recognized as king of France by the duke of Modena[7] and the printer Pompeius in Glatz, and Zachow was never recognized as ruler by the lieutenant colonel.

His biggest enemy, however, was his neighbor, Lieutenant Lange, who had the bad habit of playing the fiddle at all hours of the night. People said that Lange once fiddled Zachow to death and fiddled Däms back into the hands of the grand duke. This last was not too surprising, because Zachow had no heir to succeed him.

That's what Däms looked like at three o'clock on an afternoon in the month of June in the year one thousand eight hundred and thirty-nine as I crossed the city bridge and the gendarme paid the bridge toll. — As soon as we had arrived at the hostel I put on a brand-new black dress coat and black trousers. — I had just had them made in Graudenz in order not to be a disgrace to my Grand Duke Paul Frederick and so that he shouldn't think that a vagabond was gaining admittance to his country. — I then ran away from my gendarme and went to visit an aunt of mine,[8] a widow who lived here in Däms. She received me with all possible kindness. — I was really somebody now! — Wearing a dress coat and with money in my pocket! — Do you still remember, Franz? — I was mindful of the royal Prussian oath I had sworn and now I had a good aunt just for an emergency, but I still had the Prussian gendarme on my neck. He recaptured me and now there was nothing else that could be done except to go to the fortress.

Now it happened that the sexton's clock was just striking four and the little schoolboys were coming from school. It was such a novelty for them to see a Prussian gendarme that they did us the honor of following us. After we had lost our way and had gone to the left instead of to the right, we managed to collect another group of fine little fellows from the area around Elbe Street, and with loud hurrahs and shouts of joy they escorted us to the fortress.

As we entered, the commandant in a green summer jacket was sitting in front of a black cabinet, which he called his work desk, and reading some of those damned old stories which Henriette Hanke[9] had written especially for women. When I said "good day" he threw Henriette Hanke aside and asked me, "Oh, is it you?"

I said that it was.

"Well," he said, "we have been waiting for you for a long time. I have selected a good billet for you, and your aunt has been here and has arranged everything very nicely for you."

With that he got up, opened one door of his cabinet, took out a bottle and a beer glass and poured out a liberal amount of claret into the glass. He handed me the glass and said, "Here, have a drink."

After I had emptied the glass and expressed all due thanks to him he refilled it for the gendarme: "Here, would you like to try it too?"

The gendarme said that he would.

"Well," he said, as he again turned to me, "how was it over there with the Prussians?"

"Pretty bad," I answered.

"I can well believe it," he said with a smile. "The Prussians don't shilly-shally around too long."

He looked the gendarme over from head to toe and in doing so he caught sight of his sword knot. "Tell me," he said, "are the Prussians using this sword knot now?"

The gendarme then had to show him how the ribbon was tied and fastened to the sword hilt.

Then the commandant said, "Now I want to tell you something; go to Captain von Hartwig[10] and tell him I have seen this sword knot and like it very much. I want him to look at it too, because I think we should introduce it here for our troops. And you," he said to me, "may now go to your quarters. After you have gotten settled I want you to return here, because I want you to tell my family what they did to you over there in Prussia."

This was a good beginning; the old gentleman was very friendly, and even though he looked as though he had his share of quirks, one could hardly object to that, because he was approaching eighty years of age[11] and had been commandant in Däms for a long time, and that in itself was enough to make anyone self-willed.

I went to the guard house, where I was to have a billet free of charge.[12] Just as I was about to walk up the staircase a tall, old, superannuated veteran in a long, old, superannuated lieutenant's uniform stood before me and asked, "I beg your pardon; are you, that is to say, Herr Reuter?"

I said that was my name.

"Then I must tell you that you have committed a serious breach, that is to say, a serious breach of local guard-house regulations. You should have reported here first, that is to say, before you went to the commandant, that is to say, the lieutenant-colonel."

I said I was sorry, but I had to go where the gendarme took me, and if anyone was at fault, it was the gendarme.

"Oh, it doesn't make that much difference," said the old man; "please come in, that is to say, come in here," and he invited me into the officers' guard room.

Well, he was so polite that I entered and asked with whom I had the honor.

"I am, you see, First Lieutenant König," he said. "His Royal Highness, that is to say, Grand Duke Frederick Franz of blessed memory,[13] was kind enough to promote me to the rank of first lieutenant on the occasion of my fiftieth anniversary in the service."

I wanted to be polite; so I said, "Probably not for your long years of service, but rather for your merits."

"Oh no!" said the kindly old man. "I don't have any merits."

"Well then, because of your service in military campaigns."

"I haven't taken part in any campaigns," he said very calmly, "except in 1812 when I once had to escort a herd of oxen to Poland. You see, I was with the cavalry in Ludwigslust; our colors were blue and yellow, and there were, you see, fifty of us, but we had, you see, only twenty-five horses. We had to take turns riding the horses, and, you see, because there were not enough horses, the naughty boys in the street used to shout at us: 'Hay-rack! hay-rack!' You see, they said that because half of us always had to ride on the framework of the hay wagon."

This was very amusing and so I continued to converse with the old man. "Yes," he said, "my job with the cavalry in Ludwigslust was more profitable than my present one. I was, you see, a sergeant and in addition to my regular pay I also received something extra for all the petitions which I referred to His Royal Highness. Once I was fortunate enough to secure an unusual stipend for an old woman. — You see, it was the practice of His Royal Highness to have people feed and take care of his old 'retired' hunting dogs, you see, for one taler a month, and the old woman was next in line for such a stipend. Now I had learned that one of the grand ducal hunting dogs had died and I applied, you see, for the stipened on behalf of this old woman and — sure enough — she got it!"

"Well," I said, "then you did perform a meritorious service."

"Yes, possibly," he answered, "but there were also all kinds of vexations. For example, once, you see, the hereditary Grand Duke Frederick Franz of blessed memory had passed away and I was on the death watch. However, I was given the order not to admit any children or servant girls. Now just think of this; along came the Chief Medical Councillor Sachse with his young daughter! Was she a child or wasn't she? You see, I couldn't ask how old she was; that would have sounded too unrefined. So I took courage, you see, and asked, 'Pardon me, miss, have you already taken holy communion or not?' And if a young girl came along who, you see, looked like a servant girl, I would ask, 'I beg your pardon, miss, but are you a maid or a lady's maid?' — In that way I solved all my problems."

"That was very good," I said, "but here in Däms you certainly have had peaceful days."

"Nothing but vexation," he answered; "there are naughty people everywhere and especially here." Then the honest old fellow pointed to his mouth and said, "I'm an old man and have lost my front teeth, so that I can no longer pronounce the letter 'R' distinctly. In the evening when I made my r-ounds and the guard calls out: 'Who's there?' I answer: 'R-ounds' and then these bad people always answer: 'Hounds pass!' "

The poor old fellow! He had lived for some seventy years and was still a child. In the first half hour he related his whole life history to a total stranger. — "No," I thought to myself as I climbed the stairs to my new quarters, "a thousand times better to be in chains than to be a first lieutenant at the age of seventy-six."

Praise and thanks to God! My cell had no iron bars. I quickly straightened out my few belongings and then returned to the lieutenant colonel.

There things had changed very much for the better. My lieutenant colonel had a whole house full of daughters,[14] one just as beautiful as the other. His wife was a kind and friendly woman, and I spent many a happy afternoon and cozy evening in that hospitable home. Even today as I look back I feel sincerely grateful to those people for the happy times I spent in their home.

With the old gentleman, however, one had to be very careful. As I have said, he had his peculiarities, and because he had few friends and time therefore on occasions hung heavy, he sometimes became very cranky. He could not get along with his officers. "They send me nothing but wiseacre sergeants," he said, "and that's what they call officers! — What does a lieutenant like Lange know about the science of warfare? At that time when Diebitsch was in Turkey[15] this Lieutenant Lange said that Diebitsch would never be able to get over the Balkan mountain range. However, Lieutenant Th . . . told him that Diebitsch would be able to, and indeed he did. But then Th . . . was a real officer."

My old lieutenant colonel was right; a very unique collection of war heroes was assembled in Däms and it would have been very difficult for him to accomplish anything with such a motley assortment of stupid and unqualified officers. It was impossible for him to select any capable adjutant from among them. I still remember the time when a new officer was sent to him from Wismar.[16] This man had been recommended as one who was supposed to be especially outstanding. The lieutenant colonel decided that this officer would henceforth be his adjutant. In order to show him immediately how friendly disposed he was toward him, the lieutenant colonel gave a very special dinner to which the new adjutant and his wife were invited as guests of honor. Both of them did full justice to the food and drink, but after dinner it was impossible to get any conversation started. One of the lieutenant colonel's daughters suggested that they should have Quartermaster Plötz[17] come over from the fortress, because he knew how to perform all kinds of feats of legerdemain. Well, the man came and performed his sleight-of-hand tricks, in one of which he placed a ball under a hat and had it turn into a canary. Seeing this, the new adjutant said, "Lieutenant Colonel, I have seen this trick done before, but at that time it was a toad and not a canary."

"My dear," said his wife, "it wasn't a toad; it was a mouse."

"No," he insisted, "it was a toad."

The old gentleman, who was somewhat hard of hearing, thought he had missed something and asked me, "What did he say about a toad?"

I answered, "Lieutenant Colonel, I think he meant a frog."

"And he calls a frog a toad? My adjutant calls a frog a toad? — a toad?" he remarked, and with that he left the room.

No, Däms certainly did not have the best adjutants at that time, but possibly things may have improved since then.

I was detained at Däms for more than a year and a quarter.[18] There is still much that I might tell about this time, but I can sum it all up by saying that the Mecklenburg government did for me everything it possibly could and that I was treated by my fine old commandant just as though I were his own son. But what good did it do? I didn't have my freedom, and where freedom is lacking, the spirit is broken.

Frederick William III died in 1840 and his son Frederick William IV declared an amnesty[19] for all "demagogues." The newspapers reported that the prisoners were set free everywhere, but I was forgotten; I was still being held at Däms. The Prussians gave me no thought and the Mecklenburgers were not allowed to release me.

Oh, how the next four weeks dragged on! — One day, however, — I had just returned from a walk — a sergeant came running up to me: "Herr Reuter, you must go to Judge Blankenberg right away. There is something in the mail for you; you are being set free."

I went back and walked past a picket fence. The late afternoon sun was shining through the black staves with such a glare that my eyes became blurred and I had to hold on to something. I went to the judge and he gave me a letter. "Here," he said, "you are free; you may leave the fortress whenever you wish, and no one is to give you any further orders."

Paul Frederick had taken it upon himself to set me free without asking the Prussians.[20] A week later as I was sitting at the table with my old father a letter arrived from the Minister of Justice Kamptz[21] in which he informed me that I would soon be permitted to return home. It was very kind of him, but the letter arrived a little too late.

I said good-by to my lieutenant colonel and to other good people in the town, packed my few belongings and had them sent home by freight. At four o'clock the next morning I strapped my little knapsack to my back, tied my little dog[22] to a leash so that the soldiers couldn't coax it away from me, and as a free man walked out the gate in the direction of the Fenzir mill.

After I had passed the mill I came to a heath — a cheerless and dreary region! Sand and scrub pine and Scotch heather and juniper trees as far as one could see. There were paths everywhere, but which was the right one? I didn't know what to do; so I sat down and thought of many things.

Seven years lay behind me, seven difficult years which at that time weighed on my soul like a heavy burden, even though I have now for the most part told of them in a light-hearted vein. Nothing had happened in those years which could have been of any help to me on this earth, and whatever help they might have given was lost because of the hate and feeling of abomination which ate into my soul. I tried to erase the memory of those years from my mind; otherwise, it would be as though I were digging up graves and having my sport with the skulls and bones of the dead. — And what lay before me? — A heath with sand and scrub pine. — Paths? — Oh, there were many paths which led through the heath, but which was the right one? — I went to the right — nothing but sand and scrub pine. — I went to the left — nothing but sand and scrub pine. — Wherever I went — no prospects! Even the people had changed. — Many a one extended a friendly hand, but I felt that for the most part we no longer belonged together. It was as though I were a tree whose top had been lopped off while the other trees around me were growing and flourishing and depriving me of all air and light.

I would not have minded having my crown lopped off, because I still felt the urge to shoot forth leaves and branches, but in the course of time my roots had also been cut off. — While I was at Däms my father had come to visit me.[23] He was the same good old father as formerly, but if in those seven years I had lost all hope, so too had he. He had been accustomed to looking upon me as I looked upon myself — as a victim of misfortune. For the future he had made new plans and I no longer played a leading part in those plans. We had become estranged. It was more my fault than his, but I didn't have to look beyond those seven years to find the chief cause of this estrangement.

Oh, what thoughts ran through my mind! — What was I? What did I know? What could I do? — Nothing. — What business did I have in this world? — Absolutely none. — The world had very calmly continued on its old aimless course without paying any attention to me. As far as the world was concerned I might just as well have remained in prison and, as I sat there in the pine thicket, I too thought it made little difference where I was. — But you are free! You can go wherever you wish! The path is open! — Yes, but which path was the right one?

"Schüten, come here!" I said and I untied my little dog from his leash. "Go ahead! Go ahead!" I was playing blindman's buff with the world. — Chance and instinct were the only two pitons which I could hammer into its bare walls. At the fortresses they had enslaved me. They had given me a cloak, the fiery red cloak of fierce hate. Now they had removed this cloak and I stood there — free! — but stark naked, and that's how I was supposed to go walking into the world.

There was still something, I felt, which might restore my place in the world, and that was love. But that too was lost; it lay somewhere far removed from the sand and scrub pine upon which my eyes now rested. — "Schüten, little puppy, run on ahead!"

He did and I followed. At that moment the little dog was the only creature which could offer me its love. He was off his leash, and in high spirits he ran back and forth and jumped up on me — that was love. The warm bright light of God's sun shone down upon my little dog and myself, and where God's sun shines, it cannot remain dark very long. My spirits too were now raised.

Schüten had found the right path; I came to Grabow and to old friends — Franz, do you still remember? — But how strange everything seemed! Probably no one noticed it, but I felt as though I were standing among trees that were growing and becoming green, whereas my branches had been cut off.

At school Franz and I had taken our final examination together and on that occasion his uncle had given him a bottle of champagne. After we had successfully passed the examination Franz like a good friend had shared this bottle with me. Now he was the mayor in a beautiful little town, had a lovely and friendly little wife, and a home in which he could be happy for the rest of his life. — He probably didn't notice how I must have felt — it certainly was not envy — but it seemed to me as though I had stepped into a neat and tidy room with my muddy boots.

I visited another old school friend of mine, the town official Prehn.[24] The same friendly reception. — Yes, it was so friendly and cordial that this good old friend even escorted me all the way to Ludwigslust. There I met my good cousin August.[25] — He wanted to do me a favor; so he took me over to the home of the Court Artist Lenthe[26] who showed me his paintings. When I had seen them I said to myself, "Now you can forget about that too. You have sketched and painted for seven years, and now what you have done is all worthless stuff!" — Thus another branch fell to the ground.

I came to Parchim and to the school which I had once attended.[27] My former teachers were very friendly to me — they have always been friendly, before and afterwards. — The director[28] took me into the senior class. — The pupils of this highest class looked like children to me, and yet if I stopped to think about it, I at the age of thirty had progressed no further than these eighteen-year-old boys, that is, except to the extent that I had forgotten more. — What had happened to these, my best years!

I came home. — With my knapsack on my back I came out from the Pribbenow pine forest[29] and looked over to my little hometown, but I could hardly recognize it. It was so different from the old town as I had always remembered it. New streets had been built and the town had been extended on all sides. I entered my father's house — that was a joyful reunion, but it was not without a touch of sadness, for in my mind the joy was tempered with the painful question: "What now?" I could tell by looking at my father that this question was running through his mind too. I said "good day" to my sisters and brother-in-law.[30] Our family had also grown and to me it seemed just as strange as the new streets. — Berger and his city musicians played a serenade for me. People said that it was only fair-to-middling, but it made me happy. At least the people were still thinking of me.

The next morning when I awoke I asked myself, "What now?"
When I came to my father he also asked, "What now?" For years I
went around confused and bewildered because I was always faced
with this frightening question. I tried this and I tried that, but
nothing seemed to work out well. I know it was my fault — other
people said so too — but what difference did it make as to who was
at fault; I was unhappy, much more unhappy than when I was in
prison.

My father died[31] and now I was the only one to ask this same
terrible question. I became a farmer[32] and that was work which I
thoroughly enjoyed, but to be a farmer I lacked the most essential
requisite — money. — I had many good friends and *one* particularly good friend,[33] but the good friends just shrugged their shoulders
and the *one* particularly good friend couldn't help me. He himself
had little money.

One day I said to myself: Your boat is beginning to take in water;
it is too heavily laden. You have on board all that rabble that once
came to you with hopes and promises and expectations, and now
none of those scamps is willing to raise a finger to help you; you
have to row the boat yourself. Out with the ballast! — I grabbed the
first one by the collar: "Who are you?"

"A lawyer,"[34] he said.

"Is that so?" I said. "Did I call you?" — And — splash! — he
was in the water.

I took hold of the second one: "Who are you?"

"A civil service official,"[35] he answered, "at your service."

"What kind of an official?" I asked.

"Oh, just a councilman or a town treasurer or a registrar in a
small backward town," he said.

"And do you think I'm going to be bothered any longer by a
tramp like you?"

"At your service," he said.

"I don't need you," I answered and then he was in the water too.

Then came the third one. — "Who are you?" I asked.

"An artist,"[36] he answered.

"What do you mean?" I asked.

"A painter," he replied.

"Well, I should have known that right away just by looking at
you," I said. "Why do you have to cut your loaf of bread lengthwise

instead of crosswise as all other people do? I can't stand such an outlandish way of doing things. — Into the water with you!" — Well, he splashed around for a while; he didn't want to give up, but in the end he too had to swallow water.

"Now the fourth one," I called. — A boorish-looking figure stood up. He had no polish, but considerable weight, and that was just what I was most concerned about. — "Where do you come from?" I asked.

"From the grand duke's estate," he answered.

"And who are you?" I asked.

"A tenant farmer,"[37] he replied.

"I can't have you here any longer, my friend," I said; "you're much too big. — Into the water with you!" — Well, fat rises to the surface; he may possibly still be floating around.

When I caught the fifth one by the scruff of his neck he began to whine most pitifully, "Let me be! — I am a supervisor[38] on a large estate and I have so much to put up with. I receive about two hundred talers pay, the free use of a horse and then a little extra money on the sale of grain."[39]

"Oh, you get that money too," I said. — "You scoundrel! And you want to make all this trouble for me?"

He tried to resist, but neither that nor his entreaties were of any help. — Overboard with him!

Then came the last one, a little shriveled-up old man: "Well, brother, who are you?"

"Don't take it amiss," he answered, "I am a schoolmaster[40] with a salary of ninety talers and free housing in the schoolroom. I also write all the letters for the pastor and for that I get some potato acreage. I'm just like you; I was once a student too. You're not in accord with the world, and I'm not in accord with the members of the church council. You certainly should let me live."

"Yes, old fellow," I said, "your hopes and promises and expectations will not overload my boat too much, but when we come ashore, I'm going to borrow your coat."

"But it's all patched up," he protested.

"Makes no difference."

"But it's too tight," he added.

"Makes no difference; I'll manage to squeeze into it."

And when we came ashore I put on the schoolmaster's coat, and even though it was tight, it protected me from wind and storm, and even though for years I gave private lessons for two pennies an hour, I always felt very comfortable in that coat. And even though I didn't have to do any writing for the pastor, I did write *Läuschen un Rimels*[41] during the evening hours, and that was my potato patch. Our Lord let His sun shine on my potato patch and He blessed it with the dew and the rain — and sometimes the most stupid people grow the biggest potatoes.

Notes and References

Introduction

1. Low German as distinguished from Standard or High German is the language spoken in North Germany in an area extending from the Netherlands in the west to Slavic territory in the east. It includes many dialects, among them Westphalian, Eastphalian, North Low Saxon, Mecklenburg-Pomeranian, and West and East Prussian. All of these dialects have many further subdivisions. Reuter wrote in the Mecklenburg dialect.

2. Named after Arminius or Hermann, the chief of the Cherusci, who defeated the Roman legions under P. Quintillius Varus in the Teutoburg Forest in 9 A.D.

Chapter One

1. The fortress at Glogau (Polish Glogów) on the Oder in the western part of Poland. Reuter was imprisoned there from the end of February to the end of March, 1837.

2. Friedrich Schult (his real name was Johann Müller) worked for Mayor Reuter in various capacities for many years beginning in 1818. It is possible that he took part in the campaign against Napoleon and fought at the Battle of Leipzig in 1813. He appears also in *Meine Vaterstadt Stavenhagen (My Hometown Stavenhagen)* and *Ut de Franzosentid (In the Year 1813)*. In the latter work Reuter changed his name to Schult probably to avoid confusion with another figure, the miller (Müller) Voss.

3. Reuter was held on remand in Berlin jails from October 31, 1833, to November 12, 1834. He was then transferred to the military fortress of Silberberg in Silesia (2,200 feet above sea level) where he was imprisoned until February, 1837. He was sentenced to death by the Supreme Court on August 4, 1836, but did not learn of the verdict until January 28, 1837, at which time he also learned that the death sentence had been commuted to thirty years of fortress imprisonment.

4. At Silberberg.

5. The provost marshal was First Lieutenant Kurz.

6. Major General Leopold von Lützow (1776–1844).

7. The commandant's brother was Adolf von Lützow (1782–1834), a Prussian officer who commanded a volunteer corps against Napoleon in

1813—14. The German poet Theodor Körner has glorified the daring exploits of the corps in his poetry. Several of Reuter's teachers at Friedland and Parchim, among them Karl Horn, who later founded the *Allgemeine Deutsche Burschenschaft*, and possibly also Johann Zehlicke, were members of this volunteer corps, but no uncle of Reuter fought under Von Lützow.

8. The second commandant was Lieutenant Colonel Karl Friedrich Andreas von Wichert (1789—1861). He came to Glogau as a major in 1826 and was promoted to lieutenant colonel in 1837 and to colonel in 1839.

9. The Low German dialect spoken in North Germany.

10. Reuter's father became mayor of Stavenhagen in 1808.

11. Without the knowledge of King Frederick William III, the Prussian Major Ferdinand von Schill led a band of hussars from Berlin through Mecklenburg to the Baltic coast in the hope of arousing the populace to a national uprising against Napoleon. Von Schill was killed in battle at Stralsund.

12. There were 30 silver pennies ("Groschen") to the taler.

13. Probably charwomen at Silberberg or Glogau.

14. Höpfner, *Kommentar über die Heineccischen Institutionen.*

15. Thibaut, *System des Pandektenrechts.*

16. Ohm, *Die reine Elementar-Mathematik.* Mayor Reuter had Professor Ohm of the University of Berlin send the first part of this book to Fritz in the magistrate's jail.

17. G. A. Fischer, *Anfangsgründe der Hydrostatik und Hydraulik.*

Chapter Two

1. Works of Johann Wolfgang Goethe.

2. *Wilhelm Meister's Apprenticeship*, Book II, Chapter 13.

3. Schnabel was condemned to death for killing one of his captors during a robbery. He was executed at Glogau in February, 1837.

4. The reference is not to the daughter of Commandant B. (Lieutenant Colonel von Wichert), but to Frida von Bülow, one of the five daughters of the commandant in Dömitz (Mecklenburg) where Reuter was imprisoned from June 15, 1839, until his release on August 25, 1840.

Chapter Three

1. Reuter attended school in Friedland from the fall of 1824 until Easter 1827.

2. Hans Ludwig Count von York (1759—1830), a general trained in the school of Frederick the Great, distinguished himself in the Polish War of 1794 and again in that of 1806. He was in command of the Prussian aux-

iliaries in the Russian campaign of 1812.

3. Hans von Zieten (1699–1786), a general of Frederick the Great, fought with the light cavalry at Prague, Kolin, Leuthen, and Liegnitz.

4. Frederick William, the Great Elector of Brandenburg, defeated the Swedes at Fehrbellin near Berlin in 1675.

5. According to popular belief Field Marshal George Derflinger had been an apprentice tailor.

6. The colors of the *Allgemeine Deutsche Burschenschaft* — black, red, gold.

7. Judge Schröder was a good friend of Reuter in Treptow. His children, Hedwig and Richard, were two of Reuter's private pupils. With the help of a loan of 200 talers from Judge Schröder Reuter was able to publish his first work, *Läuschen un Rimels (Rhymed Anecdotes)* in 1853.

8. On January 28, 1837, Reuter learned that the death sentence had been commuted to thirty years of fortress imprisonment. Cf. chapter 1, note 3.

9. Frederick William III, King of Prussia (1797–1840).

10. Henry VIII, King of England (1509–1547).

11. Peter the Great, Tsar of Russia (1682–1725).

12. Nicholas I, Tsar of Russia (1825–1855).

13. Duke Karl of Brunswick because of his repressive rule was deposed in 1830.

14. A member of the ministerial commission appointed to bring revolutionary "demagogues" to justice.

15. Heinrich Rudolf Dambach, director of the magistrate's jail ("Hausvogtei") in Berlin.

16. That is, not until May 11, 1837, after Reuter had been transferred to Magdeburg.

17. Councillor Kunowski was Reuter's defense lawyer. At the final hearing in Berlin on September 15, 1834, he advised Reuter not to lose time by appealing the verdict, but to let himself be transferred to Silberberg because he would undoubtedly be extradited to Mecklenburg very soon.

Chapter Four

1. At Silberberg.

2. Exner is included in *Der neue Pitavel*, a collection of stories about well-known robbers and murderers (edited by Hitzig, Leipzig, 1844).

3. Victories of Frederick the Great over Austrians at Prague and Leuthen in Silesia in 1757.

4. Battle of Kulm on August 30, 1813.

5. Colonel B. (Von Wichert) was sentenced but soon pardoned.

6. Reuter wrote this letter to his father on March 11, 1837.

Chapter Five

1. Reuter's years as a farmer ("Stromtid") from 1841 to 1850 at Demzin with Franz Rust and at Thalberg with Fritz Peters.

2. Johann August Bank (1801–49), a shoemaker in Stavenhagen, could not have been a schoolmate, as he was ten years older than Reuter.

3. Stavenhagen.

4. C. E. Stürmer (1773–1849). In *Meine Vaterstadt Stavenhagen* Reuter writes about the theater which Stürmer and his wife opened in Stavenhagen.

5. Frederick the Great, King of Prussia (1740–86).

6. Friedrich Adolf Count von Kalkreuth (1737–1818), a field marshal in the War of German Liberation (1813–15).

7. Before her marriage Reuter's mother had worked as a housekeeper in the home and inn of postmaster Toll.

8. In May, 1840, Ernst Reuter, Fritz's cousin and foster brother, had married Sophie Reuter, Fritz's half-sister.

9. This passage like others also is meant merely as pure nonsense.

10. Malchin just north of Stavenhagen and Güstrow about twenty miles to the northwest.

11. Major General Diedrich von Schuckmann (1785–1856) came to Glogau as commandant in 1841.

12. An estate with a beautiful deer park and a grove of thousand-year-old oak trees located near Stavenhagen.

13. Reuter's father was district judge and registrar as well as mayor in Stavenhagen.

Chapter Six

1. Reuter was imprisoned at the fortress in Magdeburg on the Elbe from the end of March, 1837, to March 10, 1838.

2. The correct name was Schür.

3. Bohl was a member of the Greifswald *Burschenschaft*.

4. This may possibly be the B. to whom Reuter refers in two later letters (to his father on January 20, 1836, and to a former fellow prisoner on June 2, 1868). Braun later became the owner of an estate in Pomerania.

5. Possibly Döhn who is also mentioned in several of Reuter's later letters.

6. The grand ducal administrator ("Amtshauptmann") Johann Joachim Heinrich Weber (1757–1826). This splendid old gentleman lived in the "castle" across the square from the Reuter home and often came to have tea with Reuter's invalid mother. Weber is one of the main characters in *Ut de Franzosentid* and also appears in *Meine Vaterstadt Stavenhagen*.

7. Adelheid Wüsthoff, Reuter's schoolboy "love" in Parchim.

8. Reuter was a student at the university of Jena from May, 1832, to February, 1833.

9. Anhalt.

10. Probably Ziesar in Saxony.

11. A reference to Reuter's excessive drinking.

12. Not quite accurate, for on October 6, 1837, Reuter's sentence was reduced to eight years.

13. During a visit of the mayor to Berlin in December, 1833.

14. Reuter was probably referring to Minister of Justice von Kamptz whom he considered to be one of the most bitter enemies of the imprisoned students. The official acts, however, reveal that Von Kamptz in contrast to the other minister of justice, Mühler, constantly recommended that Reuter be released. It was Von Kamptz who succeeded in having Reuter transferred from Magdeburg to Graudenz.

15. These escapes took place at the end of September or the beginning of October, 1837.

16. This centigrade reading is the equivalent of about zero Fahrenheit.

Chapter Seven

1. The provost marshal was Captain Singer. In his letters to his father Reuter makes frequent reference to Singer's kindness to the political prisoners.

2. The warden's name was Maass.

3. In Berlin. Reuter was held in the city jail ("Stadtvogtei") from October 31, 1833, to January 1, 1834, and in the magistrate's jail ("Hausvogtei") from January 1 until his transfer to Silberberg on November 12, 1834.

4. General Count von Hacke was first commandant at Magdeburg from 1834 to 1837.

5. Colonel von Bieberstein was second commandant at Magdeburg until 1835.

6. Von Rochow was on ministerial commission with Von Kamptz and Mühler.

7. Not the shield of Achilles, but of the Telamonian Ajax.

8. Hermann Grashof, a close friend of Reuter in Magdeburg. Reuter dedicated *Ut mine Festungstid (Seven Years of my Life)* to him.

9. Colonel von Busse, who succeeded Colonel von Bieberstein as second commandant, was transferred to Wittenberg shortly after Reuter's arrival in Magdeburg.

10. One of frequent references to bribes paid by prisoners to members of prison staff.

Chapter Eight

1. Johann Liborius Ernst, a Westphalian, was appointed pontifical commissioner in Magdeburg on March 1, 1834.

2. Ferdinand Kämpf showed Reuter many acts of kindness at Magdeburg and also later at Graudenz. However, it is not likely that Mayor Reuter was unaware of this as Fritz seems to indicate.

3. Mayor Reuter had money transmitted to his son through Müller and Weichsel without the knowledge of the warden. This is evident in a letter of acknowledgment which Reuter sent to Müller and Weichsel on August 15, 1837.

Chapter Nine

1. Heinzmann later became an assistant judge in Trier and Elberfeld. After taking part in the Revolution of 1848 he fled to London.

2. Messerich had been a member of the *Burschenschaft* in Heidelberg and like Reuter was at first condemned to death. Later he became a lawyer in Trier and a member of the National Assembly.

3. Drinking bout ritual in strict conformity with the students' code.

4. Albert Schulze, the "Captain" of the *Festungstid* studied law at the university of Halle where he was a member of the *Burschenschaft*. He was condemned to death, but the sentence was commuted to thirty years and later to ten years imprisonment.

5. Duke Karl of Mecklenburg-Strelitz (1785–1837), an absolutist and reactionary, was the half-brother of the very popular Queen Luise, the wife of Frederick William III of Prussia.

6. Z. refers to Johannes Guittienne, the "Frenchman" of the *Festungstid*. Guittienne had studied law at the universities of Bonn, Munich, Heidelberg, and Berlin. He was sentenced to death because of his membership in the *Burschenschaft* and yet at the same time having been an officer in the Prussian militia. After the general amnesty he became a member of the National Assembly in 1848 and in 1870 he supported Bismarck and the National Liberals in the *Kulturkampf*.

7. A mental hospital in Berlin.

Chapter Ten

1. Albrecht Breyer, a member of the *Burschenschaft* at the university of Halle, was sentenced to six years imprisonment. Later he became a doctor in Liège, Belgium. He was not a writer nor did he ever live in Vienna.

2. For placement in an appropriate class in French at school Reuter was asked about his earlier study of that foreign language. He replied that he had read Voltaire's *History of Charles XII* in the original. However, when

he made a mistake in elementary French grammar his schoolmates were quick to nickname him "Charles douze."

3. It is doubtful that Reuter wrote such a letter.

4. Scania, the southernmost part of Sweden.

5. The provost marshal at Silberberg was Second Lieutenant Berg.

6. Wilhelm Cornelius, the "Don Juan" of the *Festungstid*, was a book dealer from Stralsund. Because he had made a revolutionary speech at the Hambach Festival on May 27, 1832, he was arrested and imprisoned in Stralsund, Magdeburg, and Graudenz. He was freed in 1839 and emigrated to America in the 1860s.

Chapter Eleven

1. A quotation from a popular drinking song.

2. That is, the colors of the *Allgemeine Deutsche Burschenschaft*.

3. Lieutenant General von Thile replaced General von Hacke who died on January 28, 1838.

4. In a letter to his father on March 17, 1838, Reuter wrote how grateful he was to Pastor Leist and to Herr Kämpf for all the kindness they had shown him at Magdeburg.

5. Reuter and Schulze (the "Captain") left Magdeburg in March, not in February.

6. Cf. Chapter 9, Note 4

Chapter Twelve

1. Reuter had been held on remand in the magistrate's jail from January 1 to November 12, 1834.

2. Karl Krüger of Malchin, a friend of Reuter in schools at Friedland and Parchim and also at the universities of Rostock and Jena. He too became a member of the *Burschenschaft* at Jena and was sentenced to 15 months imprisonment at Dömitz (Mecklenburg). He later became a senator in his hometown. Reuter visited him in Malchin in July, 1854, and dedicated *Hanne Nüte un de lütte Pudel (Handsome Hans and the Little Curlyhead)* to him.

3. Fritz Peters, the "best friend" at whose estate Thalberg near Treptow (Prussia) Reuter lived for the greater part of the years 1845–50.

4. On August 10–12, 1861.

5. An important fortress site in Brandenburg since 1232; later it became a dread political prison.

6. To Eisenach.

7. Called "Uncle" because of his sly and ingratiating manner of drawing information from the political prisoners.

8. Wintersberg, whom Reuter remembered from his earlier imprisonment in the magistrate's jail. At that time Reuter had given him a pen sketch which he had made of the courtyard as seen from his cell window.

9. About 75 degrees Fahrenheit.

10. According to Reuter's letter of August 16, 1836, it was his defense lawyer Kunowski, and not Dambach, who had made this recommendation.

11. In Treptow.

12. According to letters of March 17 and 22, 1838, Reuter and the Captain spent only two nights in Berlin.

13. In the letter of March 17 Reuter laments the fact that he was not allowed to see his father who was visiting a relative in Berlin at the time (March 11−13), nor was he allowed to send a note to that relative. Reuter points out that he had not seen his father for five years and that there would be less possibility of seeing him now that he was being transferred to Graudenz.

Chapter Thirteen

1. Cf. Chapter 12, Note 4.

2. The Vistula.

Chapter Fourteen

1. Graudenz (Polish Grudziadz) located on the Vistula about 50 miles south of Danzig. Reuter was imprisoned there from March 15, 1838, until he was extradited to Dömitz (Mecklenburg) on June 15, 1839.

2. Colonel Ludwig Johann Philipp von Toll (1775−1851) was appointed commandant at Graudenz in 1834. He was made major general in 1838 and was retired as lieutenant general in 1843.

3. Karl Schramm was an officer in the *Burschenschaft* at Jena. Like Reuter he too was condemned to death with the sentence later being commuted to 30 years imprisonment. On March 26, 1838, the sentence was further reduced to 10 years. Schramm served most of this time at Graudenz. During a visit of Schramm's father, a physician, the commandant recognized the man who had bandaged his wounds at Waterloo and had him removed to Brussels. Schramm later became a member of the National Assembly where he belonged to the extreme left. In 1852 he emigrated to America.

4. At Silberberg.

5. Schramm had always wanted to play an important role in the *Burschenschaft*.

6. The official acts support Reuter's statements concerning Schramm.

7. The provost marshal was Captain Baumüller.

Chapter Fifteen

1. *Paulus*, a poem in six cantos in iambic pentameter. Schramm also wrote a shorter epic *Hermann*.

2. Johann Heinrich Voss (1751–1826), a Mecklenburg poet especially known for his translations of Homer and other classical writers.

3. The quartermaster was named Kucke.

4. The quartermaster's step-daughter was the twenty-year-old Aurelia Schöneich.

Chapter Sixteen

1. Friedrich Wilhelm Vogler, the "Copernicus" of the *Festungstid*, had been a member of the *Burschenschaft* at the university of Halle. His death sentence was commuted to 10 years of fortress imprisonment at Magdeburg and Graudenz. His engagement to Aurelia Schöneich was dissolved and he later became mayor in his hometown of Könnern on the Saale.

2. Cf. Chapter 10, Note 6.

3. At the meeting at Hambach near Neustadt in the Rhenish Palatinate on May 27, 1832.

4. Anton Witte, the "Archbishop" of the *Festungstid*, was a printer who had fled to Switzerland. In 1835 the Bundestag had forbidden students to study at the universities of Berne or Zurich, and had also forbidden all journeymen to visit countries where there were political workers' unions. Witte became a member of the liberal organization "Young Germany." When he returned to Germany in February, 1838, he was sentenced to 20 years imprisonment. After two months in Magdeburg he was transferred to Graudenz.

5. Cf. Chapter 9, Note 6.

6. Cf. Chapter 9, Note 7.

7. Martin von Dunin (1774–1842), archbishop of Posen, was opposed the Prussian government's position in the matter of mixed marriages. He was removed as archbishop and imprisoned in 1839, but released by Frederick William IV after 10 months.

8. Orell Füssli, famous publishing house of Zürich, was founded in 1524.

Chapter Nineteen

1. Many German states including Bavaria, Württemberg, Baden, and both Mecklenburgs as members of the Rhine Confederation fought on the side of France and Napoleon.

2. In 1865 while in America Schramm learned of the role which Reuter had given him in the *Festungstid*. He reproached Reuter in a letter; Reuter

answered very politely, without, however, taking anything back. In the fall of 1867 Schramm returned to Germany and came to see Reuter in Eisenach, but Reuter's wife would not let him enter the house to see her husband.

Chapter Twenty

1. S. Löff in Berlin, the manufacturer of a self-patented coffee maker.

Chapter Twenty-one

1. Frau Bütow may have been the Reuters' charwoman in Treptow. She appears also in Reuter's short story *Woans ick tau 'ne Fru kamm (How I found My Wife)*. This work is not autobiographical as the title might suggest.

2. The "Stadtvogtei" in Berlin.

3. The correct name was Major Michaelis. The festival of St. Martin of Tours (November 11) and of the archangel Michael (September 29) are close together in the calendar. Reuter very often interchanges proper names in this manner. Cf. Altmann and Neumann in *Dörchläuchting (His Excellency)* and Weis and Schwarz in Chapter 25.

4. Guillaume Guizot (1787–1874) was opposed to the reactionary government of Charles X and leader of the "juste-milieu" (the rule of the conservative-minded bourgeoisie) under Louis Philippe.

5. Louis Philippe, King of France (1830–48), although a liberal in form, became more reactionary and was deposed in the Revolution of 1848.

6. Cf. Chapter 6, Note 7.

7. This friend of Reuter is otherwise unknown.

Chapter Twenty-Two

1. Christiane Ölpcke, the stepsister of Reuter's mother, lived with the family in Stavenhagen.

2. Albrecht Thaer (1752–1828), a professor of agronomy at the university of Berlin (1810–18) and an authority in the field of scientific husbandry. Reuter here refers to his book *Grundsätze der rationellen Landwirtschaft*.

Chapter Twenty-Three

1. There were 48 shillings to the taler.

2. A cold drink made with white wine, sugar, and usually pineapple.

Chapter Twenty-Four

1. Instead of "melancholy."

2. A measure of wine of about 30 quarts to the full anker.
3. Cf. Chapter 7, Note 3.

Chapter Twenty-Five

1. Reuter's father had appealed to Grand Duke Paul Frederick of Mecklenburg-Schwerin on two occasions and in May, 1837, both Reuter and his father appealed directly to King Frederick William III of Prussia.
2. Reuter mentions Wieck (Schleswig) and Kleekamp (Holstein).
3. Actually the sentences were more severe.
4. In the War of German Liberation (1813—15).
5. The merchant Weise. For interchange of names cf. Chapter 21, Note 3.
6. Däms is Low German for Dömitz (Mecklenburg).
7. Paul Frederick, grand duke of Mecklenburg-Schwerin (1800—42), was married to Alexandrina, the daughter of Frederick William III, King of Prussia (1797—1840).
8. The penalty would have been two years in jail.
9. Reuter had become a "naturalized" Prussian while living in Treptow, but at Easter, 1856, he had moved to Neubrandenburg in Mecklenburg-Strelitz without giving up his Prussian citizenship.
10. Frederick William III.
11. A red champagne.
12. The château or "castle" wines are excellent brands usually from Burgundy.
13. Refers to period of reaction after 1815.
14. Prussian village on the Mecklenburg border.
15. In later years Reuter corresponded with Wuthenow, the husband of Alwine Wuthenow, some of whose poems Reuter included in a literary journal which he published for a short time (1855—56).
16. A small town in Mecklenburg-Schwerin about 25 miles northeast of Dömitz.
17. At Parchim.
18. Franz Flörcke, a lawyer in Parchim, became mayor of Grabow in 1839. He was made privy councillor ("Hofrat") that same year.
19. Rather than "Sie," the formal term for "you."

Chapter Twenty-Six

1. Däms or Dömitz in the southwestern corner of Mecklenburg-Schwerin. Cf. also Chapter 2, Note 4.
2. Bokup and Eldena are two grand ducal domains to the north and northeast of Dömitz.

3. Hostel located outside the town on the way to the Elbe ferry.

4. Lieutenant Colonel Christian Dietrich Karl von Bülow (1767—1850).

5. Konrad Ludwig Zachow was the town's grand ducal administrator ("Amtshauptmann") until 1835.

6. The *superficies* is the legal right to make use of one's own possessions located on the property of another. It implies use of such land, but not ownership of it, as Reuter would seem to indicate, although in a humorous vein.

7. Franz IV of Modena (Upper Italy) was the only prince in Europe who did not recognize Louis Philippe as King of France.

8. The widow of Mayor Reuter's oldest brother, Peter Reuter. She was the mother of Ernst and August, the cousins of Fritz who were brought up in Stavenhagen. Cf. also Chapter 5, Note 8.

9. Henriette Hanke (1784—1862) wrote novels which were read mostly by women.

10. Von Hartwig became major in 1841.

11. When Reuter came to Dömitz the commandant was 71 years of age.

12. Only the room was free; Reuter had to pay for food, light, and heat.

13. Frederick Franz I (1756—1837) became duke of Mecklenburg-Schwerin in 1785 and grand duke in 1815 at the Congress of Vienna.

14. The commandant had five daughters and one son. Frida (1822—94) was Reuter's "love" at Dömitz.

15. Iwan Iwanowitsch Diebitsch-Sabalkanskij (1785—1831) was of German birth, but became field marshal in Russian service after 1801. He was commander in chief in Turkey in 1828.

16. On Baltic coast about 50 miles east of Lübeck.

17. Probably Quartermaster P., a prisoner to whom Reuter refers in a letter of March 4, 1840.

18. From June 15, 1839 to August 25, 1840.

19. On August 10, 1840.

20. Two weeks after the announcement of the general amnesty.

21. Cf. Chapter 6, Note 4.

22. The dog (Schüten) was probably given to Reuter by the Von Bülow sisters.

23. At the end of August or beginning of September, 1839.

24. Prehn later became the grand ducal administrator in Bützow, located about 25 miles south of Rostock.

25. Cf. Chapter 26, Note 8.

26. While in Dömitz Reuter had corresponded with Lenthe who had sent him some sketches and oil paintings as models.

27. From Easter, 1827, to September, 1831.

28. Johann Zehlicke. Cf. Chapter 1, Note 7.

29. Three kilometers south of Stavenhagen.

30. Cf. Chapter 5, Note 8.

31. Mayor Reuter died in March, 1845.

32. Cf. Chapter 5, Note 1.

33. Cf. Chapter 12, Note 3.

34. In deference to his father's wishes Reuter had studied law at the universities of Rostock and Jena.

35. Reuter might have become such a city official if he had completed his law studies.

36. At school Reuter had shown great interest in art. Many of his portraits and sketches were made while he was in prison.

37. While at the university and also in prison Reuter in his letters to his father continually indicated his preference for farming as a vocation.

38. It had also been one of Reuter's hopes that he might become a supervisor ("Inspektor") of a large private or grand ducal estate.

39. The purchaser of 25 bushels of grain paid the "Inspektor" of the estate a fee of one or two talers.

40. Reuter earned his livelihood as a private teacher in Treptow 1850–56.

41. Reuter's first published work (1853). Cf. also Chapter 3, Note 7.